CASS SERIES ON INTELLIGENCE

Studies in Intelligence

A DON AT WAR

CASS SERIES ON INTELLIGENCE AND MILITARY AFFAIRS

Studies in Intelligence Series
Editors: Christopher Andrew and Michael I. Handel

Sir David Hunt by Karsh, 1946

A Don at War

SIR DAVID HUNT
K.C.M.G., O.B.E.

With a Foreword by
Field Marshal the Earl Alexander of Tunis
K.G., P.C., G.C.B., O.M., G.C.M.G., C.S.I., D.S.O., M.C.

FRANK CASS

Published 1990 in Great Britain by
FRANK CASS & CO. LTD

Reprinted 2004 by Frank Cass
2 Park Square
Milton Park
Abingdon
Oxon
OX14 4RN

Transferred to Digital Printing 2004

First Edition 1966
Revised edition with additional material 1990

British Library Cataloguing in Publication Data

Hunt, Sir, David 1913–
    A don at war.
    1. World War 2. Army operations by Great Britain.   Army.
    Biographies
    I. Title
    940.548141

    ISBN 0-7146-3383-6 (Hardback)
    ISBN 0-7146-4374-2 (Paperback)

Library of Congress Cataloging-in-Publication Data

Hunt, David, Sir, 1913–
    A don at war / David Hunt.
        p.   cm. — (Cass series on politics and military affairs in
    the twentieth century)
    Reprint, with new introd. Originally published: London : Kimber,
    1966
        ISBN 0-7146-3383-6
        1. Hunt, David, Sir, 1913–   . 2. World War, 1939–1945—Secret
    service—Great Britain. 3. World War, 1939–1945—Personal
    narratives, British.   4. Great Britain. Army—Biography.
    5. Intelligence officers—Great Britain—Biography. 6. Military
    intelligence—Great Britain—History—20th century. I. Title.
    II. Series.
    D810.S7H85   1990
    940.54'86'41092—dc20   89-71272
                                                      CIP

Printed in Great Britain by Biddles Ltd, King's Lynn, Norfolk

CONTENTS

E.G. Morton

Foreword to the 1990 Edition

THIS BOOK was first published in 1966. What I had principally in mind in writing it was to entertain two young sons by telling them what I had been up to during the war. This accounts for the predominantly anecdotal style. I don't in fact regard anecdotes as beneath the dignity of history. Nor did either Herodotus or Macaulay, who are the historians I most enjoy and admire. I also thought it might be of value to future historians if I put down my view of the events of which I had personal experience during the time I served abroad, from 1940 to 1945. With this in mind I did take a good deal of trouble to ensure, from such papers as I had preserved and from official publications, that the narrative of events was accurate because it seemed to me that an enormous amount of what had been written about the campaigns in Africa and Italy was seriously misleading, either romanticised or distorted to suit the particular prejudices of the writer. The publication of the official histories has now provided a standard against which those earlier works can be judged; but when I began writing, which was before 1960, there was not much available that was authoritative outside the official despatches. When the final draft was ready I showed it to Field-Marshal Lord Alexander, my old chief. He was good enough to encourage me, and to write a Foreword, and William Kimber accepted it.

The first edition was exhausted fairly rapidly. Reviewers were generally benevolent. What pleased me even more as time went by was to find that the book was very frequently quoted as an authority in the footnotes of the official history of the war in the Mediterranean and Middle East and also in Professor Sir Harry Hinsley's four-volume official history of British Intelligence in the Second World War. More recently it has acquired readers in the United States Army War College, the equivalent of our Staff College at Camberley, from where Michael Handel, Professor of National Security Affairs, has informed me that he has found it useful for his lectures on deception, particularly in the Italian campaign. (The official account of deception by Sir Michael Howard, which will without doubt be a magisterial work of final authority, has not yet been published.) Accordingly when Frank Cass proposed to me to publish a second edition, 24 years after the first, I was glad to agree.

For the benefit of any bibliographers who may be interested I should add that a Portuguese translation was published in 1973 by the publishing house Paz e Terra of São Paulo under the title *Um Professor na Guerra*. I was Ambassador in Brazil at the time, which is probably sufficient explanation.

This new edition, at the suggestion of Frank Cass with which I fully concurred, is a straight reprint of the original except for a very few typographical corrections. I feel sure this is right. The text goes back to the period immediately after the war and reflects the work I had done on the first draft of the official history and on Lord Alexander's despatches. It has at least the merit of representing a consistent point of view formed at a certain time and with a single exception that I am about to mention there is little of importance that it is necessary to add or to correct.

The principal purpose of this Foreword is to make good that one great omission: the fact that the British were able to read German high-grade ciphers. These were produced by special machines called Enigma and the Germans were convinced, right up to the end of the war and after, that the texts they produced were indecipherable. In consequence of this success, during the whole period I am dealing with, signals passing between the senior commanders of the enemy forces were intercepted, deciphered and sent to our commands abroad. There were naturally many gaps but generally speaking a remarkable degree of continuity was maintained. It was this more than anything else that accounted for the accuracy of the forecasts that British Intelligence was able to make of enemy strategic intentions; in addition, because it was also possible to read the traffic passed between German Intelligence stations, we were able to assess the effect on the enemy of our programmes of deception and to protect the security of our operations.

It was the greatest secret of the war. Its preservation must be regarded as almost miraculous. To break the ciphers encrypted by the Enigma machine was an extraordinary intellectual achievement but it would have been sterile if the information received had not been disseminated at once to the forces in the field who could use it. This meant that there were thousands in the secret. They had all been warned against any disclosure, or carelessness in handling the material. Having been selected as persons of more than average intelligence they could see for themselves the value of the work they were doing and how easy, and how fatal, any betrayal would be.

Some may have believed the widely-circulated story that Churchill personally had threatened that the person who lost us this great advantage would be sent before a firing squad; but it was not necessary. Even more surprising is the fact that the secret continued to be kept after the war. I have heard many stories of wives who had spent four years of their lives at Bletchley Park, the centre for decipherment, and never told their husbands what they had done there. They were horrified and felt cheated when the great secret appeared in the bookshops.

It was in 1974 that it was given away, in a book by F. W. Winterbotham called *The Ultra Secret*. There had been hints earlier, especially from French sources, but for the English-speaking public this was the first explicit revelation. Apart, however, from that single merit, or demerit, the book was of very little value, though it lived up to the author's expectations of popular success. The accounts it gives of the use to which the deciphered material was put are quite unreliable, being based on the author's fallible memory. Very probably he did not understand half of what was going on at the time, and when he came to record his memoirs he was unable to refer to documents. His story about the air raid on Coventry, for instance, is in error in stating that Churchill took 'the terrible decision' to let the city suffer rather than compromise the secret; a story which is repeated, with equally fictitious elaborations, in the biography of himself inspired by Sir William Stephenson, *A Man called Intrepid*, a book compared with which *The Adventures of Baron Munchausen* could pass as sober and factual. In fact Ultra did not reveal Coventry as a target and Churchill thought the raid would be on London. Rather similiar inventions disfigure his sketchy narratives of the African and Italian campaigns. To take two examples, there is a fairy-story of a race for the capture of Bone between British and German parachutists, and a wholly-invented visit by Churchill to Italy in May 1944. The first really reliable and comprehensive account of the employment by all three Services of Signals Intelligence, to use the generic term covering all aspects of the exploitation of enemy radio transmissions, will be found in Professor Sir Harry Hinsley's book *British Intelligence in the Second World War* (London, HMSO, 1979–1990). It is an admirable book; I have had differences of opinion on matters of detail but it is a monument of industry and percipience. I have studied all four volumes with fascinated attention—indeed I reviewed them all in *The Listener*—

and have been careful to check what I have written in this Foreword against them.

It may be useful at this point to go into the meaning of the term 'Ultra'. It was not, as some fanciful theories have it, the name for an ingenious machine that transformed enciphered German signals into plain language. It was a code-word used to refer to the material provided by the decipherment of messages in high-grade cipher. (I shall have something to say later about the exploitation of signals on a lower level.) Originally it was used only by the Royal Navy who began sending signals based on this material to selected Flag Officers serving afloat in January 1940. For the next eighteen months these signals were prefixed 'Hydro' but in June 1941 the prefix was changed to 'Ultra'. At the same time stringent new security regulations were introduced in handling them. Later the other two Services began to use the same code-word. I am unable to give a date for this but I think it must have been some time in 1943; the RAF made the change before the army did. My first acquaintance with the material was much earlier than that. The practice then was to refer to it by the digraph which preceded the serial number of the messages. This changed periodically; I remember two successive series prefixed MK and QT. Mr Churchill had a more picturesque code-word; for his purposes the material was called 'Boniface' and was supposed to emanate from a supernaturally omniscient and highly-placed agent in the German supreme command. Another cover name was 'Most Secret Sources'. By the end of the war the use of the term Ultra had become normal and it is established now. It certainly has a more clandestine and portentous sound than the original Hydro.

In describing how the Ultra material was conveyed to those who needed it I shall restrict myself to the Mediterranean theatre and the army; the navy and the air force followed similar but slightly different systems. There was at GHQ, Middle East, a fairly large establishment for receiving signals from Bletchley Park; these were distributed only to a small selected group among the Intelligence staff. The recipients were described as 'indoctrinated', a ritual process which was supposed to include exhortations to secrecy coupled with blood-curdling threats. Outside GHQ the information went only as far down as Army HQ. A special cipher unit was attached there, known as a Special Liaison Unit, which received the material direct from Britain, not through GHQ. At Army HQ it was distributed to the Commander, his Chief of Staff and two or three other officers. As a further though rather frail measure of security the messages sent were never verbatim reproductions of the raw material; the German text was paraphrased and disguised in such a way that a single example might, possibly, be mistaken for a report from an agent though no one who saw it in bulk could have any doubt about its origin. A more important precaution was that when the message had been read by those on the list of the indoctrinated it was taken away and destroyed. The organisation was elaborate and worked perfectly. No one on the enemy side and very few on our side guessed what were the real functions of the SLUs.

It may be asked how Bletchley Park and the SLUs protected the security of their own communications, since the Germans were also active in the pursuit of Signals Intelligence and had some notable successes. They penetrated the navy's ciphers between 1939 and 1943 and a special intercept section attached to Rommel's HQ in the desert, known as the 621st Signals Battalion, was successful in reading a lot of our army traffic before it came to the soldierly end that I describe on page 113. The answer is that all their signals were enciphered on the One Time Pad system. This is the very Everest of cryptography involving completely random sets of numbers, never reused, to be added to the figure groups in the book cipher. The system survives, I may say, in diplomatic practice. In my experience it is employed almost exclusively for informing an ambassador of his next posting; he is instructed to decipher the telegram himself so that not even his cipher officer knows. It is a laborious and time-consuming process, at least when operated by ambassadors, but impenetrable.

The Germans did in fact have suspicions that their plans were sometimes betrayed, for instance when they learned from British prisoners taken in the course of the battle of Alam Halfa, on which pages 122–6 may be consulted, that Eighth Army had known the outline of the plan and the original date of the attack and that the troops had been warned in advance of the battle. On that occasion the Germans were gravely alarmed about their security and expressed it in a signal which was intercepted and deciphered by us. When this arrived at No.10 the German alarm was dwarfed by the ferocious indignation of the Prime Minister who suspected, as Professor Hinsley puts it, 'that General Montgomery had been too free with the Enigma intelligence' and sent a strong warning to the Middle East.

We were lucky that the Alam Halfa affair had no adverse consequences on our supply of intelligence. Nor did the potentially more serious leakage, shortly afterwards, of the sensational news derived from Ultra that Rommel was in bad health and leaving Africa; although it made Churchill still more indignant, to the point of instituting an inquiry under the chairmanship of the Cabinet Secretary, Sir Edward Bridges. The reason for our good fortune was that the Germans had decided it was all the fault of the Italians. They had already adopted this theory to account for the regular success of our attacks on their supply convoys. Ironically, this had led them to ask the Italian naval authorities to abandon their own book ciphers, which we never succeeded in breaking, for a variant of the Enigma machine and another cipher based on a similar Swedish machine which we called C38m; both these could be rapidly deciphered. The Germans then assumed we must have a formidable network of agents in Italian ports, aided by some highly-based treachery. The Intelligence authorities in GHQ Middle East thought this latter idea was a good one and resolved to foster it. They controlled a very large apparatus of double agents, used largely for the purpose of strategic deception, indeed they must have captured for their purposes something like eighty per cent of the agents in the area on whom the *Abwehr*, the German Secret Service, placed great though undeserved reliance. By using them they passed on a series of small hints in such a way that, if put together, they would point the finger of suspicion at a certain Italian General who had a senior position at the headquarters of the German–Italian Panzer Army of Africa. I remember his name well; but I should prefer not give it. The insinuations that we circulated against him were most certainly groundless, indeed deliberately invented, and I don't see why an honourable family should be exposed after forty-eight years even to a false association with treachery. It will be enough to say that the man exposed was certainly a non-Fascist and a strong monarchist, which the Germans would regard as sufficient reasons for giving some credence to the rumours against him. For all this well-applied camouflage there were few moments when we did not at least contemplate the possibility that our invaluable source of information might be compromised by some carelessness and lost to us. What saved us was the German conviction, based on cogent but fallacious mathematical arguments, that their machine ciphers were unbreakable.

I was let into the secret during the time I was serving at the

Headquarters of the RAF in Greece. In my case there was no elaborate introduction. I was simply shown, in the course of my ordinary duties, a series of signals, classified Most Secret, which described the movement forward into Romania and Bulgaria of the German air force units which were to support the attack on Greece. They were derived partly from the *Luftwaffe* Enigma traffic and partly from that of the railway administration. They were barely camouflaged to simulate agents' reports; in any event it must have been plain to anyone of ordinary intelligence who read them that they were based on decipherment of operational messages. The information was precise, detailed and minatory. I remember the impression of impending doom as we watched those overwhelming forces rolling towards us.

The supply of first-class information continued throughout the Greek campaign. We knew exactly the date and time when the German offensive was due to be launched and were even notified, five hours in advance, of a thirty-minute postponement of H-hour. Every night we had information about the enemy's intentions for the next day. It may be asked why in these circumstances our resistance was so short-lived; the answer is that at that stage of the war however valuable it was to know what was going to hit us it was painful to know also that we were too weak to do much about it. The sole advantage—no small one, indeed—was that we were able to duck under the blow. General Wilson, commanding British troops in Greece, won a good reputation for a skilfully-conducted withdrawal. I thought him lucky in this, as in future appointments which brought him eventually a Field-Marshal's baton and a peerage; to me he seemed, if I may borrow Churchill's cruel and unjustified verdict on Wavell, to be qualified to make a good Chairman of a Conservative Constituency Association.

General Freyberg in Crete was equally well served by Intelligence. As a special exception he was allowed to receive Ultra messages. As a result he was aware of the enemy plan and of the date of the attack. It might be thought that with our information so good and the enemy's so rotten—for everything I have written on their Intelligence about Crete is correct and supported by later publications—our side would have had a decisive advantage. There were other unfavourable factors, besides the crushing German domination of the air. Bernard Freyberg was fervently admired in all theatres of the Mediterranean war. He was a man of legendary courage, the best trainer of troops in the entire army and a thoroughly competent divisional commander; but he was not a great strategist. He felt his responsibility for the defence of Crete deeply. As I learn from his son Paul, the present Lord Freyberg, he also felt burdened by his responsibility for guarding the Ultra secret, which had been entrusted to him personally by Wavell; so much so that, according to the same source, he refused to reinforce the west end of Maleme airport with a Greek regiment as he had planned because he feared such a step might somehow give away the fact that he knew it was the enemy's principal objective. If he had stuck to his original intention he might well have succeeded in holding Maleme, the key to the whole battle. And this, for I stick to the views I expressed earlier, might have led to a worse strategic result for us since retention of Crete would certainly have involved us before long in greater perils than did its loss. The Germans recorded with dismay that the Allied garrison had been between three and five times stronger than their Intelligence confidently asserted and that the objective chosen for their initial attack had been well prepared beforehand for defence; they ascribed this to our 'efficient espionage system in Greece'.

I still feel sad about our defeat in Crete, more so than I can account for rationally. I can hardly bear to read the lucid and eloquent account of the battle written by Ian Stewart, who was Medical Officer with the Welch. The only consolation, and it is a serious one, is that the parachutists against whom we fought, the 7th *Flieger-division*, suffered so heavily that the Germans made no attempt to rebuild their airborne arm. It was never used again except for a very few small-scale operations. In this respect the loss of Crete meant the saving of Malta.

During the period that I served, in succession, with the Headquarters of the Western Desert Force and 13 Corps the Intelligence branch there was not supplied with Ultra material. I naturally knew, however, that such a source was available at Eighth Army headquarters and as our relations with them were close and cordial it was possible to assess correctly the reliability of the information they gave us about the higher levels of the enemy command. For our part we were content to base the advice about enemy dispositions and intentions that we gave to the Corps Commander for his guidance in tactical operations on reconnaissance, especially air photography, prisoners and captured documents, and the interception of tactical wireless traffic. I have called these the bread and butter of Intelligence and they were of vital importance not only in the field but also at the highest levels in our own Intelligence system. Even at Bletchley Park, which in army matters at least dealt mainly with high strategy, much of the Ultra material would have proved very difficult to interpret if the analysts had not been supplied with the essential mass of materials about order of battle, personalities and methods of operation which derived from these humbler techniques.

The system of intercepting and interpreting enemy wireless traffic in lower-grade codes and ciphers was known as Y. It was organised in sections known as Special Signals Units of which one was attached to each of our two Corps Headquarters and to the Headquarters of Eighth Army. Ours at 13th Corps was 101 SSU and the head of the operational side was the John Makower of whom I speak with such enthusiasm in Chapter X. It was by far the best, and John Makower had a wonderful flair, together with long experience which is one of the most important requirements for Intelligence. We had met first in Greece, in March 1941, and when I went to Tunisia just two years later I insisted on having him with me. We went together to Sicily and Italy and finished the war together.

When this book was first published Y was still almost as great a secret as Ultra and even those best acquainted with it would only have noticed an occasional allusion. Strictly speaking it had not needed quite so rigid a protection as Ultra because ciphers used in the field were only expected to remain unbroken long enough to deprive them of immediate use whereas machine ciphers such as Enigma were supposed to remain impenetrable indefinitely. However this expression 'low-grade ciphers' must not be taken as meaning that they were easy to break; they required a lot of hard brain-work and much figuring on paper which were made more irksome by the heat and dust of the desert, not to mention the frequent danger of a sudden raid by German armoured cars. The results were stunningly worthwhile. For the actual conduct of a battle Y was of greater value than Ultra. I call in evidence 'Bill' Williams, now Sir Edgar, the greatest Intelligence Staff Officer of the war who, speaking of the summer of 1942 in the desert, has claimed: 'We did not think we had done our work properly unless we had beaten the Ultra.' The fact is that Ultra gave the strategic intentions of the enemy command, its reports to Rome and Berlin and the directives it received; Y gave the actual operation orders to the formations under command and, often more important, situation reports issued in the course of the fluctuating battle. I mention Major Maclean 'of Coll', the German officer from an ex-Jacobite family whose nightly returns showed how many of the 15th Panzer Division's tanks were in workshops; I could have added that from Rommel's other Panzer division, the 21st, we intercepted and deciphered the nightly strength returns so that we could tell our own commanders precisely what numbers they could expect to face every day. Signals such as these were enciphered; but plain language was also freely employed in moments of crisis and especially by Rommel when he was more than usually muddled and lost. Also in plain language, exactly as I have described it, was the sombre signal in which Rommel announced that he accepted the unconditional surrender of Tobruk. Perhaps he intended us to intercept that message.

The omission of Y in most accounts of the desert campaigns (I except Professor Hinsley's) means that there is almost a missing dimension between Ultra and the British operational reports. At the time, too, it had its effect. Churchill read all the Ultra, with obsessive enthusiasm. He used it as an excuse for lashing commanders in the Middle East into action when he thought they were too slow or too conventional. He gave the fullest credit to whatever he read in the buff-coloured boxes in which the Ultra messages circulated whereas he scrutinised sharply the signals he received from his own commanders. Perhaps he was dazzled by the scientific miracle which produced the 'golden eggs', as he called them, and discounted information from other sources. He should have realised, for example, that although Rommel was an honourable and honest man he was not averse to exaggerating his difficulties if he thought it would speed up the despatch of reinforcements. Churchill always took his cries of despair literally. Throughout July 1942, for example, during what some have called the First Battle of Alamein, he constantly encouraged Auchinleck in the counter-attacks which the latter was only too willing to undertake. As I remarked at the time and have recorded in the book, Churchill appeared to think all generals required the spur. This was rarely true and sometimes he applied the spur on the basis of information which was indeed authentic and valuable but which he partly misunderstood.

The Germans too had their successes in radio interception in the African campaigns. I have mentioned the 621st Signals Battalion, which was a most valuable source of information for Rommel; it was virtually destroyed in July 1942 near Alamein and not reformed until

March 1943. In addition he had for a time a source resembling our Ultra, which he owed to the Italians. By burgling the Ambassador's safe in Rome, in August 1941, they had obtained American diplomatic ciphers which enabled them to read the telegrams sent by the American Military Attaché in Cairo, Colonel Bonner Fellers. He was exceptionally well informed because he constantly visited the desert, where he was treated with full confidence. I met him several times and was impressed by his knowledge, though I disagreed with his pessimism. To the Germans his telegrams were known as '*die gute Quelle*' or the good source; I mention on page 107 the sensationally pessimistic telegram referred to in Ciano's diary entry for 23 June 1942 which seems to have played a large part in persuading Mussolini to permit Rommel to carry out his great raid into Egypt in full expectation of reaching the Suez Canal. This involved abandoning the planned assault on Malta. If so Colonel Fellers' unconscious intervention may have turned out to our eventual advantage. He was awarded the Distinguished Service Medal for his work in Cairo, but this was on other grounds.

I need hardly say now, though I dared not say it then, that we were alerted to this dangerous leak by deciphering Enigma messages in which the information from 'the good source' was forwarded to the Panzer Army Headquarters in Africa. Fellers changed his ciphers. There was naturally a danger that this might suggest to the Germans that we were reading their ciphers. Fortunately this was about the time that we captured near Tell el Eisa the papers of the 621st Signals Battalion and it was easy to put about a story that references found among them had given us a clue.

The practice of deception began earlier in the Middle East than I have mentioned. It was something very close to the heart of Wavell, an intellectual General who had studied the use of deception in the Palestine campaigns of the First World War. He appointed Colonel, later Brigadier, Dudley Clarke to run it; he was so successful that his functions were extended to the whole Mediterranean and his influence guided the deception plans for 'Overlord', which have received a lot of attention from historians. Their Mediterranean and Middle Eastern parallels will have to wait for the publication of the definitive work. I have done a certain amount of research into the subject recently in the Public Record Office, for the purpose of a paper for the US Army War College, and have studied some of the papers which will have formed the basis for Sir Michael Howard's book. What would really interest the general reader would be the detailed story of how the false information was fed to the enemy through the numerous double-agents, many of them highly picturesque characters. The general strategic concept of deception is more easily intelligible. The main point to grasp is that the original object was to exaggerate our strength. In the early and desperate days this was an obvious defensive ploy against the Italians; later the aim was to tie down ever-increasing numbers of German troops in the Mediterranean and especially in the Balkans. The reasons why the Germans went on expecting a Balkan invasion right up to the time they themselves withdrew from there were partly that they regarded the retention of the Balkans as 'decisive from the point of view of winning the war for tactical, military-political and economic reasons' (I quote from an OKW document) and partly that they were convinced we had large numbers of unemployed divisions available in the Middle East and they could not imagine any other use to which we might put them. Most of these divisions were bogus, invented by Dudley Clarke and his organisation. They were given a spurious half-life with divisional signs, simulated radio exercises, a few personalities and a pedigree. Two successive false orders of battle were constructed, code-named 'Cascade' in 1943 and 'Wantage' in 1944. The result was that at the crucial moment of the war, on D-Day for 'Overlord', at a time when there were in the whole Mediterranean theatre 38 Allied divisions the Germans credited us with having 71. This was the highest level of exaggeration that we ever put across them. On the same day the Germans had 55 divisions in the area. They thought, therefore, that they were containing larger numbers of ours but in truth, had they known it, we were containing them.

So great an error must prompt the question: why was German Intelligence so bad? Not all of it was, particularly at lower levels in the field; but certainly at the higher strategic levels it was a monument of inefficiency. The simplest answer is that they started with all the wrong ideas, ideas which they thought they were borrowing from the dreaded British Intelligence Service. I sometimes fancy that MI5 acted more shrewdly than they knew when they prosecuted Compton Mackenzie under the Official Secrets Act for publishing his *Athenian Memories*. He was fined £100. This convinced the *Abwehr*, the secret service that was just getting into its stride under Admiral Canaris, that they could find the basis of British success if they studied the conceited and ineffective posturings of Compton Mackenzie in Greece during the First World War. It was all done by spies: such was their conclusion. Another deadly weakness was that Canaris had far too much money. Hitler believed that that was one of the secrets of the success of the British Intelligence Service, which was really rather a parsimonious organisation, and lavished ridiculous amounts on the *Abwehr*. Much of this was embezzled by its members, for the newly-recruited and fast-growing service had a higher than normal level of corruption; but the bulk was used to pay spies by results. This can be guaranteed to be always fatal. Canaris himself was indecisive and liable to be fooled to the top of his bent – the Hamlet of the *Abwehr*, as Lord Dacre has brilliantly described him – but when the SS took over Schellenberg did no better. The fact that the British were so much more efficient is to be ascribed simply to the use of commonsense, or inductive reasoning if you like. Military matters, as Napoleon admitted, are essentially simple: to understand them all that is required is reason, not mythologising. Thereafter, as he went on to say, there arises the question of what do you do on the basis of your knowledge; but that is another story.

Talking of mythology, nothing in the book attracted more criticism than my judgments on Field-Marshal Erwin Rommel. My remark about his having a talent for snatching defeat from the jaws of victory was thought peculiarly shocking. Rommel became early on and has remained to this day a great favourite with the British public. The press wrote him up at the time with care-free exaggerations and inventions. Popular writers on the desert campaigns loved to picture him as a chivalrous opponent and an infallible military genius. About his moral character I am happy to concur; it seems to have deserved the highest praise. It is his military competence that I am calling in question. Perhaps because I studied his personal signals for so long I could never escape the impression of a dashing cavalryman who gambled deep and lost in the end. Even though I knew he came from the sober ranks of the Wurtemberg professional classes, and was an infantry officer, I could not help regarding him as a reincarnation of such princely captains of horse as Rupert or Demetrius who threw away the day at Naseby and at Ipsus. His spectacular failure in his first attack on Tobruk, due entirely to his own carelessness and lack of thought, must have weighed with me also. Further consideration over nearly 50 years leaves me unshaken in my judgment. I am glad to see it confirmed by Field-Marshal Lord

Carver who fought in the desert and rose to be Chief of the Imperial General Staff. Moreover we now know that Rommel's superiors took exactly the same view of him. Fritz Halder, who was by far the ablest of Hitler's Chiefs of Staff of the Army, wrote in his diary in April 1941 that he was simply not up to the job, charging around the desert aimlessly and staging reconnaissance raids which only frittered away his own strength. Next year and in the first part of 1943 the criticisms continued, as I learn from my friend Ambassador von Plehwe who was Assistant Military Attaché in Rome during all the time Rommel was in Africa. (He later wrote a first-class account of the Italian armistice.) His period of command in France in 1944 was too short to allow a serious judgment. Since the war he has become a German hero as well as a British one and a father-figure to the new German army. There are two main reasons: that he was anti-Nazi and lost his life in consequence of his involvement in the army plot, and also that since the desert was an affair strictly between soldiers without any civilians to speak of being affected, it was free from any of the atrocities which, rightly or wrongly, tainted the reputations of commanders on the other fronts. He fought a clean war, in fact, and this is an excellent reason for his reputation today. He was certainly a good man; whether he was a good general is something I would rather leave open, being of the opinion that we had one or two better generals on our side.

What I wrote about Lord Montgomery's accounts of operations in which he was involved raised some comment at the time of publication but my views are now much in line with those generally accepted. I mean such points as his unfair criticisms of Auchinleck before the battle of Alam Halfa and his laughably false claims about the part played by him in Tunisia. I attribute this change of attitude to the publication of a three-volume biography by Nigel Hamilton, based on Montgomery's papers. Mr Hamilton, though an admirer, is an independent-minded historian. He allows that Montgomery's egotism and conceit make his testimony wholly unreliable. Lord Carver has revealed a significant instance of an attempt to doctor the evidence: when Montgomery was CIGS he removed from the War Office files all papers connecting him with the Dieppe raid, of which he had been in command up to almost the last minute, and destroyed them. (This was not very clever since duplicates existed in the files of Combined Operations and the other two Services.) The crushing blow to the reliability of the Montgomery Memoirs was delivered by Mr Hamilton in his third volume when he printed some hilarious extracts from the account given by Sir Edgar Williams of how his efforts to bring some regard for the facts into them were received. Sir Edgar, too, is a devoted admirer but he is also a historian. He records how Montgomery stubbornly resisted attempts to bring his narrative into line with the truth and preferred versions which he thought reflected more glory on himself. In an epigram which reveals an affectionate exasperation he declares that 'evidence was not Monty's approach march'. By now nearly all military historians would take it as a canon that no statement in the Memoirs, and particularly no statement reflecting credit on the author or discredit on others—such passages are frequent throughout the work—should be accepted as true unless fully corroborated from an independent source. So I think I shall have no cause for regret in leaving unaltered my exposures of Montgomery's imaginative reconstructions of events.

One point of detail deserves correction. The change of thrust-line for the new plan at Alamein, 'Supercharge', was attributed on page 138 to Montgomery's Chief of Staff, General de Guinguand. It now appears that it was General McCreery, Alexander's Chief of Staff, and, though he was certainly clever enough to have thought of it himself, I feel it was Alexander who inspired him to put forward the idea. Nothing of this, naturally, appears in the Montgomery Memoirs which are perversely committed to the author's unlikely claim that his 'masterplan' for Alamein remained unchanged throughout the battle.

One thing I do rather regret, and would modify if I had not determined to keep the original text unaltered, is that I think now that it was rather too hard on the Italians. In this the book reflects a frame of mind that was much more typical of the troops in the Middle East than of the British in general who in normal times are steadfastly Italophile. It was the declaration of war on 10 June 1940 that determined the mood of disgust. It seemed like the action of a jackal on the part of Mussolini, and that was what Churchill called it in a well-remembered speech. The reproach should not have been applied indiscriminately although, as I noted at the time, there was a widespread expectation in Italy at the time that the war would be both short and successful and for that reason it was not unpopular. Then came the crushing defeat at Sidi Barrani. This made the ordinary British soldier look down on Italian military competence, though I knew many who refused to join in the general disparagement and deprecated boasting. No doubt the more prevalent opinion was largely the result of relief—we had been feeling beleaguered in our Eastern Mediterranean dead-end—but some allowance must be made for the comic contrast between present performance and the pompous boasts by Fascist leaders before the war, a contrast so sharp that it must produce laughter as inevitably as plunging a red-hot bar into water produces steam. As the campaigns went on a more proper respect for Italian military virtues became common. I myself always attributed shortcomings to 20 years of fascism which both perverted morale and failed to provide the troops with adequate armaments, partly because of corruption, partly because of bureaucratic incompetence.

With the start of the Italian campaign a juster idea of the Italian people prevailed. They were all on our side against the Germans, to begin with. (Not quite true; the Italian Social Republic, under the resuscitated Mussolini, had its adherents though we never met them.) They had shown great courage in helping escaping Allied prisoners of war. The Partisans rapidly acquired a splendid reputation. Alexander in particular showed an imaginative sympathy towards them and understood what they could do and could not do. He had always been an instructed student of the principles of irregular warfare. After the Partisans in Upper Italy had been put under his orders he arranged the most lavish supply of arms for them that could be transported by air, without discriminating among the bands according to party allegiance. He called them to special efforts when needed and warned them when our offensive was about to halt and, for a brief time, would be unable to assist them. He treated them, in other words, as troops under his command for whom he felt the same responsibility as for his own armies. Nor did he neglect to give a chance to the Italians on our side of the line to share in the honour and credit of liberating their country by raising and equipping regular formations. Five of them participated in the final victory along with the other Allies. Memories of this period, and of the traditional friendship between Britain and Italy, ought to outweigh the temporary bitterness brought about in June 1940 by a miscalculating dictator; certainly they do so in my case.

I must not omit a more general tribute to Alexander. Thirty years ago it would hardly have been necessary. He was by the almost universal judgment of men of experience in senior stations acclaimed as the foremost British Commander of the Second World War;

certainly this was, for example, the view of three Prime Ministers whom I served, Attlee, Churchill and Macmillan. The last-named used to compare him to Marlborough. In the last twenty years or so, as those who knew him have departed, the general public has been more influenced by less judicious accounts of the war which reflect the spirit of the popular press in its worst bandwagon-following style. I think it is time for that earlier opinion to be restored; future historians will vindicate it.

It is not easy for me to avoid affection pressing upon judgment, as Lord Justice Crewe said in the de Vere case. I am certainly biased in his favour, as a man, above all by the year I spent with him in Ottawa when he was Governor-General of Canada. He had remarkable intellectual depths. He was interested in everything from archaeology to geology and always happy to learn more. His manners were engaging and courteous without being stiff; he had a discriminating sense of humour. He had an unusual gift for languages; fluent in German, Russian and Polish before he was thirty he later added to them Italian, French and Urdu. His greatest skill was painting. He was far above the ordinary talent of the amateur, even so advanced an amateur as Churchill, and only just fell below the professional. It had been his intention in 1914 to resign his commission shortly, go to Paris and make art his profession; war frustrated him in this and having survived, and having commanded a brigade at 27, he decided for the profession of arms. He won rapid promotion over the heads of older men and became the youngest Major-General in the army. Having served throughout the First World War in the front line and never on the staff he thought it his duty as a commander to be close to the men who were doing the actual fighting. He was constantly to be seen with the forward troops, since he considered it far preferable to gain his knowledge of the battle by personal presence on the spot than through the reports of liaison officers.

Of the quality of his generalship I have spoken in the course of the book, laying emphasis on his brilliant grasp of manoeuvre and deception. I could have added that he also had a very sound understanding of the realities of military supply and administration. Instead of repeating what I have written it will be more convincing to quote from the memoirs of one of the greatest American commanders of the war, General Omar Bradley. Bradley was a better general than writer but he knew excellence when he saw it and could rise above national prejudice. He wrote of Alexander: 'He not only showed the shrewd tactical judgment that was to make him the outstanding general's general of the European war, but he was easily able to comport the nationally-minded and jealous Allied personalities of his command. In each successive Mediterranean campaign he had won the adulation of his American subordinates.' I knew Bradley, and should not have expected the word 'adulation' from him. It is a fine tribute from one outstanding commander to another. I shall cap it with one from Attlee, made casually to me at Chequers after dinner: 'He was a man who had experienced what war was like and he understood it.'

Finally the reader may well ask whether the story here set out has stood the test of time. Is it accurate, apart from the omissions and distortions that were necessary in 1966 to conceal the secrets of Signals Intelligence? I can only say that for the last 23 years I have kept abreast of all the publications there have been on the military history of the war. I am a member of the British Committee of Historians of the Second World War. I have read all the official histories, from the proof stage onwards in the case of those on the Sicilian and Italian campaigns. I have noticed one apparent error, from comparison with Professor Hinsley's Intelligence history: on page 155 I have antedated the sinking of that fatal ship the *Ankara* by some three weeks, from 18 January 1943 back to Christmas 1942. And yet I have a strong memory of Group Captain Mapplebeck's confidential whisper over Christmas dinner in Algiers; perhaps he did tell me she had been sunk but was wrong, and she had only been closely missed; and in the confusion of my return to Cairo I did not notice the genuine sinking. Otherwise I have not come across a mistake as to facts. When it comes to opinions the text gives what is, I hope, a consistent picture of what I thought at the time and I am content to let it stand.

D. H.

Foreword to the First Edition

by

FIELD MARSHAL THE EARL ALEXANDER OF TUNIS

K.G., P.C., G.C.B., O.M., G.C.M.G., C.S.I., D.S.O., M.C.

I AM glad that this book is now available to the public. When the author showed me the original manuscript of his war memoirs I read them with the greatest interest and advised him to have them published in book form. The author was on my staff during the North African and Italian Campaigns and tells his story of those stirring times with great lucidity and indeed humour.

Major David Hunt as he then was, joined my Staff as an Intelligence Officer in August 1942 when I took over command of the Middle East and he remained with me until the final surrender of the Axis Forces in May 1945.

Here I should like to pay a tribute to our military Intelligence Service of which Major Hunt was a valuable member. The fog of war is one of the greatest difficulties a commander in the field has to contend with. No successful plan of campaign can be made unless there is adequate information about the enemy's positions, strength, morale, likely reinforcements, reactions and so on.

To obtain this vital information is the task of the Intelligence Service. It is gained from a countless number of sources. The art is to make the right deductions and present them to the Commander in clear and logical form. From my own experience I could not have been better served in this respect, with the result that the so-called fog of war was seldom more than a mist.

After the end of the war when I was Governor General of Canada, I asked for David Hunt to come and help me in the preparation of my official War Despatches—which he did in a most capable manner.

There is no person I know of who has more knowledge of those days from August 1942 to the final victory in May 1945 as seen from the headquarters of a Commander-in-Chief in the field, than the author of this book.

I hope the general public will enjoy Sir David Hunt's memoirs as much as I have done.

Alexander of Tunis
f.m.

CHAPTER I

Oxford

"ARCHAEOLOGIST?" said the clerk. "That's the same as a marine biologist." I was trying to enlist. For the second time I had come up against the Schedule of Reserved Occupations and it began to look as though I should have to go somewhere else again.

I find it a little difficult at this distance of time to recapture precisely the reasons and the feelings which led me to the second floor of the Town Hall in Oxford. I begin to suspect, from the fact that I am conscious mainly of a blank in my introspection, that they were not particularly elaborate. In the first half of the 30's I was taught to consider war as the greatest of all evils, both to suffer and take part in, and in the second half I had observed for myself that it was evidently approaching. Some of those who had been my mentors in the earlier stages now began to give evidence of some doubt whether there might not be worse things than war. However, these two tendencies had left two impressions firmly rooted in my mind, and I suspect many other minds. On the one hand to join one of the services in peacetime could obviously not be contemplated except by someone cursed with inborn blood lust—it helped also, I believed, to be rather stupid. On the other hand all but the pacifist fringe acknowledged that there were circumstances in which it was excusable to spurn the more natural role of conscientious objector and to take part in a war. But for an educated and civilized person such a decision could only come as a climax to a long period of mental stress with a sudden violence of conviction similar to a religious conversion.

Peering backwards over the interval of 26 years I realise that I have lost touch, and perhaps even lost sympathy, with the person I then was; but I am sure that I was not experiencing any moral compulsion. I could no doubt have defined my position intellectually and would have been ready to do so at the drop of a hat. For that matter I was to a certain extent caught up in the consequences of an attitude which I had adopted and which I had gradually grown into over the last couple of years. Passions had run high in 1938, as high in the Senior Common

Room at Magdalen as in the House of Commons. It was a year which, for the first time, gave English people some idea of how it had felt to live in France at the time of the Dreyfus affair. When I was living in Ottawa on the staff of Lord Alexander, Lord Avon, then Mr. Anthony Eden, came to stay as a guest—this would be in late 1946. I remember the fierce expression he had when he spoke of the great schism in the Conservative Party that year. "There was far more bitterness and hatred," he said, "than I ever remember in politics. The feeling between us today and the Socialist Government is the warmest friendship compared with it." Dons, though less extroverted than politicians, delight to bark and bite. I had many times been reminded (the epigram I think comes from Cambridge) that no one is infallible, not even the youngest of us. When, a year later, the weight of the argument began to sink fairly heavily to one's own side, it would have seemed improper to decline into some civilian employment. However, I feel fairly sure that the main reason was that I did not think of anything else but enlisting. The same cogent reason I feel sure must have held chief place with 99 out of 100 other people.

When I had made up my mind by this simple but not particularly commendable process I began to notice that there was rather a difference from what I had been told about 1914. Nobody seemed particularly interested in my services. My first thought was of the Navy. For the last few years I had been amusing myself most summers by cruising in small boats and even had some idea of coastwise navigation. I soon discovered that I might as well have been trying to enter the Athenaeum at a month's notice. A distinguished naval officer did indeed visit Oxford and even dined at Magdalen but his interest in me was languid and the best he could do was to suggest I should come along in another six months. His view seemed to be that a few more ships had better be built first. And then, as he apologetically remarked, there was the complication of the Schedule of Reserved Occupations. I do not think I ever read this vital document in full though I had a good chance of studying chunks of it in my first two efforts at enlisting. One thing at any rate seemed certain: dons were well on it.

Oddly enough, the fact of my being a don had something to do with the war. My original idea, after taking Greats in 1936, was to enter the Home Civil Service; but I was suggestible, and when the Warden of Wadham, that great man, suggested that I might put in for a Fellowship of Magdalen one of the arguments that weighed most with me was that, since a disastrous war was certainly coming in two or three years' time, it would be much pleasanter to pass the intervening period in the Senior Common Room at Magdalen than in a Government office. There was an eighteenth-century Duke of Norfolk, in the days before Catholic Emancipation, whose private life was badly thought of even in those lenient days. "I know," he said, "that I cannot go to Heaven; and if a man is to go to the Devil he may as well go there from the House of Lords as from any place on earth." So he joined the Church of England and took the oaths and his seat. These were very much my sentiments too. A Fellowship at Magdalen would be a pleasant place to go to war from. Nor was I thinking only of the pleasures of High Table, the port after dinner and a fine set of rooms in the cloisters. As I intended to specialize in Greek archaeology I meant to use the endowments of Magdalen to finance my travels in Greece which both then and now I account the ideal place for travels. The dons of Magdalen were as good as Maurice Bowra's word and elected me in the summer of 1937. I had two fine trips to Greece travelling continuously with mule pack or by caique and the nearer the war approached the more I congratulated myself on having chosen a good method of awaiting it.

In those days archaeology was not so respectable, indeed popular, a pastime as it is today. The reason why, when faced with the Schedule of Reserved Occupations, I was insisting on my archaeological character was that I had read about demobilization at the end of the First World War. Assuming for the sake of the argument that I managed to survive this war I felt I should be keen to leave the Army as quickly as possible. Last time, so I had read, priority in release was determined by profession. I therefore thought it would be a good thing to be as accurate as possible at the outset, for I supposed that my record of enlistment would be magically preserved and play a key part in my last scene as in my first. I wonder now what happened to it; certainly the subject never came up when I eventually did leave the Army seven years and six months later.

On my first attempt I described myself as a Fellow of Magdalen College, Oxford. This led to my being rejected on the spot by a well-informed man in the Territorial Drill Hall. At my second shot I thought 'archaeologist' might be vague enough to get me in without difficulty, but potent enough to get me out as easily. It was certainly not on the list, but equally certainly, according to the clerk, it ought to have been. Too tired to argue any more I wrote myself down as 'scholar'. Five minutes later I was swearing allegiance to his Majesty King George VI, his Heirs and Successors, and pocketing four shillings.

CHAPTER II

Aldershot

MY O.C.T.U. was at Aldershot. I thought this a splendid idea. After all, if you had to join the Army it was surely best to go the whole hog and nothing could be more quintessentially Army than Aldershot. The actual experience was less agreeable, though not so bad as I had been given to believe. I was prepared for some very savage and uncontrollable sergeant-instructors but in fact they were a mild lot, easily placated with a few drinks for which a whole platoon would cheerfully subscribe. Most of them were reservists and I am not sure that they were really very well qualified. The officers, I found, were a superior lot. Prominent above all was the C.O., a Lieutenant Colonel Bingham of the Coldstream who presided over our fortunes with suavity and penetration. Not many months after I had passed out from under his charge to the accompaniment of some civil and well-turned remarks, he got into trouble by writing a letter to *The Times*. This was a technical offence. It was made much worse by what the letter said. Appearing at a moment of great national exaltation, in the crisis of the aerial attacks on Britain, when the ideal of national unity stood above every other consideration, this letter had the audacity to suggest that not every inhabitant of the country was a suitable person to be made into an officer. A properly scandalized public opinion saw that he was removed by the Secretary of State for War from the command of the 168th Officer Cadet Training Unit.

I think at that time there may have been a number of commanding officers who thought it their duty to demonstrate their democratic feelings by sending up for commissions people as far removed as possible from the normal run of pre-war officers. This may have been a spiteful reaction to what were alleged to be the extreme views of Mr. Hore Belisha, then Secretary of State for War. It may more likely perhaps be part of a phenomenon which I soon noticed in other connections as well; a certain lack of self-confidence among regular officers. They had been under attack so long from the intellectuals, with Low and his Colonel Blimp marching at their head, that some of them began to have doubts about their firmest opinions. Many times in the coming years I was surprised at the way in which regular officers whom I knew to have keen and acute brains would allow themselves to be put upon by bogus intellectuals. The waste of time, materials and manpower, for example on the excesses of psychological warfare, must have been obvious to many intelligent commanders, but the dread phantom of Colonel Blimp deterred them from doing anything about it. They knew they were supposed to be hidebound, conventional and set in their ways; it was less trouble in the long run to allow a little waste to take place rather than get themselves written down as unimaginative. A good deal of the proliferation of special forces, private armies, separate intelligence-gathering organizations, was due to the same fear. Senior regular officers of the Indian Army were among the keenest in this way. General Auchinleck, for instance, was determined to show himself as unconventional as possible.

Blenheim Barracks in the Marlborough Lines were rather short on comfort. I was told that they had been condemned as unfit for human habitation shortly before 1914 but had been reprieved by the First World War. I suspect that this is an old army joke but, unlike most army jokes, it was perfectly plausible. However, a fair amount of discomfort was all part of the general background of every one of us and it was certainly recompensed by some extremely pleasant company. I think we must have been a rather exceptional barrack room. The man in the next bed to me was already known as a dress designer, but with nothing of the fame which now surrounds the name of Hardy Amies. He dispelled a cheerful, even cosy, atmosphere over what was rather a strenuous course. Without being exemplary he was so competent a cadet that all I remember, apart from various convivial evenings, is a weakness of memory when it came to the barren but frequently repeated exercise called 'Naming the parts of a Bren gun.' For some time I remembered the unofficial and coarser names but even those have now disappeared, leaving as a sole relic of what was once an encyclopaedic knowledge the words 'barrel locking nut'.

One bed further along was occupied by the present Member of Parliament for Wolverhampton South-West, then Professor Enoch Powell, late of the University of Sydney. He was reserved, taciturn and generally believed in the platoon to be modelling himself on the Prussian Great General Staff. This belief was reinforced by his practice of reading Clausewitz's *Vom Kriege* in the original German before lights out. Our days were so full that he could never have had more than 10 minutes per night for these studies. It is not a short book; his knowledge of German, though sound, was not fluent; I doubt if he found our four months' course long enough.

January 1940 had a record for cold, snow and general beastliness that stood unrivalled until the great freeze-up of February 1947. It was a harsh introduction to the facts of Army life after the cushioned Victorian ease of Magdalen. It also brought my first acquaintance with regular Army doctoring. One of my platoon, whose bed was in the same barrack room, complained one morning of feeling ill. He was allowed to miss the morning parade and stayed in bed. At 11 o'clock or so the M.O. was actually called to his bedside. This, I was carefully told, was an exceptional privilege and he should have got up and gone to the M.O. himself. Indulgence was carried so far that the M.O. at parting said that he should stay in bed all day and only get up the next morning if he felt better. Instead of being properly impressed by this the patient looked gloomier than ever, but the doctor's parting words were "Cheer up, you won't die of it". Six hours later, as a matter of fact, he was dead. It is interesting that whenever I have told this story later in Army circles it has been received with bursts of laughter but in civilian circles it apparently passes as less funny.

By the time my course closed events in Europe were taking on a more stirring air. We were all given what were known as emergency commissions and the greater and more obvious the emergency the less self-conscious we felt about dressing up as officers. One of my fellows in the same course took me to his tailor in Savile Row for my first officer's uniform and my first Savile Row suit. Eleven months later it sank in six fathoms of water in the Aegean and my next and only other full 'service dress' uniform bore the less patrician name of Ali Baksh. At this stage my past began to catch up with me again. Ever since I joined the Army I had been conscious of a watchful eye being kept on me by Stanley Casson, sometime Reader in Classical Archaeology, who blossomed at the outbreak of war into a Lieutenant Colonel in the South Lancashire Regiment in which he had distinguished himself in the First War on the Macedonian front. I had been Casson's pupil, and later examined by him, for the diploma in archaeology. He was aware of my thorough acquaintance with Greece and with the modern Greek language. I had owned to this knowledge, and of various other languages, on enlisting. I was therefore not surprised to be summoned to the War Office as soon as I got my commission. I was told that there was a possibility that a military mission of some sort might be required in Greece and that I should spend some time studying the papers in the Military Intelligence Branch on Greece, Jugoslavia and on the Italian Army.

The War Office was an agitated place in those days with people dropping in from Dunkirk or other odd spots on the French coast. For a few days I was in rather a backwater, reading long but not very valuable reports by military attachés. Suddenly on the 4th June my existence appeared to be remembered. I was hastily summoned and told that it now seemed certain that Italy would enter the war very soon and that if I was to go to the Middle East I had better go now. I was introduced to three other second lieutenants who were to go with me, two of whom spoke Greek and the other Serbo-Croat. The Serbo-Croat speaker, who had been a merchant in Zagreb, had a civilian jacket with him and we all borrowed it in turn to have our photographs taken for new passports, for as Greece was still neutral we had to travel as civilians. I was described on my passport, pro-phetically, as a civil servant. The same night we were put on the train for Poole and next morning took off in a flying boat. It was my last sight of England for over four years and this was the last civilian flying boat to do the trip.

We had to take a devious route. The Germans had already overrun northern France as far as the line of the Somme and it was impossible to say how soon Italy would enter the war. We flew therefore first to Arcachon, south of Bordeaux, where the oysters come from. Here we refuelled. We intended to spend the night at Marseilles; but an air raid had caused such disorganization that we went on instead to Ajaccio in Corsica. So far it might have been a Mediterranean cruise. From Ajaccio next morning we flew down the Sardinian coast to Bizerta and then to Malta for a night; next day to Corfu and Athens. It was a pleasure to see Athens again and the Greeks were as friendly as ever in spite of the badness of the news from France. In general the Greeks are not fair-weather friends. They like to be on the winning side but they will cling obstinately to the losing side if honour or friendship require it. However it quickly appeared that there was no employment for us to be found in Athens as yet and so we were sent on next day via Suda Bay in Crete to Alexandria. It was a delightful journey and I retraced almost all the steps at some time or another in the next four or five years.

CHAPTER III

Alexandria to Athens

Two days after my arrival the Italians declared war. For some reason the date, 10th June, has always stuck in my mind, and I think the same is true of many others who were in the Middle East at that time, as a more significant date than 3rd September. Nothing much happened on 3rd September or for many months after; but from 10th June there were constant active operations. Sir Archibald Wavell, Commander in Chief in the Middle East, had no intention of allowing a period of 'phoney war'. He might have been excused from coming to a different conclusion since his forces were so immensely outnumbered that a gallant defensive seemed his only possible strategy. No doubt it was for that very reason that he decided that it was necessary to take the offensive. On the morning of the 11th June the 11th Hussars, his only armoured car regiment, broke through the long barbed wire barrier on the Libyan frontier in the first of many raids into enemy territory. Simultaneously the R.A.F. made an attack on the aerodrome of El Adem, to the south of Tobruk. It was very successful. The entire garrison had been paraded early, to take advantage of the freshness of the morning, and were listening to a harangue from their commanding general. They were lined up remarkably neatly and provided an admirable target. A few days later the 11th Hussars sent a patrol onto the road between Bardia and Tobruk, the two principal towns of Eastern Cyrenaica, and picked up a prisoner, General Lastrucci, Chief Engineer of the 10th Army. He was accompanied by a woman who was not his wife and who gave birth to a baby in the forward casualty clearing station. The comments of the troops can be imagined but were unjustified; she was merely an acquaintance whom he was taking to hospital in Tobruk.

It sometimes seemed as though the Italians in Libya never wholly recovered from the shock of the first day. This would be going too far; they were confident, in fact, as they should have been, in their great superiority in numbers and in armament; but they did take it rather amiss that we should have been willing to make a fight of it. Their view was that the war, to all intents and purposes, was over. Having come in at just the right time there would be a few more formalities to comply with before they could settle down and enjoy the fruits of victory. They considered therefore that it was rather in bad taste for us to spoil this agreeable picture.

Some three and a half years later I arrived in Italy, having had the pleasure of playing a small part in the negotiation of the Italian Armistice. Like all other members of the Allied Forces I was deafened by a continuous murmur of Italians assuring me that no-one in Italy had ever wanted to take part in the war, at any rate not on the German side. The thesis found wide favour among the Allied troops. The English have always had a tradition of friendship with Italy, and there are large numbers of people of Italian origin in America. It is now almost canonical. I share the general English affection for Italy, but I have never believed this story. I believe, on the contrary, that the war of 1940 was the most popular war the Italians were ever engaged in. The average man was convinced that the war was won already; and even the anti-fascists had a strong suspicion that the Duce was going to pull it off again. Like the German generals at Munich, the anti-fascists thought that their calculations were being once more overthrown by the errors of the British and French. Naturally it is almost impossible to prove this. The press and radio admittedly spoke with one voice of exuberant rejoicing but it could be argued that this did not represent the true feeling of the country as a whole. I base myself mainly on prisoners' letters and on the attitude in particular of officer prisoners whom I met in Greece shortly after. For the first five months of the war at least, all the prisoners we and the Greeks took spoke with great confidence of a successful outcome and boasted of the future greatness of Italy, victorious at the side of Germany.

At any rate for the moment it looked as though in Africa the Italians were on to a good thing. In East Africa they had something around 300,000 troops, well provided with reserves of equipment and munitions. In Libya there were two Armies, the 5th and 10th, composed of between fourteen and fifteen divisions. Their strength was usually calculated at about 300,000. They were excellently, even luxuriously, equipped and supported by a large and apparently formidable air force. At this time the forces available under General Wavell amounted to some 36,000.

With the entry of Italy and the departure of France from the ranks of the belligerents, the likelihood of a British Military Mission being welcome in Greece receded. I was accordingly put at the disposal of the nearest British unit which happened to be the First Battalion of the Welch Regiment in Mustapha Pasha Barracks. I regarded this step at first with some bashfulness but I never regretted it. The Welch were immensely friendly, extremely professional and abounding with confidence. It was a regular battalion and there were not more than four or five non-regular officers. They had gone out to Palestine in 1938 to protect the Jews against the Arab rising and had stayed there ever since. Since this was a peacetime move they had with them all the regimental plate, a full band and of course a male voice Welsh choir. We were one of the only two battalions available for the defence of Alexandria and we took it reasonably seriously to the extent of providing anti-parachutist pickets at appropriate places, but otherwise we lived a fairly peacetime and regular existence. Every Sunday the officers gave a cocktail party lasting from 12 to 3 (champagne cocktails only) to the youth and beauty of Alexandria. At 3 o'clock, incidentally, we all sat down to roast beef and Yorkshire pudding, although the temperature was fairly steady in the 90's.

It was rather a strange feeling in those summer days of 1940 being locked away at the end of the Mediterranean while such stirring events were going on at home. In some ways it was odder still to be in Alexandria with all the pleasures of a great and beautiful city. It is too late now to try to draw a picture of Alexandria in its great days. It has been done for all time by E. M. Forster, by Cavafy and lately by Laurence Durrell. It still retained then its largely Greek character. It was still a great city of world trade and world civilization. The presence in the harbour of the Mediterranean Fleet added to its animation —particularly at night when a few rather half-hearted Italian planes would come over to be received by a most spectacular fireworks display from the Fleet. By day it seemed to be more given to pleasure than to work. I cannot claim to have made much acquaintance with its curious and cosmopolitan population, though I remember a Jewish baron who had a unique collection of coloured diamonds and also played the recorder. I spent a few weeks on loan to the Area H.Q. which lived in the middle of the city in an old fort on the top of the artificial mound of Kom el Dik which is supposed to hide the burial place of Alexander. It all felt rather like being in a beleaguered garrison and one result was that there was a feeling of belonging together. Everybody knew everybody else.

At the time when the Italians declared war the Commander-in-

Chief and Governor of Libya was Italo Balbo. He is probably still remembered for his square beard and for having led a formation flight across the Atlantic in the thirties. In the usual way of rumour he was supposed to be at enmity with Mussolini; the rumour mongers scarcely explained why in that case he should have been given the most important military command. It suited Balbo in his talks with Italian journalists to represent himself as having a difficult and almost impossible task because of the Duce's jealousy. Speaking to a friendly journalist shortly before the declaration of war, Balbo declared that for a satisfactory defensive he required three times as many troops as he had at the moment, leaving it to be imagined what he would require to take the offensive. As he must have been fairly well aware that as things stood he already enjoyed a superiority of 10 to 1 over his British opponents, this judgment must be taken as another example of that engaging sense of realism which was characteristic of Italian senior officers when considering the troops under their command. Balbo did not long survive this pessimistic appreciation. He paid a visit to Tobruk by air when a British air raid had just ended and his aircraft was cheerfully shot down by the trigger-happy gunners of the cruiser *San Giorgio*. This was, symbolically, the first success for the gunners of this antiquated cruiser since it shelled the refugees in the old castle at Corfu in 1922.

A successor was immediately forthcoming. It was Marshal Rodolfo Graziani, Lion of the Desert and Marquis of Neghelli, known to the Arabs as El Jazar, or the Butcher. He had been Governor of Libya in the late twenties and during his period of office the Arab population of Cyrenaica was reduced by over 60 per cent. He had also been Viceroy of Abyssinia, in which post he had done his best to live up to this record. His marquisate was the reward for his having commanded the Southern Column in the invasion of Abyssinia in 1935–36. His advance on the southern front was given in Fascist historiography the title of 'The March of the Iron Will' (La Marcia della Ferrea Volunta). Abyssinian opposition, which was never of a very serious character, was almost lacking on the southern front; it is significant that the South African column which covered the same distance in 1941 did it in less than a third of the time against the opposition of a European and better equipped army.

Graziani too, to judge by his subsequent apologia, made the same difficulties as Balbo about taking the offensive. He was overruled by Mussolini, who was well aware of Graziani's great numerical advantages.

It was the general belief in Rome and Berlin that the autumn at least would see the end of the war and Italy was determined to have some of the gains in hand by that time. The 15th September, a popular date for the invasion of Britain, was accordingly laid down as the date on which the advance into Egypt should commence. It was not possible to start at once. The Western Desert Command, having seized the initiative, was creating a very untidy situation among the Italian forward positions. In particular a surprise *coup de main* by an armoured car regiment, two companies of infantry and two troops of guns had captured Fort Capuzzo. This was a romantic-looking but militarily rather pointless construction a little way west of the Sollum–Bardia road and controlled a network of tracks on the Italian side of the wire. It required a set-piece attack on the Italians' part to recapture the position. However, the Italian divisions were gradually being brought forward more and more until there was, practically speaking, standing room only on their side of the frontier. Accordingly, on the 15th September, the 10th Army at last lurched over the frontier.

The British plan was now to revert to the original strategy and fall back gradually on Mersa Matruh where a strong position had been dug. This withdrawal was expected to be a fairly ticklish job since the axis of the Italian advance was split in two by the line of the Great Libyan Escarpment. The word 'escarpment' brings back with particular force a flood of memories of the Western Desert. I first set eyes on it a year after the events now described but it made an impression as great as Victoria Falls or the Acropolis. Some people have objected to the very use of the word. Mr. Ivor Brown, in one of his valuable books on English words, takes it to be a mere military fad. He supposes it to mean nothing more than a high ridge. Even Sir Winston Churchill, in his Second Volume, speaks of our troops on the coast being separated from those further inland by 'a high ridge which was crossed only by the one pass of Halfaya.' Setting aside the fact that it is only reasonable for military spokesmen to use a military word, I must protest that there is all the difference in the world between a high ridge and an escarpment, above all the Great Libyan Escarpment. A high ridge, I submit, suggests something like the Hog's Back; but for a parallel to the Escarpment at Sollum you must think of Beachy Head. The Escarpment was in fact a steep, precipitous cliff on land. Halfaya is not a pass like the Brenner or the Khyber; it is a place where a steep spur slopes down to the coastal plain looking like a ladder placed against a wall, up which a track zigzags to the top. (There is a second

Halfaya some 30 miles further east at a place called Halfway-House).
To see the Escarpment at dawn or at sunset when the air was clear and
cool enough and the low sun cast an oblique shadow was to see one of
the great works of nature. It sharply divided, by a sheer plunge of some
300 feet, the coastal plain at its foot, sandy, and near the sea marshy,
from the plain which ran back level with its crest, bare limestone
covered with gravel and a thin crust of sand, tilting away southwards
to Jarabub and the Sand Sea.

It was natural to suppose that the Italians would attack simultaneously
at both levels and accordingly there was on the coastal plain the 22nd
Guards Brigade with some artillery and on the top of the Escarpment
the 7th Armoured Division. General Maletti, who commanded the
group of two Libyan divisions, had proposed to Graziani that he should
with his forces carry out a wide outflanking movement. This would
have given us something to think about. However, in the event
Graziani decided that this was too complicated a way of doing things
and the whole force was ordered to advance along the coastal plain.
It amounted to something over five divisions, including a special
armoured force commanded by Maletti. There were the two Libyan
divisions, the 63rd Cirene Division and the two Blackshirt Divisions
known as the 23rd of March and the 28th of October. Having arrived
at Sidi Barrani they went immediately on to the defensive. We were
expecting them to push on to Matruh and had to make a fresh
appreciation.

While this was going on I was living the life of a regular subaltern
in barracks in Alexandria. Thoughts of revisiting Greece had faded,
though a hint of what might be coming was given when an Italian
submarine torpedoed a Greek cruiser off the port of Tinos on August
14th. In spite of the fact that the two countries were still at peace this
passed off remarkably quietly. No one could be blamed for not
knowing that the Italians intended an invasion of Greece since they were
careful to keep it concealed even from their allies the Germans.
However, very shortly after the Italian invasion of Greece, which
began on 28th October 1940, I discovered that someone in Cairo had,
after all, an efficient card index system. I was hastily summoned and
informed that a British Force was being sent to the assistance of the
Greeks and that I would be seconded from the Welch and attached to
this in the capacity of an intelligence officer. For this purpose I was
at once promoted captain. The code word for the move was Barbarity.
I was told that I was to have under my command a remarkably mixed

collection including some cipher operators and an entire field security section, the latter commanded by Mr. Geoffrey Household whose memoirs are as good as his novels.

Barbarity Force sailed from Alexandria. It spent a couple of days first of all in the harbour there, during which time it was bombed with rather more pertinacity than the Italians had recently shown, though without much success. My part of the force was on a Dutch ship belonging to the Royal Mail and called the *Nieuw Zeeland*. My admiration for the Dutch was increased by the result of a clash between the captain and the G.H.Q. orders for the troops on board. The theory of Cairo was that we should take with us hard rations, i.e. bully beef and biscuits, on which we should feed for the duration of the trip, drawing from the ship only hot water to make tea. The captain and the purser, when informed of this, expressed horror and said they could not agree to such a thing on one of the ships of the Royal Mail Line. They would feed all on board from their own stores and trust to be repaid in due course. As a result all the way across we fed on rijstafel and other Javanese delicacies, served in great comfort by polite and efficient Indonesian stewards. It was a delightful trip with no sign of any enemy and we arrived well fed and contented in Athens.

As we tied up on 22nd November someone shouted from the quay below that the Greeks had captured Koritsa. There had indeed been stirring doings on the borders of Albania and Epirus. The principal motive behind Mussolini's invasion of Greece was the desire to score some success off his own bat. He had been enraged by the fact that the Germans had sent troops into Rumania on 21st October without giving him any warning although he always regarded Rumania as within the Italian sphere of interest in the Balkans; now, as he told Ciano, he wanted it to be Hitler and not himself who had to read in the papers of some fresh move by the Axis. The enterprise did not strike him as likely to be arduous but, partly for form's sake, a council of war was held beforehand on 15th October 1940. The minutes of this meeting fell into our hands together with a mass of Mussolini's more private papers in 1945. Marshal Badoglio was among those present and his advice was characterized by the same pessimism, or perhaps sense of realism, which I have already noted in Balbo. He took the line that for a successful invasion of Greece there would have to be concentrated in Albania at least sixteen divisions; lest he should seem to be treating the subject too lightly he added hastily that this was on the hypothesis that the Bulgars should also simultaneously declare war and employ eight divisions against the Greeks. As the Greeks had at the moment under four divisions mobilized in the whole country, of which only two were on the Albanian border, this might be considered as showing either undue caution or an unduly low opinion of the value of Italian troops. Certainly Badoglio had a name for caution but otherwise the odds, reckoned in men and materials, seemed fair enough. Mussolini said he would 'resign from being an Italian' if anyone made any difficulties about fighting the Greeks. As far as material went, the Italians were well supplied, with a particularly lavish equipment of light automatic weapons. The Greek equipment was a mixture. The basis was material from the First World War supplemented with artillery and machine guns taken over as war booty from the Austrians. Much of the regimental transport, horse-drawn of course, consisted of carts captured from the Bulgarians in 1912, in the second Balkan war. They had an air force of sorts but it was equipped mainly with obsolete French and Polish types. Their only real strength lay in the great powers of resistance of the ordinary infantryman who would fight on one loaf of bread and a handful of olives a day. To this they added the advantage that they both disliked and despised the 'Macaronades'. Greeks are a mercurial race and when their spirits are up they are most formidable in battle.

The Italian attack started with the advantage not only of numbers but also of surprise. The decision to invade Greece was taken with such speed that the Italian Ambassador who delivered the ultimatum to the Greek Prime Minister at two o'clock in the morning of the 28th October was not fully briefed as to the meaning of the document which he was handing over. It was not intended to be accepted; Ciano described it as offering only two choices: either accept complete military occupation or be attacked. A bloodless victory would not have suited Mussolini. The attack which took place almost simultaneously was aimed at the centre and western end of the Albanian–Greek border. It was headed by the 131st Armoured Division, called Centauro, a source of endless proud allusions, after its defeat, to the fate of the original centaurs. It gained a great deal of ground but by the end of the first week in November it had been brought to a standstill short of the plains of Thessaly and the Greek counter-offensive was taking shape. General Papagos had concentrated his strength on his right and was prepared to allow his left to be pushed back down the spine of the broken Pindus Mountains. He now advanced on his right and in a short but violent fight captured the frontier town of Koritsa, opening the Italian left flank to a deadly encircling movement. As with most descriptions of strategy it sounds a simple enough manoeuvre; indeed Napoleon said that to know what to do in war was simple, the skill came in the doing of it. Certainly Papagos' strategy must have involved very great efforts by his administrative services and called for great enthusiasm and dash on the tactical level. It had a most decisive effect. The Italians had to withdraw their right, losing heavily in the process, and were manoeuvred out of one position after another from the north to the south of their lines.

For the moment there was only a hint of this great strategic feat. It was permissible to suppose that Koritsa was an isolated flash in the pan. Meanwhile the main British contribution was to be in the air. We were short enough in the Middle East but on the Greek request it was found possible to spare two squadrons of fighters, two of medium bombers and half a squadron of heavy bombers to operate when the moon was right. The bombers were Blenheims and Wellingtons, the fighters Gladiators. At that time all our fighter squadrons in the Middle East were armed with Gladiators, the last biplane flown by the R.A.F. It had even then a faintly archaic look, but sturdy and friendly. It was not hopelessly outclassed since a good many of the Italian fighter squadrons at the time were equipped with the CR42, also a biplane. To watch a dog-fight between these two types was like something from a film of World War I. Things took place at a reasonably low level, there was a good deal of circling and aerobatics and the two sides were easy to make out because our planes had two wings the same length and the Italians had a lower wing shorter than the upper. The Supreme Command of all British troops in Greece was exercised by Air Marshal D'Albiac. Besides his R.A.F. squadrons he also had some army units, mainly Sappers, for airfield construction and service troops for dock working and supply duties. He had as his senior Intelligence Officer Wing Commander Lord Forbes (now the Earl of Granard) who had been Air Attaché in Bucharest.

This was my first introduction to Intelligence work. It was a special sort, being concerned only with the air forces, our own and the enemy. There was also a Military Mission to Greece which arrived about three weeks later. It was headed originally by General Gambier-Parry, who was next year taken prisoner in the desert when he surrendered Mechili to General Zaglio of the Pavia Division, and subsequently by General Heyworth. The Chief Intelligence Officer was my old friend and military patron, Stanley Casson. He had a bright collection of Greek-speaking young officers under him. John May, with whom I came out to the Middle East, was one, and another was Monty Woodhouse, later well known as head of the British liaison officers in Greece during the German occupation. It was the job of these people to follow the picture of the enemy dispositions and intentions on the ground and for this they were provided with a liaison officer to Greek G.H.Q. in the form of Prince Peter of Greece. This famous traveller, one of the greatest experts on Central Asia, was then serving as a captain in the Greek Army. When the mission arrived there was a certain struggle for my body; Casson assumed I should at once come on his staff but the R.A.F. stuck out for my services and were finally successful. It suited me very well to be the only Army officer on the operations staff of Air Force Headquarters. Lord Forbes also, who was a bright and tenacious officer, and not unaware of the advantages of Empire-building, wanted to have his own liaison with the Greek G.H.Q. I was well adapted for this as my Greek was still very fluent; I was accordingly given the entrée to the big Operations Room—in better times the ballroom of the Grande Bretagne Hotel—and called daily on Colonel Hadjidakis, a cheerful and competent Cretan. After which I would pop upstairs to call on Prince Peter and my friends of the Mission.

There was plenty of encouraging news after the fall of Koritsa. Papagos' strategy continued to produce results. At the beginning of December he extended still further his outflanking of the Italian left, up the shore of Lake Ochrida, and on the 4th captured Pogradec, at the head of the lake. At this point General Soddu, the Italian C.-in-C. in Albania, who spent his evenings composing light music for the films, telegraphed that further military action was impossible and a political solution was necessary. Mussolini was temporarily crushed by this message and contemplated asking Hitler to intervene with the Greeks to grant him an armistice. This was much too drastic; however severe the Italian defeats the mere topography of Albania precludes any rapid collapse. The Greeks could only advance at a foot pace, even if unopposed. Nevertheless they were able to make some gratifying gains of territory, now on the west of the front. Himarra, Agioi Saranta, Argyrokastro were names which meant much to the Greeks. Agioi Saranta, or Santi Quaranta, called after the famous forty martyrs, a small port opposite Corfu, was a name which meant a lot to the Italians as well, because it had been renamed Porto Edda, after Mussolini's daughter, Ciano's wife. The Greeks are pious Christians one and all and prophesied no good to the house of Mussolini when the

Forty Saints were dishonoured in favour of a pagan name chosen by her atheist father from Ibsen.

This part of Albania had a strong Greek minority and had played a notable part in the Greek movement of independence in the early nineteenth century. To the Greek Government it was the *irredenta* North Epirus and there was a sanguine hope of annexing it after the war; militarily the first important objective was the port of Valona (Avlon in Greek) which was the principal Italian supply base for the southern and central parts of the front. My pre-war memories of Valona were mainly gastronomic, stressing a magnificent *fritto misto* of small fish which the crew of the boat hauled aboard in huge numbers for the mere trouble of dropping in an unbaited hook. I was now studying it in a vertical view on a splendid series of stereographic photographs, for Valona was the main target of our two squadrons of Blenheims. In those days we thought it a significant operation of war when six of these obsolescent machines hauled a pitifully small load of bombs over the jagged mountains of the Pindus and Acroceraunia to cast them on the primitive installations of Valona. Not much damage was done, but it was good for morale.

Quite early after my arrival I was approached by a middle-aged Greek who offered his services as a secret agent. He proudly claimed to have been employed in that same capacity over twenty years before by Sir Compton Mackenzie. I had naturally read Sir Compton's lively and engaging stories—which were also, I discovered later, great favourites with the German Intelligence authorities, much to their disadvantage—but my present situation seemed to me quite different from his and I declined the offer politely. Stanley Casson was more downright, having been himself in Greece at the same time, and gave me good advice to lend no credence to agents. 'Stick to prisoners' was his advice and I never regretted taking it.

The Greeks never got Valona, in spite of most gallant efforts. One of the greatest feats of arms in this war was the capture of Kleisura, in the depth of winter. It was the Cretan Division who led the attack, and they were badly missed next spring in their own island. Kleisura is, as its name indicates, a castle on a crag dominating a defile in the valley of the Shkumbi leading to Valona. From the point of physical difficulty it was probably worse than either Keren or Cassino, with the added difficulty of heavy and continuous snowstorms. The Greek troops suffered severely from frostbite. Their communications were much more difficult than the Italians', who had excellent roads in their rear leading to their main bases at only a very short distance. The Greeks had much greater distances to contend with and their services and the roads they had to use were much inferior. Even where they could use the good Italian-made roads in occupied Albania they were so short of motor transport that they were little better off. One advantage they had was that their troops were used to living on very little. This argument won't apply to guns, and often the artillery preparation for an attack was little more than a token because of the shortage of ammunition.

For all this the spirit of the Greeks everywhere was inspiring. Even though they had been for four years under the authoritarian rule of General Metaxas, a rule which caused the deepest dissensions, there was no sign of opposition except from the hidden communists, whose inspiration came from the Nazi–Soviet alliance. Indeed when Metaxas died suddenly in February his funeral was the occasion of a remarkable demonstration of national unity. It was a military funeral, passing through the centre of Athens, and as I watched it the impression grew on me that it was also the burial of our luck in Greece. The signs of the coming German intervention were increasing. It had been decided that British troops from Libya, calling off their triumphant westward advance, should come to the aid of our Greek allies. There was a fatality about the western border of Cyrenaica, so it seemed to the troops in the desert; twice when we had successfully reached it our strength had to be diverted, first to Greece and next year to the Far East. It was the sadder in that in each case the reinforcements which it cost the desert army so much to give up went straight to a heavy defeat, and their absence ensured the defeat of those they left behind. The likelihood was certainly well in many people's minds in the early months of 1941. We were sending more squadrons of the R.A.F. and, of the Army, an Australian and a New Zealand Division and an Armoured Division from the United Kingdom. Would they suffice and, if not, would they all be lost? In spite of this, most people thought it right. A war cannot be won by refusing to fight if you look like losing; certainly Wavell in 1940 had taken the opposite view and had won a great victory as a result. Besides, the Greeks would certainly fight the Germans whether we came or not; it would look bad to let them do it alone. It would be too reminiscent of the Poles. So in general the decision was approved though there must have been many who waited for the battle, like the French officers at Waterloo, 'without fear and without hope'.

CHAPTER IV

Athens to Alexandria via Crete

THROUGHOUT the pleasant and triumphant winter there was the feeling of what would happen when the Germans came to the rescue of the Italians. It seemed certain that they must do so in the Spring. During February and March I was able to follow the move forward of German divisions into Rumania and Bulgaria. To some extent it was an intellectual pastime, for we were well informed about the enemy progress and also about the carrying capacity of Balkan roads and railways so that a calculation of the time at which the Germans would be deployed in force behind the Bulgarian–Greek border was not difficult to make and if I remember ours came out fairly accurately. There was also the interest of conjecturing the likely attitude of the Jugoslavs. To begin with it seemed that they were completely cowed. They rejoiced in the reverses suffered by the Italians at the hands of the Greeks but the Crown Prince and his Prime Minister Stojadinovic had been too thoroughly indoctrinated in the belief of German greatness to allow them to do anything but repress the natural feelings of the people. The last bit of good news that Spring came when the movement led by General Simovic at the end of March overthrew the government and proclaimed the young King Peter. A month earlier it would have been valuable. By then it was too late, for the Germans were in position. Hitler's reaction to the Jugoslav coup d'état demonstrated what a thorough Austrian he was. His inherited hatred for the Serbs led him to take far more violent steps than were strictly necessary, disrupting more than he need have done the preparations for the invasion of Russia.

It was on the 6th April that the attack began on Greece and Jugoslavia simultaneously. The Bulgars joined in attacking the former and the Hungarians came in against the Jugoslavs with whom they had six weeks previously signed a treaty pompously described as 'of eternal amity'. The Hungarian Prime Minister Count Teleki, finding this action dishonourable, committed suicide; but the same scruples were not widely felt and the Hungarians were content to annex part of Jugoslavia as spoils of a war to which their contribution had not been marked. In Macedonia the Germans led the way, the Bulgars were to follow. The western part of the Greek–Bulgarian frontier was protected by a fortified line called the Metaxas Line. This resisted well and no progress was made. But when I went on the 7th to G.H.Q., Colonel Hajidakis was gloomy. 'The Serbs have played us a fine trick.' The main German effort had in fact been switched into a due westerly direction along the Strumitsa over the Jugoslav border. Caught half mobilized, the Jugoslavs were unable to make any serious resistance. Once into Jugoslav Macedonia the Germans were free to turn south through the famous Monastir Gap and come in behind the flank of the Metaxas Line. That manoeuvre sealed in effect the fate of mainland Greece. The Greek armies were split and the British forces which were to plug the gap were not strong enough to hold so extensive a front. The rest of the campaign down to Corinth mainly consisted of the Germans coming round our left flank and forcing one retreat after another.

One of my last acts before leaving Athens was inspired by memories of what had happened after the surrender of France. A fair number of German pilots and other aircrew had been shot down during the campaign, almost entirely by the R.A.F., and were in a prison camp very close to Athens. I had interrogated a number of them in the course of my normal duties. It seemed likely that the Greek Government, if not the present one then at least its successor, might find it useful, for the sake of getting better terms, to hand these prisoners back and put the R.A.F. under the tedious necessity of having to shoot them down all over again. I accordingly got hold of a number of lorries from the nearest R.A.S.C. depot and picked up a platoon of Australians who had turned up in Athens claiming to have lost all touch with their unit. With these I drove to the cage and went in to see the commandant. He knew quite well what my motives were and though he felt sure he would get into trouble for it, he readily agreed. The German airmen, who were confidently expecting that their captivity would soon be over, were very upset at being moved out at short notice. I had them loaded on to the trucks, handed them over to the Australian subaltern and told him to take them to Piraeus and put them on a ship that was sailing in a few hours' time for Egypt. Later that afternoon, but after the ship had sailed, the inevitable row began; someone in a senior position in the Greek services was demanding the prisoners back. I never heard the final stages because I took

31

care to keep out of the way, but there was enough inertia and down-right sympathy with our action at lower levels in the Greek services to make sure that nothing serious was done.

Later that evening the staff of R.A.F. Headquarters assembled in the courtyard of the H.Q. building. I had, as I supposed, fixed myself up rather well as a passenger in a comfortable car driven by T. H. Wisdom the racing driver. I had thoughtfully contributed a bottle of whiskey to the commissariat. The orders were to drive to Nauplia on the west coast of the Peloponnese, which was the main port for embarkation. Five minutes before we were due to leave, however, I was hailed from a window above me by Arthur Forbes, who enquired whether I would prefer to do the trip by air. The Greek Air Force had eleven Ansons from a naval reconnaisance squadron which they were proposing to fly to Egypt, but they had only ten pilots. The suggestion was that Forbes should fly and I would go along to man the single machine gun with which these slow and antiquated machines were equipped. As a matter of fact I would much rather have gone by sea but I could not think of a way of putting this delicately. I accordingly accepted and Wisdom drove off on what turned out to be a fairly uneventful journey.

The Ansons were at an aerodrome near Athens and the idea was to take off at first light or rather earlier in order to be under way before the usual German fighter patrol turned up. After a reasonably peaceful night we turned up at the appointed time with the usual pre-dawn qualms. The ten Greek pilots proposed to take off first so we had to wait. The tenth had just gone and we were about to taxi off when the siren went. For some reason the Germans were early. We would have had little chance either of escaping notice or avoiding being shot down so we tumbled out of the plane and into a slit trench close beside it. It was the deepest slit trench I have ever been in in the whole course of the war, being a good six foot deep in hard soil. This turned out to be a good thing. The six Messerschmitt 109 fighters lost no time in shooting up our Anson which roared and crackled some 20 yards away from us, but they also, and this I thought mere spite at the lack of suitable targets, machine gunned our slit trench. After they had gone away, fortunately without shooting up the car we came in, we took breakfast with the aerodrome commander and considered the next move. Fortunately Lord Forbes, who had retained his diplomatic connections, was aware that the Legation had been provided with a steam yacht which was sailing that evening; and he had been promised a berth if all else failed. We therefore returned to his flat and spent a peaceful day before going down to the Piraeus. As we were leaving, a number of Greeks, who were obviously aware of the fact that we were about to try to leave the country, came up and shook us warmly by the hand wishing us a good voyage and commiserating on the ill-fortune of the Allied arms. After we drove off I found a piece of paper in the car with the following message: 'Great Britain forever victorious! We are all with you, the whole nation, and we are waiting and looking forward to your coming back and setting us free.' I found this rather affecting and indeed magnanimous, especially as we were, after all, running away and abandoning the Greeks to their fate. It was a typical attitude and I found it even more marked in Crete.

The *Calanthe* was a steam yacht owned, I think, by a British subject living in Greece, which had been taken over by the Greek Navy as a fleet auxiliary. It had now been lent to the British Legation and was commanded by Captain Glass, the Naval Attaché. There was a distinguished company on board including the late Permanent Secretary for Foreign Affairs, Lord Caccia and his wife; Sir Charles Mott-Radclyffe, M.P. for Windsor, and a number of Greeks. The plan was to sail only by night and to lie up by day in as out of the way a place as possible. We waited therefore for sunset to go on board. 23rd April is St. George's Day in the Orthodox as well as the western calendar and, it being the King's name day, all the churches and public buildings were flagged. Athens and the Piraeus looked therefore almost gay as we prepared to leave. As the sun set behind Salamis the *Calanthe*, darkened all over, steamed out into the Saronic Gulf.

It was a warm night, there was no room below and I spent the night in a chair on deck. Next morning at first light *Calanthe* slid into a convenient bay in the small and uninhabited island of Polygos. The name is strictly speaking Polyaigos, meaning 'many goats', and on some charts it is called Polinos, but in spite of these numerous names I have never been able to find any reference to it by any writer ancient, mediaeval or modern. It is separated by a fairly narrow strait from the island of Kimolos which is larger and inhabited and is referred to once in antiquity in connection with cheese. Kimolos in turn is close to Melos which is more in the main stream of Greek history with its massacre in Thucydides and its statue of Aphrodite in the Louvre. The plan was that the passengers should disperse on the island by day, rejoining at night. I had made the acquaintance, one of those rapid shipboard acquaintances, of a young woman who had the name of

Belinda and a large and well chosen hamper. My own provisions were more austere but she very civilly agreed to a pooling arrangement. After an agreeable day spent in bathing and exploration of the island, the *Calanthe's* siren sounded as warning to return on board. Before we had gone very far two German aircraft came low over the island. After one dummy run they returned and the foremost dropped a stick of four bombs, the third of which caught the *Calanthe* amidships. She was the other side of a low ridge from where we were, about 20 minutes walk away. By the time we got there she was already settling low in the water and blazing with a fierce crackling sound. Two people had been killed instantly but for the remainder of the few on board injuries were slight. She was close in shore so most of them were able to swim to land.

We were not long marooned on this uninhabited island. As soon as night began to fall the people of Kimolos just across the strait put across in two motor caiques and transported us to their island. As with most Aegean towns Kimolos is built on a height above the harbour and it was a long way up carrying one or two stretchers. We were given a school for a refuge and fed and looked after most tenderly by the islanders. We were five days altogether on Kimolos. Remote as it was from the rest of the world, we got news from time to time of the German advance. Arthur Forbes had been aboard *Calanthe* when she sank and had swum ashore with nothing but a pair of trousers ruined by oil. I had still a fair number of drachmae on me and I spent a few on buying a suit for him off the peg in the only tailors shop on the island. It was mauve in colour.

We were lucky when a caique turned up from Crete. It was large enough to take the whole party; but its best speed was six knots and it could not be expected to do the whole trip to Crete in one night. There were numerous discussions about the best course. One possibility would have been to make our way through the islands to the Turkish coast and thence, relying on the well-trained benevolent neutrality of the Turks, down to Cyprus. A simpler course was to make first for Santorin, the most southerly of the Cyclades and the nearest to Crete. It was 80 miles from Santorin to Heraklion which was more than could be done in one night; a few hours of daylight would have to be risked. The Germans entered Athens on the 28th April and we decided to make for Santorin the next day. There was fairly frequent enemy reconnaissance so it was important not to assemble on the quay in a noticeable manner. We all went down by day to the harbour and hid under cover on the hill above it or in some small warehouses. It seemed a long wait. I had borrowed a copy of *Alice in Wonderland* from one of the fellow passengers and felt remarkably like *Journey's End*.

We actually weighed anchor before sunset and cruised smoothly away into that violet light which bathes the Aegean in early summer. The beauty of the Cyclades comes almost entirely from sharpness of outline and not from colour, but in the evening and in the morning for less than half an hour the islands suck up some colour from the sun. However beautiful the effect was, and with me it is one that never fails, the dark was welcome. There was little wind and no sea and we made good progress, entering the harbour of Santorin just after dawn.

This was not my first visit to Santorin but even at second sight it remains an astonishing spectacle. The island is a fragment of the rim of a volcano shattered by some violent explosion whose date is conjectured by archaeologists to be about 1400 B.C. You sail into the crater; the town of Santorin is perched up on a precipitous cliff above you and on your other side is the still active cone, a small island looking more like a reef except for a continuous wisp of steam and smoke rising from it. It is a long way up from the tiny harbour to the town since the path has to zigzag up the steep side of the crater. Just as we were entering Santorin town I was delighted to see two extremely smart British Military Policemen and just beyond them, also beautifully turned out, their C.O. Captain Oxborrow of the Wiltshire Regiment who had been a member of our mess in Athens. He had been supervising the embarkation of the New Zealand Division at Lavrion and after they were all aboard he and his detachment of M.P.s had commandeered a ship and sailed off. I was even more delighted to discover that the ship he had collected in this way was a motor ship capable of something like 12 knots. She was very small but there was room for all of us and Oxborrow was delighted to take us. With the prospect of getting to Crete under the kindly cover of darkness all the way I was able to enjoy to the full the excellent wine of Santorin which is famous throughout the Aegean. Volcanic soil is of course particularly good for grapes though in some vintages in Santorin the whiff of sulphur is slightly overdone.

We sailed that evening just as it was getting dark having picked up a number of other people who wanted to go to Crete. In fact there was such a demand that I was put up to harangue the mob in my best Greek and assure them that there would be room for all. I spent the night on deck and slept well as the old ship pushed on, with much rattling, but steadily and at an encouraging speed. A good deal of the advantage of this, as it happened, was thrown away by careless navigation, for when the dawn rose it showed plainly that we were aiming at a point on the coast of Crete some five miles to the west of Heraklion. However, for some reason enemy air activity was a bit slack that morning and we entered harbour without being attacked.

Heraklion should be an encouragement to anyone in the position that the British forces on the island were then in. In the seventeenth century it stood a siege of sixty years from the Turks, the longest siege of which there is historical record. The very soil of Crete speaks of war; the character of the Cretans is warlike, romantic and fanatical. Their whole history is one of resistance to foreign invaders. They tend to be rather taller than the average Greek and normally of a fine physique, as is usual with mountaineers. I have mentioned that it was the Cretan Division which captured Kleisura in a raging blizzard. Alas, the stalwart survivors of the division were still far away in Albania and about to share the fate of the whole victorious army, surrender to the German invaders. Apart from the seventeenth century siege the main associations which Heraklion aroused in my mind came from Kazantsakis' book *Freedom or Death*, a story of the Turkish period. Others, from peace-time visits, concerned the Palace of Minos, just inland. These associations too are of battle and violent action, the gloom of the labyrinth and the blood lust of the arena and the final sacking of the Palace, with the King's remains found where he was struck down by the invaders beside his most sacred altar.

The garrison of Heraklion was the 2nd Black Watch; the Welch were at Canea, the capital, at the other end of the island. I was under orders to report to the Air Officer commanding in the island, George Beamish, then a Group Captain, who was also at Canea. He was in a rather anomalous position. He had no aircraft under his command and it was unlikely that he would get any because all three Cretan airfields at Maleme, Retimo and Heraklion were within the range of German single engined fighters operating from the southern Peloponnese and from Melos. Compared with the very great German air resources in the theatre the whole of the R.A.F. in the Middle East was absurdly small. An attempt to keep aircraft in Crete would therefore have meant the gradual destruction of all our forces without any advantage. German aircraft were already ranging the island freely, particularly fighters, shooting at anything they saw moving.

I was not with George Beamish for long. I was sent off on one expedition to find and destroy a crashed Gladiator somewhere on the slopes of Mount Ida and on the way back came off my motorbicycle rather too quickly to avoid a strafing fighter and fractured my right shoulder. Shortly thereafter it was decided that my most useful field of action would be on General Freyberg's H.Q. where my knowledge of Greek would help with liaison and my German and Italian could be used for interrogation.

General Freyberg, who commanded the New Zealand Division or rather, as he always insisted, the Second New Zealand Expeditionary Force, had just been appointed to command all the troops in the island. It was my first acquaintance with him, but I was lucky enough to see a great deal more of him between then and the end of the war. His qualities of personal bravery and endurance are almost legendary; less well known, but equally if not more striking, were his gifts in the training of troops.

The garrison of Crete consisted of the two British battalions which had gone there in November 1940, the Black Watch and the Welch, a force of Royal Marines known as the Mobile Naval Base Defense Organization under General Weston, plus the survivors of the Greek campaign from the 2nd New Zealand Division and from one brigade of the 6th Australian Division. The Australians and New Zealanders had got away from Greece with little more than their small arms. In addition there was a troop of the 3rd Royal Tank Regiment, sent hastily from Egypt, and something like ten scratch battalions of Greeks, the over-age and the under-age and a few others retained in the depots.

It was soon evident that the Germans intended to mount an operation against Crete. Their gradually increased air activity was one proof and information received about movements in Athens and on the way down to Greece made the matter quite clear. It must be an air operation, for in spite of the enemy's best endeavours the Mediterranean Fleet could still command the waters around Crete. The Germans had devoted much attention to the development of parachute troops and had already used them on a small scale in the opening phases of their campaign in the west. They now had a complete division, the 7th Air Division, and the whole of this was known to be concentrating in the Athens area. To back it up they had the 5th and 6th Mountain Divisions which were intended to come in in transport aircraft and by sea. These latter two divisions were chosen no doubt because they were already trained to operate in small groups when necessary, in mountainous country, and their equipment was to some extent adapted to be man-handled. After the landing grounds at Molaoi in the south-eastern Peloponnese and on Melos were completed, by about 14th May, dive bombers and fighters were engaging in very heavy attacks on the anchorage in Suda Bay, and in particular, on all fixed anti-aircraft positions.

This air attack was plainly working up to a crescendo and on the morning of the 20th May it reached its greatest intensity. General Freyberg's H.Q. was established in a stone quarry on the hill east of Canea town, just off the road from there to Suda. It commanded a fine view over the old city with its Venetian harbour works and its few remaining Turkish minarets, then westwards along the coast to where the aerodrome at Maleme lay at the foot of the northward pointing peninsula of Cape Spada. By about 8 o'clock on that morning the whole scene was alive with German aircraft in numbers greater than ever. They were operating singly or in pairs, dive bombers making attacks on gun positions and fighters shooting up not merely any movement they saw on the roads but even any place that looked like good cover purely on the speculative chance that troops might be hiding there. In fact in view of their numbers the German aircraft must have been very hard up for targets. This continuous bombing and machine gunning was to continue by day for the whole of the rest of the battle. It replaced the artillery which the Germans were unable to bring with them. Up to that time the dive bombers had enjoyed the greatest reputation with our troops as a weapon of terror but I think that my own view was widely shared, that the machine gunning by fighters was more damaging and certainly more frightening. The point about dive bombing is that ninety-nine times out of a hundred you yourself are not the target, in which case you can sit up and watch with interest or sympathy, or *schadenfreude*, according to temperament. For that matter the bombs carried by the Ju. 87 were not heavy and even if you were in the target area you had quite a good chance of escaping damage. The Messerschmitt fighter on a machine-gunning run, however, was the more frightening because it could appear at any time and with very little warning. Moreover it always seemed much more accurate. We had plenty of this sort of thing later on in the desert and even, for a time, in Tunisia; but I never saw anything to touch the numbers that were continuously visible in the sky over Crete. Complete absence of opposition was one of the reasons and it added of course to the general feeling of annoyance. I remember on one occasion being shot at by a slow flying and obsolete-looking seaplane, and unexpectedly, because it was a two-seater and the observer in an open cockpit behind the pilot stood up and took aim deliberately with a machine gun on a swivelling mount. He was only about 20–30 feet up and going quite slowly so I could watch it all. For that matter I was once fired on also by a Bulgarian aircraft which was joining in the fun. To make matters worse it was an early type of Blenheim which we had sold them.

All this excitement was obviously the prelude to something big and at about 9 o'clock the steady drone of heavier aircraft could be heard. It was a beautifully clear day and from where I stood I could see easily to Maleme though it was some eight miles away. All at once, as it seemed, there appeared over Maleme and between there and Canea a close formation of heavy, black-painted aircraft and no sooner had they crossed the coast line than a cloud of many coloured parachutes blossomed underneath them. It was a sparkling and stirring sight. George Beamish, who was crouching beside me, stood up in unabashed professional jealousy. At least I think that was what he was feeling; what he actually said was "What a remarkable sight—looks like the end of the world". Very shortly after we had something more to think about; some strange-looking aircraft wheeled slowly over our heads and began to descend further up the road towards the Akrotiri Peninsula. They had almost disappeared before I realized they were gliders. The battle for Crete had been joined with a rousing dramatic opening.

As I was for the next ten days to be concerned with the enemy's movements rather than our own, I might perhaps set out shortly now how the picture seemed to the Germans. The battle has often been described, in particular in the excellent New Zealand Official History. A German book giving the tactical picture from that side has been published by Colonel von der Heydte who commanded a battalion in the battle and later a regiment at Alamein. What follows is based on my own interrogation of enemy prisoners at the time, on study of the numerous captured enemy documents and on a note which I compiled on my return to Egypt, a copy of which I came across recently.

The invading troops were, as usual, weighed down with documents of all sorts; in particular they had conveniently brought with them the latest divisional intelligence summary issued on 19th May, the day before the attack. It gave the garrison of Crete as no more than 5,000 men, of whom there were 400 at Heraklion, none at Retimo and the remainder in the Canea area. It asserted bluntly that all the Australian and New Zealand troops who had been engaged in Greece had gone straight back to Egypt. It added that there were no Greek troops on the island. In fact there must have been over 20,000 British troops and about 10,000 Greeks. The Greek Government was said to be either at Heraklion or Retimo, whereas in fact it was at Canea. This was my first introduction to the extraordinary badness of German military intelligence. It may be objected that the Germans had only recently arrived in Greece and that Crete was an island with which they had had no contact. This is fair enough though I must be permitted to draw a contrast, for the honour of the British Service, with the case of the island of Pantellaria. We had had no contact with that either, beyond air photographs, but our estimate of the strength of the defending forces was only 50 out in a total of over 11,000. The fact is that the Germans had all the wrong ideas about intelligence and hitherto had not felt the need of improvement. Whatever errors they might make about the forces opposing them, they had always been strong enough for these errors to make no difference. One result was that the operations branch tended to pay no attention to what their intelligence branch told them. The time was coming when this could be a serious handicap. What struck me most at the time was the cool certainty with which these appreciations were presented. Any British Intelligence Summary, even at a later and more self-confident period of the war, would undoubtedly have hedged with a few 'probablys'. Although we had good reason as time went on to believe in the accuracy of our appreciations we never, so far as I can remember, allowed ourselves to err on the side of underestimating the opposition.

It may seem rather jejune of me to be concentrating on these themes instead of on the battle for Crete, one of the hardest fought and most dramatic battles of the war. I must plead in excuse that for the first part I was rather perched above the battle, my only contact being with German prisoners whom I interrogated. Contrary to what has so often been said, the ones I met were far from fanatical or indoctrinated Nazis, but rather for the most part sensible, good soldiers and above average in training and intelligence. Many had taken part in the attacks in Holland and Belgium. The theme of the battle was a simple one. The German aim was to seize an airfield and by its use bring in ever increasing numbers of reinforcements until they were strong enough to drive us off the island. Our object was to recapture the airfield.

What happened in the rest of the island was incidental. As soon as the Germans discovered our real strength they abandoned all idea of reinforcing Heraklion or Retimo and concentrated on Maleme. Here again they demonstrated a difference to the character given them at my O.C.T.U. We were assured there that the Germans were fiendishly clever and worked out schemes of the utmost ingenuity based on full and accurate information provided by a superhumanly efficient intelligence service. But, my instructors would insist, the moment their plans began to run into difficulties they were at a sad loss. The British, I was told, were always at their best in these circumstances; but the Germans were quite unable to improvise and floundered about trying to get back on the hard and fast lines laid down in their preliminary planning. This may, for all I know, have been a German characteristic of the First World War, though it sounds to me more like an intellectual construction; but in the Second World War, in all my experience right up to the end, the pre-eminent German characteristic was brilliance at improvisation. Some generals, Rommel for example, seem to have enjoyed improvisation almost for its own sake; in his case, I admit, the result was usually to end up in a worse state than before. Kesselring on the other hand was a master. He was almost always wrong about our intentions and our strength and the opening day or days of an offensive would plunge him into a mess from which it seemed he could never get out; but he was so fertile in expedients that he was time and again able to extricate himself from the most desperate situation. As Lord Alexander says in his Despatches: "Although he could often be outthought he could only with the greatest difficulty be outfought." The same thing was certainly true in the Italian campaign all down the line to unit commanders. Crete showed this characteristic to a high degree. The local commanders, often isolated and up against heavy odds, showed enormous initiative. The German command in Athens, faced at the end of the second day with an almost complete breakdown of their plans, showed a determination and forcefulness which brought them success.

For all that the battle of Crete was essentially a soldiers' battle. It was also, like Waterloo, a very near run thing. By day the German air force dominated the scene and movement was almost impossible. Our tactical necessity was to drive the enemy off Maleme airfield at night leaving enough time to be able to dig in before morning. Twice it was cleared but neither time could it be held next day. Then, on the 22nd, the Germans began landing troops from aircraft on the aerodrome. This was an extraordinary sight. Aircraft landed in groups of three at a time at intervals of not more than ten minutes. The regularity had a depressing effect on morale. The airstrip was actually under fire from our side but not very effective fire. The New Zealanders had been obliged to leave their guns in Greece and all we had was some captured Italian guns from the Western Desert which had been sent over for the use of the Greek Army. The six tanks, on which a great deal of hope had been placed, proved mechanically unreliable. One success cheered us on the night of 21st-22nd May. A force of German troops, some 2,000 strong, which sailed from Melos for the island in caiques, was intercepted by the Navy and all destroyed. Part of this action could be seen from General Freyberg's H.Q. Burning ships were visible all along the horizon. In spite of this and in spite of the losses in aircraft it proved impossible to stop a continuing build-up of German troops through Maleme, and the New Zealanders were pushed back at first to the outskirts of Canea.

We moved back that night to an olive grove on the slopes of the hill above the south shore of Suda Bay. With Maleme and Canea lost and the whole west end of the island open for the Germans to land at will it was clear that, as long as the Germans were willing to pay the price, we should be unable to hold Crete. The price had already been heavy in trained parachutists. To us the loss of the New Zealand Division was not to be contemplated. We had hoped to hold Crete and Tobruk as two anchors or advanced posts of the Middle Eastern position; we had nearly succeeded in holding Crete but nearly is not good enough and it was plain we should have to go. It was ironical that just as this decision was becoming inevitable further reinforcements in the shape of two British battalions were being landed in the S.E. of the island, intended to reinforce Heraklion.

To get away from Crete the only method for the forces fighting in the western end of the island was to be taken off from somewhere on the southwest coast. The Navy would endeavour to send smaller forces to remove the troops from Retimo and Heraklion which were already cut off by the enemy from the bulk of our troops round Canea. The main body must fall back on the fishing village of Sphakia. There was a road running from Suda almost to Sphakia; it was a new one, the first motorable road to pierce the Ida mountains, though it stopped, unfinished, about five miles short of the coast. General Weston, commanding the Royal Marines, was to have charge of the rearguard which consisted of his own men and the Welch Regiment.

It was a difficult operation to disengage, though at this stage of the war one with which British troops were not unacquainted. General Freyberg moved his H.Q. back to a point near where the Sphakia road joined the coastal road. He chose a kind of dell in a cleft of the rocks, thickly wooded. By contrast with most of Greece, Crete is fairly well watered and grass, trees and flowers grow profusely. The H.Q. was entirely hidden from view but in spite of this on one or two occasions it was shot up by German fighters who plainly did so merely as a speculation and for want of worthwhile targets. I was interested to read in *The Times*, after I got back to Egypt, an account of this period which owed something, I think, to a conversation between the correspondent and Geoffrey Cox who was also on Freyberg's staff. He had already made a start in journalism before the war and has since distinguished himself still further. The episode I have just mentioned appeared in the following form: "For two hours General Freyberg and all his staff lay motionless under a hail of machine-gun fire. To move meant instant death". It is always interesting for the amateur writer to see how the professional does it.

I almost missed the move from here to Sphakia, having been sent off on a mission by Freyberg's Chief of Staff, Brigadier Hargess, to locate an M.T.B. and give the Captain a thousand pounds' worth of drachmae. I set off on a motorcycle, although I still only had the use of one arm, and spent a frustrating afternoon in the search. As it was beginning to get dark I thought I saw what might be a motor launch close inshore down a fairly steep descent below the main road. By the time I got back from the shore to the road, having once more drawn a blank, the road was fairly full of traffic moving towards Sphakia and someone had helped himself, understandably though annoyingly, to my motorbicycle. I set myself rather ruefully to trudge in the direction of where H.Q. had been and within two minutes, implausible though it may seem, I saw coming along the road one of the H.Q. lorries with some signallers and orderlies on it. They stopped at my wave and hauled me on, though I was the last one they had any room for, and off we went. I owed the lift to the efforts of an orderly from the Welch who recognized me. This splendid man's name was 04 Jones (the Welch as might be expected, had so many Jones that they required to be identified by the last two figures of their regimental number). He even offered me later on a pull at his water bottle, but I had to decline this because he had injudiciously filled it with condensed milk. Most private soldiers are fond of condensed milk but it has to be recognized that if you have a thirst it merely increases it. However he had saved me a forty-mile walk and I was most grateful.

The road wound upwards into mountains through the night. The truck was packed with tins of bully beef. It is odd under what circumstances one can get to sleep but I certainly did until we paused for a moment just before dawn on the inland plain of Lasithi. This is a strange saucer-like depression in the heart of the mountains. Many times it formed a haven of refuge for the Cretans in revolt against the Turks and it was the scene of one of the main actions of our retreat. The people of Lasithi, as a result of their history, claim to be the purest bred Cretans and have a reputation for bravery and haughtiness. A shepherd came and spoke to me as we were filling the radiator of the truck from one of the many springs of the plain. He had no word of reproach for our running away though he knew well enough what the fate of the island was likely to be, for he called the Germans worse than the Turks. He seemed, indeed, to have the idea that some of the blame might rest on the people of Canea and district for whom he had a quite unjustified low opinion. I remember, when we first arrived in the island, a Major in the gendarmerie who offered me his condolences on our being 'let down' by the mainland Greeks, assuring me that Cretans would do better. An Australian friend of mine making the same journey slightly later in the day was received with open arms at a farm house by the elderly farmer who insisted on killing his last three remaining chickens for him, explaining that he himself intended taking to the hills. He then pulled out his old Mauser rifle from under the rafters, slung two ammunition belts round his shoulders and strode off northwards in the direction from which the Germans were coming.

An hour or so after dawn we reached the edge of the last escarpment where the cliff plunges sharply down to the sea. Far below we could see the village of Sphakia. The road turned sharply to slide down in a series of hairpin bends which broke off halfway at the place where road work had stopped. There were many lorries which had come to their last stop at this point. They were to prove a useful source of forage in the next few days. General Freyberg and his H.Q. were in two large caves down the mountainside about three miles above Sphakia village.

The bulk of the troops were to be evacuated on the night of the 29th May. The H.Q. was to leave on the night of the 30th. General Freyberg eventually stayed till the 31st when he was taken off in a flying boat. I had therefore two days in my cave. There was nothing to do but wait. I had lost the books, the select few, with which I had set out for the wars, when the *Calanthe* went down. Fortunately among our number was a former colleague of mine from Magdalen, Ellis Waterhouse, now Professor of Fine Arts at Birmingham University. He lent me from his store a volume of *La Comédie Humaine*. It was a good choice under the circumstances: as Ellis said when he handed it to me "It's all about nothing but money". A calm and steady contemplation of the miseries arising from not having enough money, from failing to get the money you expect to get, or frittering away money you used to have, is an admirable antidote for one fleeing before his enemies. I had just handed back the thousand pounds' worth of notes and was about to crawl up the mountainside to see what I could loot from a broken-down lorry on the road above. It turned out to be two tins of marmalade, and they were very welcome.

When the time came for us to be taken off the rearguard action was rattling away at the top of the cliffs at the road's end. In fact the Germans had pushed forward at one point in a threatening way towards the beaches. However the embarkation went off without a hitch. It was rather like an extra long theatre queue, very orderly and well-behaved. The beach at Sphakia was narrow and the ships had to lie some distance off. Those embarking were taken off by motor launches. I found myself next in the queue to Major Guy Thomson, the Security Intelligence Officer, who was accompanying one of the Ministers of the Greek Government. Our launch headed towards a civilian-looking ship. It was in fact the *Glengyle*, one of the famous Glen ships which had been fitted as infantry landing ships. There was an amusing altercation as we came alongside. The Minister, whose name I forget, insisted in fair English that in view of his status he ought to be going in a battleship. It looked like developing into a wrangle until the young sub-lieutenant at the entry-port, having apologized for there being no battleship in the convoy, assured him that the *Glengyle* had been commissioned into the Royal Navy, and was therefore a warship at any rate for ceremonial purposes. No sooner had we got aboard than I was handed a mug of cocoa and introduced to a comfortable cabin with sheets on the bunks. The Navy, God bless it, has at least this advantage, that it cannot fall below a certain minimum standard of comfort—unless of course the ship goes down. The Army officer may vary from Shepheard's Hotel one night to a damp slit trench the next but the Naval officer at any rate has some approximation to home comforts. I say this with a full realization of the hardships and losses of the Navy, never greater than in the Mediterranean, and never greater than precisely at this time when it was suffering such grievous losses in the fighting round Crete and in the task of bringing off the Army. They did a magnificent job and they knew it. I was told that the popular toast in the Mediterranean Fleet at that time was 'To the three Services, the Royal Navy, the Royal Advertising Federation and the Evacuees'. My main thought however was how pleasant it was to sleep between sheets and to wake up at the gentlemanly hour of 8.30 to have bacon and eggs for breakfast. To stroll on deck thereafter with a pipe well lit was like a Mediterranean cruise. An hour after breakfast, it is true, we were attacked by dive bombers, but the *Glengyle* was in the centre of the convoy next to an anti-aircraft cruiser, and the Stukas very sensibly went for the fringes. As I have already mentioned, the person who is not the actual object of attack by dive bombers tends to take a very philosophical and disinterested view.

Many times since leaving Crete I have pondered on the balance sheet of the whole operation. The question to which I have not found an answer is what would have happened if we had been successful, as we very nearly were, in retaining the island? To begin with, its supply would have been bound to have cost the Navy dear. The north coast, where the only harbours are, lay completely within the control of the German Air Force. The Navy's losses in the ten days of the battle were already so heavy that this would have been a commitment desperately difficult for them. For the Army to have garrisoned the island properly would have involved locking up troops without which our position in the desert approaches to Egypt would have been much weaker. I know that this is an argument which can be pressed too far; Sir Winston Churchill has commented with bitter irony on the argument which excuses our abandoning of our position in the southern Irish ports by saying that we were thereby relieved of an expensive commitment. For all that, we never had too many troops in the Western Desert, and to have subtracted a division—less than that would have been useless—would almost certainly have made the difference between success and failure in 1942. Turning from speculation to facts, it can be said that the German victory had been purchased very dearly in the terms of the loss of picked and specially trained parachutists. After Crete the Germans never again, throughout the rest of the war, carried out a large scale parachute attack.

I saw Crete again in May 1945, when I went to supervise the arrangements for the surrender of the German garrison. It was an agreeable example of the wheel turning full circle. At that time the Germans were all concentrated at the west end of the island, and our main concern was to keep the Cretans from falling on them. The solution was to move them all into the Akrotiri peninsula, where I had watched the gliders landing four years earlier, and put a cordon of British troops across the neck. From there they were taken away by ships and sent to Suda Bay. I was glad to have seen the day.

CHAPTER V

The Western Desert

O N THE morning of 1st June the *Glengyle* steamed into Alexandria Harbour. It seemed a long time since I had steamed
out on the *Nieuw Zeeland*; I was richer in experience but
poorer in kit. In fact all I had was a shirt, shorts, stockings, boots, a
steel helmet and a pistol. I kitted myself up fairly quickly at an
Ordnance Depot, signing away large drafts on future pay. When the
wheels finally ground out an answer to my application for reimburse-
ment for loss of kit I got the sum of £18 10s. 4½d., with a footnote
saying that if I could produce written authority for having taken two
pairs of shoes to Greece I could have another 17s. 3d.

I was next ordered to Cairo where, in a corner of G.H.Q., I put down
some observations on the battle of Crete which I have no reason to
suppose were ever taken any notice of. However it did appear from
them that I had interrogated prisoners of war both in German and
Italian. German linguists were wanted; we were about to attack on the
Libyan frontier. Two days later, after buying a little more desert kit, I
took the overnight train for the Western Desert. I was posted to H.Q.
Western Desert Force, under General Beresford-Peirse. The railway
had been hastily pushed forward in 1940 as far as Mersa Matruh; H.Q.
Western Desert Force was at Maaten Baqqush, about 30 miles east of
Matruh. My feelings as the train pulled out of Cairo were decidedly
mixed. On the one hand I was undoubtedly going to the most interesting place (though there is a lot of point in the Chinese curse 'May
you live in interesting times'); on the other hand I felt fairly sure that
I should not like the desert. I had seen its easternmost fringes outside
Alexandria and thought it disagreeable. As a matter of fact I never did
like the desert though I grew to like the life there and the people.
As the train, after passing through Alexandria, puffed reluctantly
westwards next morning I got a good view of one sort, the most
familiar, along the coastal strip. Here the sand was very light in texture
and almost white in colour and lay around in wind-blown dunes not

unlike the kind of desert beloved by films. Southwards from this strip, still in the coastal plain below the escarpment, the desert was more hummocky, dotted every four or five yards with a thorn bush; this gave a black and white impression from close to, while in a distant view the dark of the scrub predominated over the light colour of the sand. Then came the great Escarpment on top of which was a hard limestone plateau with for the most part only a sprinkling of sand. In large areas, and increasingly so as you went further south, the surface was composed of gravel. It was dotted here and there with little white snail shells. Wherever you looked there seemed to be hundreds; for there were not only the present generation of living snails but there were also the empty shells of all their forebears. The newcomer always wondered how they got enough water, but once he had slept out in the desert, even in the height of summer, he realized that every night there was a heavy and soaking dew. These gravel tracts some 50–60 miles south of the sea always struck me with a peculiar sense of desolation; 'the naked shingles of the world' was the phrase that always came into the mind. Strangely enough they were so dark in colour that at noon, when all the colours in the sky were swallowed up by the white blaze of the sun, the general impression was one of gloom, not brightness. Still further to the south, in the latitude of Siwa and Jarabub, the real sand sea began, billows of wind-blown sand, tall dunes 50–60 feet high as though made for a background to a chain of Hollywood camels. In the sand sea only the Long Range Desert Group moved at will.

The maps of the desert were therefore like charts. Apart from major features such as the Escarpment, their surfaces were dotted with information about the type of 'going'. Later on maps were produced in which four different grades of 'going', ranging from good to impassable, were distinguished in different colours. The main difference from a chart was that the surface was thickly scattered with names. Every tiny feature had an Arabic name and these were nearly always descriptive. Sometimes indeed they merely recorded the name of a supposedly holy man who was buried thereabouts. More often they were meant as useful tips for the next comers, for example the name of Halfaya Pass reveals that at certain seasons good pasturage of alfalfa could be found there. Bir is a very common ingredient in these names and means a cistern in which rainwater can collect. Maaten means a larger and more sophisticated form of underground cistern, probably dating from Roman or Byzantine times. Maaten Baqqush, where

I arrived shortly before lunch, was alleged to have a very elaborate underground construction but I never saw it. By way of compensation the whole of the H.Q. was underground. An elaborate system of corridors and offices opening off them had been dug out of the sand dunes about two miles in from the shore. They were perfectly hidden from view even at short range. They also had the advantage of being cooler, though they had the disadvantage that when the wind blew, which it did almost all the time, clouds of sand came down the ventilating shafts. It was a particularly clinging variety of sand, almost as fine as talcum powder with a lot of mica and coral dust in it. However the June climate, though extremely hot and with temperatures well into the hundreds, was not so very unpleasant near the sea. At that time of year there are steady north and northeast winds which blow all day long on the northern coast of Africa. These are the winds once known as Etesian which the Greeks now call Meltem; three years before they had given me perfect sailing among the islands of the Aegean. The sea was invigorating though its currents were dangerous. The surf came rolling in and Ordnance could be persuaded to make surf boards.

There was a line of defences round Maaten Baqqush, mainly consisting of barbed wire and minefields, but there were no troops to speak of. At Mersa Matruh was the Polish Brigade. This was a force originally formed in Syria under General Weygand's command. When the French there accepted the armistice the brigade broke away and marched over into Palestine to join us. The men were mainly drawn from the elements of the Polish Army which had escaped over the border into Rumania in September 1939 and thence, at a time when Rumanian neutrality was rather more friendly towards us, through Turkey to the Levant. They came to Alexandria in the late summer when I was helping the Area H.Q. and it struck me as an example of how the Army expected you to know everything when I was ordered to lay out horse lines for them in the desert—they then had two squadrons of horsed cavalry. Greatly daring, I telephoned G.H.Q. and was put on to the Director of Veterinary and Remount Services himself. He was most civil and told me all that I wanted to know. The great tip for heel ropes is to tie them round a full sandbag and then bury the bag in the sand.

In front of Mersa Matruh, watching Sollum and Halfaya, were the 4th Indian Division and the 7th Armoured Division. But I cannot write the names of these two splendid divisions without harking back to the great events of the previous winter and giving some account, however brief, of the first great Western Desert campaign. I missed this campaign myself, being in Greece, but I knew so many men who took part in it, so many stories about it became part of the common heritage of the desert, that to leave it out of any story of those years would be impossible.

The Italian force which crossed the frontier on 15th September 1940 consisted of the 10th Army under Graziani's personal command. There were the equivalent of three corps under it, the 21st Corps consisting of the 1st and 2nd Blackshirt Divisions and the 63rd Cirene Division, the 23rd Corps of the 4th Blackshirt Division and the 64th Catanzaro Division and the Group of Libyan Divisions consisting of the 1st and 2nd Libyan Divisions. There were various other oddments of which an armoured group was the most important. This formidable collection made a slow and ponderous advance towards Sidi Barrani, 60 miles from the frontier, and there, as though startled at its impetuosity, began to dig in. A large number of fortified camps gradually arose, covering a wide area of desert but not very well sited. In theory this was a mere pause in an irresistible advance and the 1st Armoured Group which had the name of 'The red flames of Italy' was assured by its commander in an Order of the Day that those flames would shortly be burning brightly at the foot of the pyramids. As the pause in operations drew on, the thought at G.H.Q. in Cairo began to change from planning a defensive battle at Mersa Matruh to a consideration of whether it would be possible to beat up the Italians in their camps.

The actual operation which was launched on 5th December was an excellent example of what could be done with a comparatively small but very well trained force. The battle was planned in the most rigid secrecy, and though no battle ever goes entirely according to plan, this one came very close to that ideal. It went so smoothly in fact that many people suspected at the time, and Graziani pleaded as an excuse, that there must be a hopeless disparity in equipment between the two sides since the disparity in numbers was heavily on the Italian side. In later desert battles the Italians did seem to be poor relations; but in the first battle they were well, not to say lavishly, equipped. The infantry had a full scale of light and heavy automatic weapons of a modern type. The artillery was a mixed lot, some of the types being rather old, but there was plenty of it in 10th Army. The main tank was the Fiat CV3, a light tank armed only with machine guns in a non-revolving turret. This was mechanically highly reliable but not very formidable;

nor, for that matter, was the Mark VI B light tank with which 7th Armoured Division's cavalry regiments were equipped. The medium tank, the M 11, was armed with an effective 47 mm. gun but it was fixed in the hull and could not be traversed. The chassis was also very unreliable mechanically—which seems odd in view of the great reputation of Italian motorcar engines. On the other hand a country that produced the Crusader tank had better be careful how it criticizes other models. In other ways, too, the Italians went to war on a de luxe basis. It had been decided that it was too much of a hardship to expect Italian troops, or at any rate Italian officers, to drink the local water which was good enough for their British opponents and thousands of cases of bottled mineral water from Reccoaro Spa were imported into Libya and carried forward in vast quantities even to the most far flung outposts. This, incidentally, disposes of another excuse put forward after the battle, the pretence that the Italians had insufficient motor transport. In fact they had so much that we were able to motorize two brigades out of what we captured; ironically, but for the captured transport, we could never have pushed on so far into Libya. Of particular value were the large 10-ton Diesel lorries of which the 10th Army had large quantities. The comfort of senior officers was looked after by the provision of motor caravans; it was from the Italians that we learnt the use of caravans which became so popular with the British forces in the desert and subsequently when we moved to Italian soil.

The attack by the 4th Indian Division and the 7th Armoured Division, who were both trained to a hair and full of confidence, fell like a thunderbolt. In the first two days both the Libyan Divisions and the 4th Blackshirt Division (the '3rd of January') were captured or killed to a man in their camps or outside them together with the whole of the 1st Armoured Group. The 64th Catanzaro Division was actually moving up in a routine relief and was caught by the 4th Armoured Brigade undeployed near Buqbuq. After a brief palaver almost the entire division surrendered without a fight. All the divisional artillery fell into our hands and a very large amount of corps and army artillery. All the camps were certainly bristling with guns. Rear services of the Western Desert Force were overwhelmed by the floods of prisoners. The first general to be captured was General Gallina, the Corps commander of the Group of Libyan divisions. He was given a bed in the caravan occupied by Air Commodore Collishaw and startled him in the middle of the night by crawling on the floor of the caravan looking for his false teeth. Like all his colleagues he arrived with his kit well packed; it included a tin uniform case entirely full of photographs of himself in a white cloak riding on a camel. A perhaps exaggerated story used to be told by General Gott on whose staff I later served. At Sidi Barrani he commanded the Support Group of the 7th Armoured Division. Arriving in front of one of the smaller camps he sent in an Italian prisoner under a flag of truce to call on the commander to surrender. The prisoner was not long in coming back with the Italian General's reply, which was to the effect that, having been entrusted with the command of this fortified camp, he considered it his duty, for the honour of the Italian Army, to defend it to the last round and the last drop of blood. Strafer Gott replied that this reply was very clear, and of course very proper, and that he would therefore now proceed to make his dispositions for the attack. At this point he was interrupted by his emissary. "I ought perhaps to explain," he said, "the meaning of this message which is not fully apparent on the face of it. The General wishes you to understand that he cannot surrender the fort until you have at least opened fire. If however you will be good enough to fire one round he will then be only too pleased to comply with your request." This interpretation proved to be correct. Immediately after one round had been ceremoniously fired by the accompanying troop of 25-pounders the white flag was raised and the garrison filed out of the fort with their belongings all carefully packed.

It has always seemed a striking example of General Wavell's self confidence, and also an illustration of the scantiness of the forces at his disposal to meet a strategic situation threatening on all sides, that the 4th Indian Division were collected straight from the battlefield of Sidi Barrani and sent off without a pause to the Sudan. From here they were to advance to the conquest of Eritrea and to the battle of Keren, a sterner battle than Sidi Barrani, against even more extraordinary odds. Their place was taken by two brigades of the 6th Australian Division, an untried and not wholly trained formation. With these and with the 7th Armoured Division, its tanks now rather the worse for wear, the advance went dashingly on.

The positions at Halfaya and on the frontier were abandoned and four divisions locked themselves up inside Bardia. They were the 1st and 2nd Blackshirt Divisions called after the 23rd March and the 28th October respectively, and the 62nd Marmarica and 63rd Cirene Divisions. They also had a company of the latest tanks, the M 13. This was the most modern tank the Italians ever developed—they were still fighting in them at Alamein and in Tunisia. It was 13 tons in weight and had a 47 mm. gun mounted in a revolving turret. It was a good-looking tank but the engine was still desperately unreliable. Bardia was a strongpoint surrounded by a regular line of fortifications including a deep and well scarped anti-tank ditch, wire, minefields and concrete block houses. The garrison was commanded by General Bergonzoli, who had previously commanded 23rd Corps. He was a picturesque figure, bearded like so many other Italian generals, and known to the Fascist press, if not to his troops, as 'Barba-elettrica'. This got translated into English as 'old electric whiskers'. Like many of his compatriots he was an indefatigable diarist; again typically, his diary showed a festering jealousy of all his colleagues and a conviction, not borne out by his performance, that he deserved even higher rank and responsibilities.

The strong defences of Bardia called for a set piece attack. It was led by the infantry tanks followed by infantry, though not quite so closely, I was told later, as the tank crews would have wished. The artillery kept the defenders well down and four more divisions were added to the prisoners in the bag. General Bergonzoli escaped in a small boat. Before Bardia fell, the 7th Armoured Division had already cast a blockade around Tobruk. They were followed shortly afterwards by the two Australian brigades and such of our infantry tanks as remained after the last two battles, which was not many. Tobruk was an even stronger fortress than Bardia but its area was larger and the garrison was only one division, the 61st Sirte. On the other hand, our own forces were also considerably weakened by then. The Italian intention was to form a counter attack force under command of 20 Corps, General Cona, consisting of the 60th Sabrata Division and the Babini Armoured Group, which was of two medium tank battalions and a Bersaglieri regiment. This force moved forward to the line of the Wadi Derna, but Tobruk fell too quickly. Our next aim was to round up the Babini Armoured Group at Mechili, down in the desert on the southern flank of 20 Corps; however they took flight and slipped away to the north and the great retreat began.

Cyrenaica pushes out in a semicircular bulge northwards into the Mediterranean. The top of the semicircle is occupied by a mountain range known as the Green Mountains or Gebel Akhdar. From the chord of the semicircle southwards is all desert, mainly the limestone and gravel kind. The only good road goes round the arc of the semicircle and it was on this route that the Italians were withdrawing. It might well seem obvious to anyone that the clever thing to do would be to make a dash by the desert route and cut the road where it turned southwards from Benghazi. There were however plenty of arguments against this; the fact that this was all entirely unknown territory of which we had no maps except a scanty supply of captured Italian ones; that the going was likely to be bad; and that any force which could get there quickly enough to be of use, and which could then be supplied at such a distance, was bound to be a small one. Nevertheless the risk was taken. A single battalion, the 2nd Rifle Brigade, after a harrowing journey, debouched on to the coast road just ahead of the main columns coming south. Here at a place called Beda Fomm ('the white mouth'), at which point the road runs through a defile between the sea and some low hills, there began a long straggling battle which was one of the fiercest fought of the campaign. Graziani had left for Tripoli long before, handing over command of 10th Army to his former Chief of Staff, General Tellera. There was little co-ordination, however, about the battle. The Italians had the better part of four battalions of medium tanks though one of these battalions had crews that had never seen the M 13 before. General Tellera himself rode in a tank in one of the attacks and had his head blown off by a direct hit from a two pounder anti-tank gun. So the battle degenerated into a series of desperate individual assaults, many of which came as near as possible to breaking through. It lasted all day until the last efforts died down. By that time some more of 7th Armoured had arrived to help in rounding up the prisoners. Among them was old Electric Whiskers, Bergonzoli, who was found hiding in some bushes down by the seashore.

There has been a certain amount of speculation on the reasons for the poor showing the Italians made in this campaign and later on. After all, before the war they had been taken as one of the Great Powers, even though the least; they had a very large army, though not so large as the eight million bayonets Mussolini was fond of referring to; and they were both well equipped and had had recent experience of actual warfare in Abyssinia and in Spain. A popular view in later years, particularly in Britain, was that their failure was caused by a hatred of fascism and a willingness to see even the defeat of their country so long as that involved the defeat of the evil system. This is an explanation very popular in Italy also, for simple and readily understood reasons.

There is some force in this argument, but I would put it rather differently. The main effect of 20 years of fascism had been to produce in the average Italian a total apathy and cynicism about anything connected with politics. In the army, too, corruption and favouritism in appointments had produced a serious deterioration compared with the First World War. Of the first, the bad quality of captured Italian army food supplies provided an illustration—and sometimes the cases would be half filled with gravel. Of the second the example of General Nuvoloni provided an engaging example. Nuvoloni commanded the Italian force which was defeated ignominiously in the battle of Guadalajara in the Spanish Civil War. The first excuse given for this by fascist apologists was that they had been overwhelmed by superior strength; and it appears that there were in fact six Russian tanks engaged on the Spanish side against Nuvoloni's one armoured battalion. I owe this latter fact to General von Thoma, the Commander of the German Afrika Korps, who was taken prisoner at Alamein and who gave me an interesting account of the battle of which he was an amused observer. Before long the story being put about was that Guadalajara, though in itself a defeat, was only of local importance and that it had made an important contribution to victory elsewhere on the Spanish front; and by 1940 Guadalajara was being included without any further ado among the lists of the victories won by the Italians in Spain. One result of this was that it was impossible to remove General Nuvoloni to the obscurity which he had merited. On the contrary, he had to be given an important command, and he turned up in North Africa in the spring of 1941 in command of the 102nd Trento Division, a new motorized division which was supposed to be the best of the Italian formations in the theatre. It did not in fact live up to those expectations while under his command and his troops, with that wry good nature common to the Italian soldier, used to refer to the hero of Guadalajara as 'il generale sfortunato', 'the unlucky general'.

Beda Fomm was the last battle of the campaign. All Cyrenaica was cleared. We had captured 125,000 prisoners. There was a bit of mopping up to do and I like this story about Strafer Gott in the attack on the fort at Sceledeima, a strong place commanding one of the passages down the escarpment southeast of Benghazi. Like the other Italian forts in the desert it looked like something in a Hollywood film about the Foreign Legion, painted white and prettily battlemented. In the little turrets on the four corners were mounted guns, the 65/17mm. guns which the Libyan divisions had. These had a much shorter range than our 25-pounders, a troop of which were firing on the fort. As a result it was possible to stroll about and watch the leisurely progress of the attack in safety. Our guns would fire and dust would fly from the pretty little fort, the enemy guns would pop back and shells would land some 600 yards short, sending up decorative columns of sand. The scene had an animated holiday look and Strafer Gott turning to his signals officer said, "What a lovely day. I wish I'd brought the children."

A more inexplicable experience befell two friends of mine in the Rifle Brigade who were given leave after the capture of Tobruk and made off for Alexandria in a looted Lancia staff car. They made good time and drew up with an air in front of the Cecil Hotel. A number of willing porters dashed out to help them with their simple kit, which was all dumped in the back of the car. One of the porters, however, went to open the boot, whereupon there fell out the body of an Italian major in full uniform.

The boundary between Cyrenaica and Tripolitania is at the bottom of the gulf of Sirte. It is an arbitrary line in the middle of the desert and is marked by a triumphal arch across the road known as the Arco dei Fileni, but called by our troops Marble Arch. Militarily speaking, however, the real point of division comes at Agheila. This is a very strong position, defended by impassable salt marshes; and twice it marked the turning point of a desert campaign. There was a factor common to both occasions, the demands of other theatres, Greece in January 1941 and the Far East in January 1942. On this occasion the 6th Australian Division, after entering Benghazi, went off to Greece; the 7th Armoured Division went back to Egypt to refit. Their place was taken by part of the 2nd Armoured Division, a newly arrived formation, the other part of which went to Greece. Any possibility of an advance into Tripolitania was ruled out; though this was naturally not known to the Italians who were now reduced to four divisions with very little artillery. To them the arrival of German troops seemed like an unexpected salvation.

In fact the decision to send German troops to Libya had been taken before the Italian defeat. A special formation had been organized called the 5th Light Motorized Division, sometimes referred to as 'Colonial' to distinguish it from the original German Light Divisions. It was an odd collection of units supposed to be specially suited for its task; however, in spite of numerous legends that were current at the time and are not wholly dead now, the men were not specially trained for the desert. It is a pity to have to deny the stories about the glass houses built in the neighbourhood of Hamburg to accustom the troops to tropical heat and about the wind machines that blew sand all over them, but it is amusing to remember that they were seriously believed and often printed in the British and American press. When the first contingents of troops began to arrive they were commanded by Colonel Graf von Schwerin. He ended the war as a Lieutenant General commanding the 14th Panzer Corps in Italy; I still have a pair of riding breeches that used to belong to him from which he was parted at the crossing of the River Po. Immediately on arrival in Tripolitania he took a selection of men from the various units of the Division on a round tour of the Italian garrisons in the southern part of Tripolitania, partly to show the flag and encourage the rather downcast Italians and partly to provide the training in desert conditions which, in the absence of glass houses and wind machines, had hitherto been impossible. This route march was known as the Unternehmung Graf von Schwerin and accounts of it, no doubt distorted, reached G.H.Q. in Cairo and caused some alarm. Some people thought that the aim was to reinforce Vichy forces at Dakar or else to drive out the Fighting French from Chad.

By the time the 5th Light Division was complete in Tripolitania and Graf von Schwerin's boys had returned, that is about the end of February 1941, it consisted of a tank regiment of six squadrons (half of them equipped only with light Mark I and II tanks), a reconnaissance unit in armoured cars, two motorized machine-gun battalions, one battery of field artillery and one or two of heavy anti-aircraft artillery, an ordinary motorized anti-tank battalion and a heavy anti-tank battalion with self propelled guns. This last was an odd unit; its equipment consisted of Czech 47 mm. anti-tank guns mounted on a Czech tank chassis. Both the gun and the chassis were of excellent design and had been acquired as a result of the Munich agreement. The unit had distinguished itself in the attack on the Belgian fortifications of the Albert Canal. The Division was commanded by Major General von Prittwitz und Gaffron, but over him was a Lieutenant General Erwin Rommel whose title was Commander of the German Afrika Korps. This gave promise of more troops to come.

For the moment General Rommel considered, rightly as it turned out, that his one German division plus whatever Italian troops he might think it useful to add to them would be sufficient for a counter attack on the now weakened British forces. Our 2nd Armoured Division was relatively inexperienced. It was also short of tanks, in fact one of its armoured regiments was equipped with captured Italian M 13 tanks which performed no better for us than they had for their original owners. A principle which was implicit in the Italian defeat was plainly demonstrated: that to lose a battle in the desert south of Gebel Akhdar meant the abandonment of the whole of the bulge of Cyrenaica, since the defeated side had nowhere to make a stand between Agheila on the west and the Gazala-Tobruk area on the east. It was very much touch and go whether Tobruk itself could be held. The 9th Australian Division, a very recently arrived formation, was brought forward from Egypt and flung hastily into the fortress. It just had time enough to organize itself, thanks to the delaying actions of the 2nd Armoured Division. It was helped by Rommel displaying, not for the last time, the defects of his qualities.

Since time is always precious in war, there is a great deal to be said for the dashing general who pushes ahead at all costs. For all that, it is possible to combine impetuosity with the proper amount of planning and foresight as was demonstrated later in the war by General Patton. Rommel was always at his best when handling small, fast-moving formations. When later on his command increased notably in size he could usually be relied on so to mishandle the opening phase of an operation as to reduce it to the optimum size for the appropriate display of his talents. In this opening campaign he started off with the right sized command. He brought forward, in addition to his 5th Light Division, only part of the 27th Brescia Division along the coast road and part of the 17th Pavia Division across the desert route. He made good progress with both columns and on 6th April General Gambier-Parry was summoned to surrender the position at Mechili which had been hastily occupied by the 3rd Indian Motor Brigade and part of the 2nd Motor Brigade of the 2nd Armoured Division. The demand was made in the name of General Zaglio, commanding the Pavia Division, much to the annoyance of the German commander. Twice it was refused, although the post was surrounded on all sides, but the third time it was accepted. Some of the 2nd Support Group fought their way out and back to Tobruk. Almost immediately thereafter the German forces came into contact with Tobruk.

The defences of Tobruk, though the Italians had lavished great pains on them, had a number of unsatisfactory features. To begin with, the perimeter was too big; but this was unavoidable if the only adequate water supply was to be included within it. In the second place it had an Achilles heel which became only too evident from even a cursory study of the map and the terrain. In the southeast corner the ground on which the defences are built is fairly flat but it is dominated from just outside the perimeter by two hills known as Bel Hamed and

Sidi Rezegh, and the attackers are therefore at a great advantage. Inexplicably too, though not untypical of the Italians, the defences were at their weakest just here. It was at this point that we had broken into Tobruk when we took it from the Italians, at this point that our garrison broke out to make contact with the relieving force when the German siege was raised and at this point again that the Germans broke in when they captured Tobruk in June 1942. A glance at the map, or a single ride round the perimeter, would have been bound to reveal this weakness to General Rommel; but that was not his way. His line of march had brought him to the southwestern corner and he decided to attack there at once. It seems scarcely credible, but it is vouched for by the Italian Liaison Officer with him at the time, that he was not aware before he launched his first attack that there was a system of permanent defences with concrete blockhouses, anti-tank ditches, minefields and wire entanglements. After this it scarcely seems surprising to add that he chose the very strongest sector of the whole of the defences for his point of attack. Apart from the short portions of the line on both sides of Tobruk between the road and the sea, where the defences ran along steep sided wadis, the place where nature most favoured the defenders was Ras el M'dauar. Here the permanent defences had been built on top of a prominent ridge commanding the countryside for a good distance all round. Moreover the artificial defences were there at their strongest. This was a Godsend to the inexperienced 9th Australian Division because twice in March and April the Germans butted their heads against this easily defensible position. They were in fact successful, at considerable cost, in overrunning a certain number of the blockhouses and driving a salient into the defensive perimeter, but thanks to the natural advantages already mentioned the Australians were able to seal off this penetration. At this point Rommel felt obliged to call off his attacks. In his first sweep he had been successful in reaching the frontier and establishing himself in Sollum and Halfaya. By May, however, our strength on the frontier was being re-established, and there was an obvious danger that if he kept on battering at the defences of Tobruk he would be too weak to hold off a relieving force.

CHAPTER VI

The Relief of Tobruk

A T THE time when I arrived in the Western Desert plans were in train for an operation which, it was hoped, would result in the relief of Tobruk. The strategic side of this operation can be studied in Sir Winston Churchill's great history. It will be remembered that he had gone to great lengths and had caused great risks to be taken to send to the Middle East a reinforcement of tanks which he hoped would swing the balance of armoured strength in our favour. The code name was 'Tiger' and the Navy was instructed to run all risks to deliver the goods. He speaks with almost paternal affection of the tanks brought by this operation as 'The Tiger Cubs' and it is with great disappointment that he animadverts on the time taken to prepare them for battle and on the result of the battle when fought. These censures come home with much less force to those on the spot who remember that the tanks on which such hopes were placed, for which the Navy ran such deadly risks, and which Sir Winston clearly feels were misused, were nothing but those Crusader tanks which were the cause of so much bitterness. It was not so much, at that time, their lack of hitting power that was criticized since the Germans then had no tank gun bigger than 50 mm. (There were a few Mark IVs armed with 75 mm. guns but these were howitzers for close support not armour-piercing weapons). The thinness of the armour was a more legitimate complaint. But what infuriated the users beyond measure was their mechanical unreliability. In this battle it showed at its worst since, although a number of modifications had been made to fit them for use in the desert, there was still a number of defects vulnerable to the hard going and the ubiquitous drifting sand. In a powerful passage Sir Winston Churchill complains that the commanders in the Middle East seemed to want a 50 per cent margin of superiority in tanks over the enemy. His comment that 'Generals only enjoy such comforts in Heaven. And those who demand them do not always get there', may well seem majestically convincing. But if in order to arrive with 100 tanks at the end of a march of 20 miles it is necessary to start off with 150 to allow for mechanical casualties, the demand for such a margin may not seem unreasonable.

At a later stage of the war, just before the battle of El Alamein, I had an officer serving with me from the Gloucester Hussars. He had such a dislike for his Crusader that, with the full concurrence of his crew, he swopped it with a neighbouring armoured regiment, recently arrived from Britain, for a 3-ton lorry. His argument was that a 3-tonner could go anywhere a tank could, was not prone to break down and a hit from an anti-tank gun would only make a neat hole in it instead of burning it up with all the crew. His C.O., though understanding, thought that this might spread a bad example and had him transferred in a friendly way to G.H.Q. There he found another subaltern from the Bays, also then working with me, a blue-eyed and fair-haired boy of 21 who had had no less than nine Crusaders 'shot under him'. He was suffering from shell shock, not I think a very common complaint in this war, but fully justified in his case.

The other tank used in this operation was the Mark II infantry tank. It was its swan song. The Mark II had excellent thick armour and its London bus engine was mechanically very reliable; the trouble was that its top speed was four miles an hour. It was designed to accompany infantry and had performed wonderfully well in this role at Sidi Barrani, Bardia and Tobruk. It was too slow for the armoured battle and could be engaged at long range and destroyed by the German 88 mm. anti-aircraft gun. This remarkable weapon was frequently used in an anti-tank role in the desert, and took the fancy of the war correspondents so much that, as Lord Alexander observes in his African despatches: 'The press appeared to be unaware of the existence of any other calibre of artillery in the German Army.' The obsession was catching. I remember visiting an American unit at the time when the Americans were fairly new, in southern Tunisia. In reply to my question as to how they were getting on, the company commander said, "Pretty well, but those 88's are giving us hell." This surprised me in view of the fact that they were in a depression in the ground not overlooked anywhere. A moment later a mortar bomb came over the brow of the hill and fell into the position. "There they are again," said the captain. In spite of this belief in the ability of this wonder weapon to shoot round corners and over hills, in fact it had, like all anti-tank guns, a dead flat trajectory. I must admit it made the most disconcerting noise.

The operation was given the code name of 'Battleaxe'. The 7th Armoured Division, plus the 22nd Guards Brigade, was to operate on top of the Escarpment and the 4th Indian Division below it. The latter was intended to attack Halfaya and Sollum. I think there must have been some doubts in the minds of General Wavell and General Beresford-Pierse whether, even if we had won the battle on the frontier, we should have been strong enough, after the losses involved, to relieve Tobruk. In the event we proved not strong enough to win the battle on the frontier. It was a near run thing and very hard fought on both sides, and the result was determined by the failure of the infantry tank when faced with the 88 mm., the greater tactical skill of the German tank units and the repeated breakdown of our tanks. I spent the period of the battle at Mersa Matruh interrogating prisoners, of whom large numbers were captured. The main point of interest that arose from the interrogation was that the second German armoured division had arrived, the 15th Panzer Division, commanded by General von Esebeck. This was the first time that I spent long periods interrogating large numbers of prisoners. The setting was perfect. Mersa Matruh was mainly in ruins and interrogations were carried out in a single-roomed hut, badly dilapidated and hung about with dingy Army blankets. The lighting was by either candles or a hurricane lamp and the general effect was distinctly Stanislavsky. To assist in depressing the Germans the garrison was provided by the Polish Brigade. Most Germans had either a bad conscience about their own treatment of the Poles or else were convinced that the Poles had been in the habit of treating the Germans in Poland with great brutality; in either case they disliked the idea of being in Polish custody. And a hint that in return for a co-operative attitude they would be handed over to British troops to be looked after used to work wonders in loosening their tongues. As a matter of fact they all were going to be handed over to British troops anyway as soon as they left Matruh and furthermore we were obliged to get them away as quickly as possible in order to save on food supplies.

I do not remember that I particularly enjoyed interrogating prisoners. I always felt a certain sympathy for them, though most of them, and all the Italians, seemed quite pleased to be out of things. It is a hard, monotonous, and time-consuming task. On the whole, although my German is better than my Italian, I found the Italians less tiring. Ninety-nine per cent of them were anxious to help by telling all they knew. The main thing was to keep a friendly and a fairly informal conversation going and wait to hear what they had to say. If some reluctance was shown, as occasionally happened in the case of officers, the best technique was to express surprise that an officer as senior or experienced as the one you were addressing should be ignorant of the answer to your question. The main Italian obsession is to avoid appearing unimportant or stupid—'fare una brutta figura'—and a little spur to his pride would usually made him ready to show that in fact he knew the answer.

Most Germans were similarly communicative though with them the best approach was to put your questions in an easy but authoritative way as though you had not the least doubt that an answer would be forthcoming. Instincts of discipline were usually strong enough to ensure that the answer was given. The comradely approach was no good; the interrogator had to be rigidly regimental. I well remember many occasions when senior German N.C.O.'s would rack their brains in the most conscientious manner to drag up every detail about something in which we might be interested—the performance of a new anti-tank gun for example or an order for a future operation. I remember one *oberfeldwebel* making efforts which were almost physically visible to remember details of papers he had seen connected with a forthcoming operation and he did in fact do so well that he gave us practically all the essentials of the German plan of attack at Gazala in May 1942.

The trouble is that prisoners know so little. No doubt if we had happened to pick up the chief mess orderly at the enemy G.H.Q. we might have found his information of considerable value but the average man knows next to nothing outside his own small unit. For that matter, units were so scattered and the desert itself so featureless that it was hard to get from him the location of his unit. However the accumulation of stories from large numbers of prisoners could always be put together and made into something. They and the documents they carried were the basic sources of information about the enemy, the bread and butter of intelligence. They were above all valuable, indeed practically indispensable, for confirming the arrival of new enemy units and formations.

After the failure of Battleaxe the next three months were pretty quiet. Both sides were reinforcing. On the German side the 5th Light Division was reorganized as an ordinary armoured division and took the title of 21st Panzer Division. But Rommel still required some good infantry if he was to capture Tobruk and he was allotted a new German motorized division. The infantry came over by battalions at a time. The first complete regiment to arrive was rather an oddity. The 361st Regiment was formed from Germans who before the war had fought in the French Foreign Legion. The Legion always recruited very large numbers of Germans but German law made them ineligible for military service as being guilty of 'national dishonour'. By 1941 it had become apparent that this was an unnecessary waste and so they were sent out to join Rommel's forces to make use of their previous North African experience. Two of them, Alsatians I think, deserted to our lines in Tobruk fairly rapidly so that we had early knowledge of the regiment's arrival. The Division, of three regiments, was known to begin with as 'Africa (Special Purpose) Division', later as the 1st Africa Division but eventually—perhaps some of the older formations objected to this undeserved claim to priority—as 90th Light Division. Under this name it acquired great notoriety, almost popularity, among our troops. It was, until August 1942, the only German infantry division in Africa. To mark this increase, General Rommel's H.Q. was renamed 'Panzer-gruppe Afrika', 'Africa Armoured Group'.

I ought at this point to warn the reader that I intend for the future to use the expression 'Afrika Korps' to mean the Afrika Korps, a body which was commanded at this time by General Cruewell and consisted of a Corps Headquarters and the 15th and 21st Panzer Divisions only; and not in the sense, which has become popular in Britain, of all the troops under Rommel's command. My reasons are not pedantic. I have no objection to the popular usage; but for practical purposes I am up against the dilemma that if I use 'Afrika Korps' to mean the whole of the German forces, what am I to use if I want to speak of the Afrika Korps?

Under Rommel's command, then, at this time there were first the Afrika Korps of the two armoured divisions, secondly the 90th Light Division and a fair amount of army troops, particularly artillery, and thirdly the Italian 20th (Mobile) Corps. He was by now a full General. He planned to attack Tobruk in November, by which time he reckoned that he should have the requisite amount of infantry and artillery. Now that he had discovered the right way in it was likely that he would succeed in his attack, and our intention was to anticipate him. A few more troops were arriving on our side as well and it was decided that in our next offensive they should be commanded by an Army H.Q. It was to be called the Eighth Army and would have under its command two Corps, numbered 13 and 30. The 13th was to be mainly an infantry Corps and the 30th armoured. Another armoured brigade had arrived from the United Kingdom and was joined in the desert by the 1st South African Division, fresh from its Abyssinian triumphs. It was confidently expected that the terrain would be suitable for a reproduction of the tactics so successfully displayed in the South African War.

The Germans had also received another and more unusual reinforcement. After the defeat of Jugoslavia, the Belgrade wireless had been beamed on North Africa and used to have a programme particularly addressed to German troops there called 'The Young Sentry'. The main features consisted of 'answers to correspondents'; but what particularly took the imagination was the closing theme song. According to contemporary legend the organizers of the programme had come across a single gramophone record abandoned in the corner of a studio. They thought it might suit and played it experimentally at the end of their first programme. Thereafter it maintained its position by overwhelming popular demand. It was not long before the British troops too were in the habit of tuning to Belgrade at 9.45 each evening for the husky voice of Lala Anders singing *Lili Marlene*. Sir Fitzroy Maclean in his brilliant book *Eastern Approaches* has borne tribute to its unforgettable quality, rather spoilt by the fact that he goes on to misquote the first two lines. Certainly the tune has proved unforgettable. The words were nothing much, either in the original or in the Italian version—for it quickly caught on with them too, even displacing for some time the song about the young girl and the doctor. There is an amusing difference between the words: in the German song the singer has died before the last verse, which records his ghost returning to haunt the spot; this was pretty well standard with all German soldiers' songs. The Italian last verse records how much the singer is looking forward to returning to the heroine once more.

The operation for the relief of Tobruk was held up because the Australian Government insisted on the 9th Australian Division being removed from the fortress. The reasons for this are set out in Sir Winston Churchill's history which includes the impassioned appeals which he addressed to the Prime Minister of Australia, then Mr. Curtin, to reverse his decision. Mr. Curtin was adamant, basing himself on reports from Australian H.Q. in the Middle East that the health of the troops was suffering. Accordingly a U.K. Division had to be sent. This was made up principally from the various regular infantry battalions which were in the Middle East at the start of the war. It was called the 70th Division. It was a particularly fine and well-trained body of troops; from all I heard it retained its health pretty well in Tobruk. Unfortunately after Tobruk it never fought again as a Division but, on arrival in the Far Eastern theatre, it was broken up and used in General Wingate's Chindit expedition. I am not competent to speak about the merits of this operation but I have heard those who are express the gravest doubts whether the results compensated for the destruction of this fine formation. The Polish Brigade was also sent to Tobruk so that the commander of the fortress had four brigades of infantry under his command. The relieving operation was a most hazardous one for the Navy. Tobruk harbour was within gun range of the enemy and was bombed fairly continually by night and day. The Commander-in-Chief of the Mediterranean Fleet, which had scarcely recovered from the heavy losses of the battle round Crete, viewed it with great anxiety. In fact it went off reasonably well though one battalion of Australians had to be left behind because the ship that should have taken them was sunk.

Tobruk had by now settled down into a fairly steady routine as a besieged fortress. The actual investment was left to the Italians who had three divisions, Pavia, Bologna and Brescia disposed round the perimeter. Inside the fortress everything was underground. The fortress command had an admirable underground headquarters built by the Italians deep in the side of a ridge, generously protected by concrete. Everyday life was reminiscent of the First World War. The besieged were the more active and raids and minor flare-ups in no man's land were frequent. A steady stream of Italian prisoners was passed back with returning supply ships to the cage at Mersa Matruh. The Poles in particular rapidly established a great moral superiority over the Brescia Division to whom they were opposed on the Western flank of the perimeter. The C.O. of one of the Polish battalions, whose name I now forget, used to make quite a habit in the summer evenings of strolling across no man's land towards the nearest Italian positions and haranguing the enemy in good Italian on their stupidity in being allied to the Germans. On one occasion at any rate he was received with cries of 'Three cheers for the Poles'.

When Eighth Army H.Q. was set up it took over a great deal of the staff of the old Western Desert Force. The rest went to form H.Q. 13th Corps. To my surprise and pleasure I was appointed G.3 Intelligence, 13th Corps. This abbreviation stands for General Staff Officer 3rd Grade, and meant a rise in status, though not in rank, from

Intelligence Officer, which had been my previous appointment. The G.2 was a regular officer Major Freddie de Butts. If I was pleased with my new appointment I was even more pleased with my new chief; a man of outstanding common sense, hard working and quick to grasp a point, he was an excellent example of the advantage which accrued to Intelligence in the Middle East in general from the fact that the bulk of those engaged in it were people with active experience of proper soldiering. There were no doubt strong reasons for the formation of the Intelligence Corps, but officers who had spent their whole career in it, though often valuable as specialists, never seemed quite at ease as general staff officers with other members of the staff. At this period of the war there were comparatively few Intelligence Corps Officers serving in the Middle East though a certain number were beginning to arrive in G.H.Q. I always maintained that the Intelligence Officer needed no different qualities from those required of a staff officer in any other branch. It was necessary of course to have available someone capable of translating captured documents and interrogating prisoners. But on the one hand specialists and translators are not so hard to come by and on the other hand linguistic ability is no guarantee of intellectual ability. I agree whole-heartedly with Sir Harold Nicolson who says "I affirm in all seriousness that I have never met a first-class linguist who had a first-class brain. Conversely, I have met several brilliant linguists who possess no brain at all." Some of the most successful and highest placed intelligence officers whom I knew had very little if any knowledge of foreign languages. However, I must not be taken as belittling the intelligence of the Intelligence Officers, two German speaking and two Italian speaking, who made up the rest of the Intelligence branch. Although all four were thoroughly competent linguists they had a good deal of common sense as well.

The Commander of 13th Corps was General Godwin Austen. His last command had been that of the troops in British Somaliland where he had been forced to withdraw in the face of overwhelming odds. For a General commanding four infantry battalions to be defeated by one commanding eighteen plus two armoured battalions is not surprising, but such odds also heavily reduce his chances of distinguishing himself. British generals who come to high command in the early days of a British war are generally worthy of sympathy. The ideal is to take command half way through, when the tide begins to change. General Godwin Austen was shrewd and energetic and popular with the troops. He had that quality of robustness which Lord Wavell laid down as one of the prime requisites of a general. He would refuse to be rattled and would maintain his objective with the utmost imperturbability. He must be given a good share of the credit for the victory gained by 13th Corps' first battle.

His Brigadier, General Staff, was a man different in many ways and a perfect complement to him. This was none other than John Harding, later to be distinguished in command of the 7th Armoured Division, as Chief of Staff to Lord Alexander in Italy, as a Corps Commander, as C.I.G.S. and as Governor of Cyprus. He had been in the desert since 1940, as Chief of Staff to Western Desert Force and to Cyrenaica Command. It was almost entirely due to him that the decision to hold on to Tobruk in 1941 was successfully carried out. He was a man of the greatest physical and intellectual courage, strong willed and persistent in all he did; but the vigorous impression he made on me was by reason of his sheer intellectual capacity. He had one of the most lucid and clear thinking brains that I have ever known. He was not outstandingly rapid or intuitive in his apprehensions, but he was quick enough to seize the elements of a problem and from that point on his mind worked like some beautifully oiled machine to deliver the brilliant and inevitable solution. He had a reputation for bad temper, which he would sometimes half humorously accuse himself of, but I never saw it. He seemed to me from the first time I knew him the ideal of the regular staff officer and I never found anyone in that role to put above him.

The Commander of 30th Corps was General Willoughby Norrie (later Lord Norrie). He was a cavalryman who had recently arrived from England, intended as commander of the 1st Armoured Division. He had succeeded to the senior command thanks to a certain type of American transport plane. I had better not give its proper name for fear of a charge of libel, but it will be recognized by all who served in the Middle East by its usual description as the plane that was good for promotion. It got this reputation because it was used a lot for the transport of senior officers, being both fast and comfortable; it also had a strong tendency to spin into the ground a few seconds after take-off. These crashes were always fatal to all on board. The commander designate of 30th Corps and his chief of staff had just been written off in one; many other senior Army and Air Force commanders suffered the same fate, bringing unexpected, and sometimes well deserved, advancement to their juniors.

On about 20th September 1941 the new 13th Corps H.Q. moved off from Maaten Baqqush and took to the desert. From this time on, apart from a short spell in G.H.Q., I never knew a static H.Q. again in Africa. Our first camp was at a place called Ghot Wahas, near Sofafi, one of the camps built by Graziani as part of the Sidi Barrani defences, and also near 'Strafer's Wadi' which was where the 7th Support Group had lain before the battle. Rear H.Q. was at Bir Wahas which is the only place in the world where I have climbed a tree beginning at the top and ending at the roots to see a cinema show. The Bir was an unusually large affair providing room and concealment for the cinema. There was a hole in the roof and a crack in the floor, thanks to which a large fig tree had grown up inside the Bir with its top branches just jutting out of the hole at ground level. The H.Q. camp was called a laager because it was composed entirely of vehicles. The office of the Intelligence Branch, for example, consisted of a 3-ton lorry with a tent thrown over it. The body of the lorry was reserved for storage and work went on underneath the two flaps of tent at the side. The tent was camouflaged with a net though I think this was not particularly effective. The defence against air attack was dispersion, carried out to great lengths for it was rigidly laid down that there should always be 200 yards between each vehicle. Round our lorry we pitched low tents of ground sheets on sticks just sufficient to cover a camp bed. The first thing we did on stopping was to dig a slit trench each as defence against air attack. The result of this was we were only attacked once or twice from the air and never with any effect.

I had a batman called Perryman from the Essex Regiment. He was a tailor by trade which was distinctly useful because the desert was rather hard on clothes. He was also very skilled at acquiring things though I did not inquire into his precise methods: as far as I was concerned, he produced some acceptable trifles every now and then, and I never had any cause to complain. Although an "old soldier" he was not particularly clever. At an early stage of our association he was nearly the death of me. I had a short violent attack of sandfly fever which produced much the same symptoms as Asian flu. When I was at my most feverish I was presented as a treat with a bottle of soda water to drink. Perryman brought this in but had mislaid the bottle opener. I noticed him wrestling with it in a rather helpless way when suddenly there was a loud bang, a bullet whistled past me and went out of the side of the tent about two inches above my head. It had apparently struck Perryman as a good idea to use the trigger guard of my pistol as a bottle opener and he had not stopped to find out whether it was loaded or not.

The desert in Autumn, especially on top of the Escarpment, was immensely bracing. The north winds still blew freshly, there was a good soaking dew at night and the air was dry, clean and sparkling. It was a joy to drive long distances over the crisp gravel, to visit forward troops, such as the two armoured car regiments which at that time provided the forward screen, the 4th South African Armoured Car Regiment and the King's Dragoon Guards. The South Africans were an exuberant lot, most of them Afrikaners but commanded by an exceptionally English Englishman. They seemed to take to desert ways and to the job of reconnaissance as though to the manner born. There certainly is a great similarity between the air of the desert and the air of the high veldt in the Transvaal, and a job which called for acting on one's own and quick movement over wide areas seemed to speak to the heart of the Afrikaner. The King's Dragoon Guards were farther south watching the frontier near Bir Sheferzen. They had an extremely well-stocked mess and even provided some fresh meat brought up in dry ice from Alex. There was other fresh meat for a good shot in the gazelles which flitted about freely over most parts of the desert.

The major operations for the winter of 1941 were given the code name 'Crusader'. There was some controversy about their timing, as can be seen from Sir Winston Churchill's history. It was to a large extent conditioned by the enemy. We were aware that their intention was to assault Tobruk some time in the last 10 days of November; the actual date was the 23rd. There was something to be said for allowing the Germans to start first in order that they might be thoroughly engaged and therefore be unable to free their full forces to meet our offensive. The reason why this strategy was rejected is very interesting in view of the recriminations about the fall of Tobruk next year. General Auchinleck held, and the view was supported by General Scobie, commanding in Tobruk, that there was a real danger, now that the Germans had obviously discovered where they ought to make their attack, that the fortress might be captured in the first day or so, before the offensive of the Eighth Army could have any effect. It is interesting that this should be the view taken at a time when the defences of Tobruk were very firmly manned by a strong force whose defence plans were at a high pitch of preparedness. It sheds a light on the reasons for the failure of the 2nd South African Division to hold Tobruk next year.

It was accordingly decided that our offensive should start before, but only shortly before, the Germans were to attack Tobruk. The date chosen was the 18th November; the plan was that 30th Corps with three armoured brigades and the greater part of the 1st South African Division should advance and put itself in a position between Bardia and Tobruk, nearer to the latter than to the former, challenging the German army to come out and fight it. 13th Corps, with the 4th Indian Division and the New Zealand Division, was to pin down and cut off the enemy troops holding the frontier defences from Sidi Omar to Halfaya and then to advance westwards, south of the Bardia–Tobruk road, to assist 30th Corps in clearing the battlefield, leaving the enemy fortresses to be dealt with later at leisure. It was quite clear that, apart from the operations of 13th Corps, the fighting would be of a mobile fluctuating nature and that it would be impossible to make any detailed plans for that very reason.

As always, there was a thoroughly worked out deception plan and, as always, it was entirely successful with the Germans. A Brigade of the 5th Indian Division was sent to Jarabub and every means was taken to persuade the Germans that the next attack would come from there and would take the form of a broad sweeping movement to outflank to the west the forces besieging Tobruk. If this was swallowed a corollary would be a mistake about the date of our attack; the false indications that were being promulgated were designed to make it appear that the base at Jarabub for supporting the attack would not be ready until the beginning of December. The fact that the Germans did fall for this deception was confirmed to me by an excellent source later, though it could be proved quite easily at the time. The source I refer to was a Lieutenant-Colonel Mario Revetria, who was the senior Italian Intelligence Officer in Libya. His name was familiar to us at the time from captured staff lists and, for that matter, from captured copies of his intelligence summaries. These were often excellent and always better than those of his German colleagues. Before he took over, though, I remember an Italian summary which, commenting on a wireless intercept from the Support Group about a Colour Sergeant in the Rifle Brigade, drew severe conclusions about British weakness in manpower from the fact that 'even this crack regiment had been forced to recruit negroes, and promote them to NCO's rank'. Revetria took up his appointment in February 1941 and held it until after the battle of Alamein. In Tunisia he transferred to the Operations side. In about the middle of October 1943 he suddenly turned up at General Alexander's H.Q., then near Bari, and I had an extremely pleasant time discussing with him the battles in the desert in which we had been on opposite sides. He was a most efficient Intelligence officer and such success as was obtained by the Axis Intelligence in that theatre was largely due to him. Fortunately for us the Germans, who never believed in their own Intelligence, were not going to start believing in Italian Intelligence. He insisted to me at Bari that he had guessed correctly the point of our attack. This may be so or not; many Italians and Germans have made similar claims but the evidence of their actions at the time does not always support them. However, I believe Revetria when he says that German Intelligence expected the attack to come from Jarabub because it fits in very well with other intelligence, including the evidence of captured documents. I also think highly probable his story that at midday of the 18th November, six hours after 30th Corps had crossed the wire and headed northwest for Tobruk, the chief German Intelligence Officer, Major von Mellenthin, came into Revetria's office and said: "Well, everything looks quiet today." An even more important example could be quoted, for this was obviously a case in which the Chief Intelligence Officer enjoyed the full confidence of his commander. Rommel had refused to believe in the imminence of a British attack. He wasn't even in Africa when it came; he had gone off for a conference with the Italians in Rome and, it was believed by the German troops, to have a few days' leave while celebrating his birthday. The battle thus inauspiciously begun was perhaps the most mishandled of all Rommel's battles in the desert. It is significant that *The Rommel Papers*, edited by Captain Liddell Hart, contain nothing from his pen on this battle at all; he seems to have adopted the motto of the sundial 'I only count my sunny hours'. Instead there are some fugitive and rather romanticized impressions by his Chief of Staff. These give a picture of great activity, not all of it appropriate for a general, but leave rather unexplained how it came about that in the result he had to abandon the whole of Cyrenaica with the loss of 35 per cent of his force. The fact is that this battle is perhaps the best example of Rommel's ability to snatch defeat from the jaws of victory.

I shall try to justify this judgment in the course of the narrative but it may be useful to insert at this point some general observations about the man who is by far the best known of all the enemy commanders in the last war. Much that has been written about him is either myth or mere panegyric. What was written about him while the war was actually proceeding carried these characteristics to excess. It was natural that at a time when the British Army was only engaged in one theatre there should be intense interest in the enemy commander. This interest was started and nurtured by the British press; the German press paid very little attention to General Rommel, and when they did eventually start, which was not before late 1942, it was largely a reflection of the splendid write-up he had already received from the British press. In the absence, therefore, of authentic information the imagination was freely drawn on. Some newspapers, perhaps with an axe to grind, insisted that he had risen from the ranks. Mr. Aneurin Bevan, falling into the same error, declared in the House of Commons in 1942 that many people were saying that if Rommel had been an Englishman instead of a German he would never have risen above the rank of sergeant. Another popular theory was that he was a devoted Nazi who had received accelerated promotion for this reason. The facts are simpler, less romantic and more natural. He was in fact a Wurtemberger of a solid middle-class professional family who was always intended for an army career and was commissioned into an infantry regiment shortly before the First World War. He served with distinction as a regimental officer on the western, Italian and Rumanian fronts, winning among other decorations the order 'Pour le Mérite', the highest Prussian award for gallantry. He remained in the army between the wars and gained a certain limited reputation by writing books on infantry tactics. I used to have a copy of his book *Infantry in the Attack* (*Infanterie greift an*), a sensible little handbook on infantry minor tactics which is based mainly on his own experiences in the First World War. (It was borrowed from me some 23 years ago by the Right Honourable Member for Wolverhampton South-West and if he should happen to read this I should be glad to have it back.) He was a colonel in 1939 and commanded the 7th Panzer Division in France in 1940 as a Major General. This command formed the basis of his reputation. In spite of all he did in the desert campaigns and in the west and in spite of all that has been written about him since his death, I still think it could be argued that his real gift was for commanding an armoured regiment, perhaps a division, and that his absolute ceiling was an armoured corps. The same thought seems to have been in the mind of Lord Alexander writing about Rommel in his despatch on the campaign in Africa: 'He was a tactician of the greatest ability, with a firm grasp of every detail of the employment of armour in action, and very quick to seize the fleeting opportunity and the critical turning

Field Marshal Lord Alexander

point of a mobile battle. I felt certain doubts, however, about his
strategic ability, in particular as to whether he fully understood the
importance of a sound administrative plan. Happiest while controlling
a mobile force directly under his own eyes he was liable to overexploit
immediate success without sufficient thought for the future.'

The attack began at 6 o'clock on the morning of 18th November.
At that time the whole of 30 Corps began their advance. Simultaneously, but more deliberately, 13th Corps began its more restricted outflanking move to isolate Sidi Omar from the northwest. There was a
great feeling of confidence in the air. For the first time we appeared
to be about to take the offensive with a good chance. Our tank
strength was known to exceed the enemy's and it was not yet known
how far they came short in quality. One of the greatest contributing
causes of this feeling of confidence, and the thing that I personally
found most impressive, was the fact that the air was full of our aircraft
and there were no Germans to be seen. On the opening morning this
was due to the fact that the enemy was blissfully unconscious that anything was going on; but even when they woke up to the situation, and
when we began to be attacked from time to time by fighters and even
dive bombers, there was a great change in the air. No longer was it
axiomatic that if you heard an aircraft overhead it was bound to be an
enemy.

Enemy dispositions on the morning of the 18th were unchanged
from what they had been for some weeks. Around Tobruk were the
three Italian infantry divisions already mentioned, the Brescia, Bologna
and Pavia, and behind them stood the 15th Panzer Division and the
90th Light Division. On the frontier there was a line of fortified posts
stretching from Halfaya to Sidi Omar. Halfaya was held by a German
regiment, Sidi Omar by an Italian Division, the 55th Savona Division,
and the posts between by mixed Italian and German troops, the latter
including some specially organized independent companies known as
'oasis' companies. These came out with the original 5th Light Division
as an extra infantry element. I do not know what bureaucrat in
O.K.W. chose their romantic name, but they never saw an oasis in
the course of their existence. North of Sidi Omar and west of Bardia
was the 21st Panzer Division in a position where it could support either
the frontier defences or the troops around Tobruk. Finally at Bir el
Gobi, south of Tobruk, was the Italian 132nd Armoured Division
known as Ariete which means 'the battering ram'. They were so
placed as to cover the routes from Jarabub to Tobruk and to be able

to support the forces round Tobruk if necessary. The division was now up to strength and equipped throughout with the M 13 tank. These dispositions meant that the enemy armour was split into three bodies. The intention was that they should be capable of joining up quickly should the need arise, but if, as was our plan, a hostile force were to thrust itself somewhere between Tobruk and Bardia the three would have to fight separately. With this in mind the idea was that two armoured brigades, followed by the 5th South African Infantry Brigade, should make for the positions of the 15th Panzer Division outside Tobruk while a third armoured brigade, the 4th, should face northeast as a flank guard against the 21st Panzer Division. The 4th Armoured Brigade was equipped throughout with a new tank, the American light tank which we called the Stuart. It had an excellent engine and transmission which made it easy to drive and reliable over rough going. Its armour was good and it had a 37 mm. gun which was up to standard for 1941, but it had the disadvantage that it was built up too high, higher than the Crusader or the average German tank, and therefore presented in the desert a conspicuous target.

The 21st Panzer Division did not get under way until the afternoon of the 18th and the clash with the 4th Armoured Brigade came next day. On our side the attack was marked by great determination. The three regiments of the 4th Armoured Brigade had great confidence in their new tanks and pressed home their attacks with greater dash than circumspection. The Germans were more skilful in the combined use of anti-tank guns with their tanks, but for all that the result of the first battle was a German repulse. It was dearly bought, for our losses were heavy, and it was not possible to prevent the 21st Panzer Division moving westwards to concentrate at the vital point southeast of Tobruk. Here the other two brigades of the 7th Armoured Division had fought their way on to the height of Sidi Rezegh overlooking the vulnerable point of the Tobruk defences. The word was accordingly given to the Tobruk garrison to start their sortie to join hands with the 7th Armoured Division. Meanwhile the 5th South African Brigade was to be brought up to Sidi Rezegh to consolidate the position.

Rommel did not get back to Libya until the evening of the 18th. He still believed we were only conducting a reconnaissance in force—in fact he first discovered he was being seriously attacked when he heard the B.B.C. news on the evening of the 19th, D+2. Cruewell had by now ordered a concentration. The vital importance of Sidi Rezegh was as clear to him as to us and he needed both his armoured divisions and 90th Light Division to recapture it. The counter attack began early on 22nd November. It was an unusually grim and violent battle. Sidi Rezegh is a stony ridge with the limestone only two to three inches below the level of the sand. It proved impossible for the infantry or the artillery to dig in. Superior tactics, and in particular the use of anti-tank artillery, gave the Germans the advantage. By the evening of the 23rd the 15th and 21st Panzer Divisions, sadly depleted but flushed with victory, had cleared us from the whole of the Sidi Rezegh Ridge and driven us back into the desert to the south.

This was a considerable German success. It demonstrated the ability of the commanders to recover from an unexpected situation and the skill and experience of their armoured troops. General Cunningham's plan was in ruins. Rommel was exuberant at his victory and burning to make it even greater. In spite of the pleas of his divisional commanders he decided to set off, with almost all the armour that could be made serviceable, on a sweep over the battlefield and towards the frontier in which he hoped to be able to complete the destruction of our armour and, no doubt, to pick up prisoners from what he supposed to be a disorganized army. He accordingly set out in a straight line for the frontier, driving ahead himself with a small escort of armoured cars and tanks.

While all this was going on, 13th Corps had been pursuing an offensive against Sidi Omar. The defences were elaborate and our losses were heavy, but by the 21st a large part of the fortified area of Sidi Omar had been taken. This was the work of the 4th Indian Division. The New Zealand Division then advanced past Sidi Omar as far as the track which leads from Fort Capuzzo to Tobruk, now known as the Trigh Capuzzo but earlier as Trigh Enver Bey after the Young Turk leader who fought here in the war of 1911. They left a brigade to observe Bardia and with the other two brigades turned westwards for Tobruk. 13th Corps H.Q. followed them. I must confess to a pleasurable thrill on entering enemy territory for the first time, though the colour of the desert remained the same. An advance was always a splendid thing to watch and to take part in. The vehicles advanced still keeping their 200 yards apart so that miles of desert on every hand were occupied by lorries bucketing along at six miles an hour and sending up a long trail of dust behind them. On occasion there would be a burst of fire as someone spotted a gazelle escaping in fright, but when they were running they were not often shot. We camped just off the Trigh Capuzzo, behind the two New Zealand brigades. Bardia, to our east, was still in enemy hands, but they were not in any great strength there. As soon as a halt was made the lorries were rigged as offices and G.S.I. sat down to study the current haul of captured documents and collate the messages from the divisions.

We knew that the battle at Sidi Rezegh was being fiercely fought and was not going well for us, but almost the first intimation of disaster was the sudden arrival from the south, in clouds of dust, of the commander of 30th Corps with some of his officers. His Corps H.Q. had been right in the track of Rommel's advance to the frontier and it was dispersed to the four winds when the German column drove right through the middle of it. The same fate was overtaking other formations and H.Q.s as well, for the whole of the desert to the south of us was full of the rear elements of 30th Corps. Rommel held on steadily for the frontier. Our immediate guess was that there was some plan in this advance and what other plan could it be than to find and destroy our dumps? These lay in vast profusion just on the east side of the frontier, and there was nothing between them and the German columns. At this point General Auchinleck arrived at Eighth Army H.Q. General Cunningham, impressed by the magnitude of the disaster, urged that the offensive should now be abandoned and that all forces should withdraw behind the frontier to consolidate. This would inevitably have resulted in the loss of Tobruk. General Auchinleck now showed the strength of his character. The position did indeed look desperate: our plan of attack had been disrupted, our tanks had been beaten and our main attacking forces scattered. Nevertheless, he never forgot that the enemy's difficulties, though you don't know them yourself, may look as great to him as your own do to you. There were still elements in the situation on which success could be built. 13th Corps was in a favourable position, pressing on to meet the garrison of Tobruk. The armoured forces were indeed scattered but they could be gathered and there were fortunately adequate reserve tanks to re-equip them. If we could last out the next day or so the German effort might yet spend itself. He determined therefore to maintain the initiative and as a sign replaced General Cunningham as commander of the Eighth Army with his own Chief of Staff, General Ritchie.

The Rommel raid reached the frontier and crossed it, coming close to driving Army H.Q. away. He had no idea where our dumps were and he never found them, although one portion of his column actually drove through part of one of the dumps without realizing. The vast spaces of the desert gave perfect opportunities for dispersion and a Field

Maintenance Centre might occupy as much as 100 square miles. It would therefore have been a long job to destroy such a dump, though a fuel dump would have blazed well enough and its loss would have been the most serious of all.

This confused and difficult period gave rise to many of the favourite Rommel stories, for instance about how he visited the British wounded in a field casualty clearance station and chatted to the medical officers; the stories are faithfully reproduced in his Chief of Staff's account in *The Rommel Papers*. What is quite clear from this account is that he had entirely lost control of the battle. At one time he was completely lost himself, all alone in the middle of the desert. Cruewell rescued him and then got lost himself; of course all this time, about 24 hours, they were out of wireless contact with their troops. Rommel had only the vaguest idea where his two armoured divisions were and the most he could control effectively was what he had directly under his own eye at a given moment. In fact he had abdicated his position as an Army Commander. No such stories are told of General Auchinleck, but he did retain control of the battle. And what in fact did Rommel achieve? He caused a pretty panic and added to his legend; but at the end of it all he found himself in a very much worse position than when he set out on his raid. General Auchinleck is justified in saying in his despatch 'On the whole the enemy thrust inflicted little material damage, and the moral effect was almost negligible. . . . Inasmuch as the New Zealand Division was able to fight through to Tobruk, which they might never have been able to do if the weight of the enemy armour had been thrown into the scale against them, the advantage rested with us.' General Carver, writing twenty-five years later, says 'The reckless manner in which he personally conducted it [the raid] largely contributed to its failure and led almost directly to the defeat of his army.'

At this time 13th Corps H.Q. was about one-third of the way between Bardia and Tobruk. There were no British troops very close but we had two platoons of the Buffs, two anti-tank guns and two light anti-aircraft guns for protection. These soon came in useful because Rommel had now been forced to alter his plans. The New Zealand Division was pushing on towards Tobruk and that very night the 4th New Zealand Brigade captured Bel Hamed and the 6th New Zealand Brigade Sidi Rezegh. The sortie from Tobruk was also doing well and there was reason to hope that they would shortly join up. The armour of 30th Corps was reorganizing in the desert to the south and was already recovering its strength after its temporary disorganization.

In other words, so far as Rommel was concerned, there was all the weary work to be done again. By doggedly maintaining the offensive, General Auchinleck had recaptured the key to Tobruk that Rommel had had in his hands and had thrown away. Moreover, in the course of his raid many of his tanks had broken down and many others had been destroyed, for example by the heroic gunners of the 1st Field Regiment. It was a remarkable and well-deserved reversal of fortune.

It was now time for the Germans to get back to Tobruk and see whether they could repeat their earlier victory there. The circumstances were encouraging for all of us at 13th Corps; but a certain note of personal concern entered into our appreciation of the fortunes of the battle. In the Intelligence branch we had a pretty good grasp of the enemy picture. The R.A.F. continued to fly constant and valuable reconnaissances and 'Rommel, either because his constantly moving H.Q. was unencumbered with cipher staff or because he was impatient of the least delay in issuing his commands, could be heard continuously over the wireless instructing all his mobile forces to return in the direction of Tobruk. This meant that he would be coming up behind Corps H.Q., and the air reconnaissance showed large numbers of enemy vehicles including tanks moving on a wide front not far to our east. About this time we picked up a troop of 25-pounders hopelessly parted from their parent regiment and were glad to take them under our wing temporarily.

One of the disadvantages of being cut off from our lines of communication was that we had to rely for water on local resources. I see I have not yet even referred to water, a subject which comes closest of all to the heart of man in the desert. Our normal ration at this time, when on a mobile basis, was three-quarters of a gallon per man per day. Of this a proportion was supposed to go on filling the radiators of the transport. Nor could this be shirked, because a man can go thirsty but a truck just won't. However, steps were taken to make sure that the trucks' thirst was not excessive. There was an ingenious arrangement to prevent water being lost by boiling over; I have not seen it elsewhere but it worked very well. A rubber tube was led from the top of the radiator into a two-gallon petrol can fastened to the wing. The tube was sealed tightly at both ends. When the water boiled in the radiator it ran along the tube into the can where it came off the boil. At this point the vacuum created sucked it back into the radiator and the cycle started again. After paying this debt to transport what water remained had to be divided between drinking and washing.

The result was that one never got more than half a gallon a day to drink and sometimes less. This may seem little enough in so hot a climate, but I do not remember feeling thirsty on the normal rations. The main trick was to drink only at breakfast and after nightfall and to avoid drinking at all by day.

The next point concerns the taste of the water. Before we crossed into Libya we drew our water partly from some copious wells near Mersa Matruh and partly from Buqbuq. The Mersa Matruh water was quite reasonable. I think it had a little iron in it but not enough to be noticeable. The Buqbuq water was chemically pretty pure but, coming from wells on the seashore, it was liable to get brackish if there were too many people drinking it. However, the taste of salt was only slight and in fact it was better for quenching your thirst. Apart from these two there were a variety of local sources and the connoisseur rapidly acquired a discerning palate for the wells of origin of the water he was given to drink. One of the nastiest of all was the Tobruk water. This was drawn from wells in the Wadi Auda on the west of the perimeter and was extremely salty. I remember being told that at the outset of the desert campaigns an estimate was drawn up by the medical staff of the maximum amount of salinity in water which could be tolerated and that the Wadi Auda water contained eight times as much as this maximum. Whether there is any basis for this story I don't know; the truth was that this was the only water and so it had to be drunk. The Italians, incidentally, when they held Tobruk, lived on bottled mineral water imported from Italy or on distilled water from a small seawater distillery (they demolished it when they surrendered the fortress). Certainly the Wadi Auda water was very unpleasant and I am sure that if it had had just a scrap more salt it would have been really undrinkable. The main trouble about salt water is that though it may be quite refreshing when taken neat it makes very nasty tea. Nor does it mix well with whisky. As a result a popular drink was whisky and water with a dash of lime juice, a mixture called 'Blue Nile'. It sounds revolting when I think of it now but as a matter of fact the lime just killed the taste of the water.

Besides salt there were other disagreeable ingredients such as sulphur and magnesium which turned up in various combinations in different places. The Jarabub water was full of magnesium and a very debilitating effect it had; in fact it was said to take 3 months before the intestines got used to it. Constant diarrhoea is weakening to the best troops; this factor was taken into consideration in the construction by the French of the Mareth Line in Tunisia. All the wells in front of the line were stiff with magnesium and it was thought that this would be bound to have an effect on the morale and efficiency of an attacking force.

In our present position, however, there was an extra factor which made 'local supply' even more ill-omened an expression. We had held this territory the winter before and when we fell back we were anxious to do what we could to render its occupation unpleasant to the enemy. Now, poisoning of wells has been regarded askance by international law from the very earliest times. This solution was accordingly rejected; but a typical British compromise was found. All the wells between Tobruk and the frontier were contaminated with bone oil. This is not poisonous but it is so extremely nauseating that it takes away the desire to drink equally effectively. Our own experts also proudly claimed that the flavour would last. Unfortunately this prediction, when we came to put it to the test some ten months later, turned out to be only too true. For one whole day the only water that could be found came from bone-oiled wells. I remember that I was extremely thirsty; but one small sip of tea made with bone oil was all I could manage for the whole of that day. It was a pleasure on the next day to get back to the plain salt and chlorine, with traces of mud and sulphur, taken from some casual puddle.

As I have already mentioned water, perhaps a few remarks about food might round off the picture. All this time we were on 'hard rations' which meant tinned meat and biscuits. The meat was bully beef, always firmly supposed to be from stocks which had been built up in Egypt during the First World War. I do not suppose that the date in fact made much difference and it all tasted the same. The only other meat was tinned bacon which was fatty and so welcome, particularly in winter. Some mess cooks made biscuit porridge but it was not very nice. The alternative garnish to bully beef was jam and almost invariably fig jam made in Palestine. I could never bring myself to eat it. The biscuits were packed in wax paper and did not keep specially well. I remember on one occasion being issued with biscuits which were weevily. I am bound to say I found this rather sympathetic, a link with soldiers of the past, Corporal Trim in the Low Countries or Rifleman Harris in the Peninsula. The weevils were rather attractive little beetles. As long as you avoided eating them they did not seem to make much difference to the taste of the biscuit. I was also delighted to see that if you tapped a biscuit on the table the weevils put their heads out as they did for Captain Horn-blower and his crew. During the period I am writing about we were on the scale known as 'battle rations' and a little bit later when we were at Agedabia we went on to half battle rations. This was not very satisfying for a hardworking man in cold weather because it only came to half a tin of bully per man per day. I had a hoarded stock of biscuits including some South African biscuits which were said to be superior to our own, and managed well on that.

On the evening of 26th November the forces of 70th Division from Tobruk captured Ed Duda, a height adjoining Bel Hamed, and made contact with the New Zealanders. This was the first direct contact the garrison of Tobruk had had with friendly troops since March. Rommel's wirelessed instructions became more urgent than ever. That afternoon, as I was looking through field glasses at some dust in the distance, which was in fact some German armoured cars being cautious, the Corps Commander dropped into the Intelligence tent for a chat. He was in excellent form and seemed not merely confident but exuberant. I showed him some information just received about what was going on in the Bardia area and between there and Sidi Omar. This was supposed to be the Corps' lines of communication or L of C; but at that moment it was being disputed between wandering groups of our own and enemy mobile forces. Godwin Austen was interested but unaffected: "Yes, everyone tells me I have lost my L of C; but I say I have got my objective. Bernard Freyberg has got back on to Sidi Rezegh and I expect he will be joining up soon with the Tobruk garrison there. I say that Godwin plus his objective and minus his L of C is much better than Godwin minus his objective and plus his L of C."

In spite of this carefree, if militarily correct, attitude, John Harding thought it as well to move the H.Q. that night. It was a rather well carried out night move, made without lights; we covered some ten miles or so. There was a good deal of movement going on and at one point we overtook a fairly large and foreign-looking column containing some tanks. I discovered next day that this was a detachment of the Italian Ariete Division with which we had shared the track. In the dark neither side cared to investigate too closely, but like Dogberry was glad to be rid of a knave. We camped next morning in cheerful mood in a pleasant hollow and I remember I had just finished some bacon, which was the only decent thing in the tinned ration, when an enemy armoured car entered the laager. The ensuing scene was extremely noisy. I am sure that the enemy was much the more startled. Our artillery branch had collected a fair number of scratch weapons apart from the ones I have mentioned and the G2 R.A. was particularly fond of an Italian Breda 20 mm. gun. He was breakfasting beside it only a hundred yards or so from me when I saw him put down his cup of tea and open fire with some rather beautiful tracer rounds. Not knowing whether there might not be larger forces following up we got under way fairly fast. In fact the whole Corps H.Q. went bumping off within a matter of minutes and carried on for about a mile and a half before settling down again. The German made off, and if, as I believe, he was alone he was probably thankful to do so.

I rode further west that day myself to visit New Zealand Division H.Q. They only had two brigades up with them as the third was observing the enemy in the frontier area, particularly in Bardia. They had had a very severe fight to capture Sidi Rezegh. The enemy were strongly entrenched and 90th Division had fought extremely well. They owed their successes entirely to their attacking by night where their great superiority in night operations had carried them on to their objectives. They were firmly on Bel Hamed and Sidi Rezegh but they could do no more than hold them. It was accordingly left to 70th Division to widen and consolidate the long corridor which they had driven out to meet the New Zealanders. John Harding flew in a small aeroplane into Tobruk that same day to co-ordinate the operation.

Next day the fruits of this visit were seen in a combined attack during the afternoon by the New Zealand Division and 70th Division, which cleared up the three hills Bel Hamed, Sidi Rezegh and Ed Duda. The enemy were now, however, returning in greater strength and 13th Corps H.Q. was in the position of defending the rear of the New Zealand and 70th Division position. This is an unusual role for a Corps H.Q., although by now we had acquired quite a useful, though varied, collection of arms. On the afternoon of 28th November it became clear that the enemy were preparing to deliver a serious attack. This was no longer an affair of raiding armoured cars or tanks, but a proper infantry assault. We therefore temporarily ceased work on preparing estimates of enemy strength and took the clerks off typing casualty returns and deployed them fully armed in a tactical position round the office lorry. The infantry strength of Corps H.Q. was to be under the command of the Commander Royal Engineers and the Brigadier Royal Artillery commanded our scratch collection of guns. Unfortunately the crust of sand on top of the limestone was too shallow to allow any positions to be dug, but we disposed ourselves hopefully on the outskirts of the H.Q. laager on a little ridge. The enemy position was on another fairly steep ridge about a thousand yards away. The German artillery preparation was not heavy; but in the event we did not wait for their infantry to attack. General Godwin Austen, reflecting that his job was to retain control of the battle as he had throughout, and not to break off to fight a private engagement, 'decided', as the H.Q. diary put it, 'to set up Corps H.Q. in Tobruk.' We did a properly phased withdrawal, got into our transport behind the ridge and made off through the gathering darkness. About a week later, incidentally, I was reading a captured diary of a soldier in the 115th Regiment (15th Panzer Division) which revealed that he had taken part in the attack. We were described as a large mixed unit of infantry and artillery in prepared positions and the writer was surprised at us withdrawing.

It was a twisting difficult drive between extensive minefields, barbed wire and entrenchments and we spent most of the night on it. It was surprising that enemy artillery fire dropped away practically to nothing that night. We arrived before dawn and pitched our camp close to the airfield on the first escarpment. General Austen, in his report to Eighth Army ended as follows: 'The corridor to Tobruk is perfectly secure and open to the passage of our troops and will be kept so. Have arrived there without incident. Press may now be informed that Tobruk is as relieved as I am.'

Most battles end with an anticlimax and it was not until the final battle in Tunisia that we came to an example of a really decisive battle. Tobruk was in theory relieved, but the two New Zealand brigades were still in a hazardous position. Heavy enemy attacks continued all next day against the 70th Division positions in the corridor. Ed Duda was lost once and recaptured. Next day, 30th November, Rommel tried again with his favourite manoeuvre of a tank attack in the late afternoon with the tanks coming out of the setting sun. Although the 7th Armoured Division was harassing the enemy's southern flank and the 1st South African brigade was moving forward to support, the attack was successful in recapturing Sidi Rezegh. Next morning the Germans took Bel Hamed and so severe were the New Zealand losses that Divisional H.Q. and the two brigades had to break out south-eastwards. Tobruk was once more sealed off.

For just over a week therefore I had the experience of sharing in the first siege of Tobruk. The garrison were not particularly pleased to receive a collection of refugee staff officers instead of the relief or at least reinforcement that they had a right to expect. For us newcomers however the place was fascinating. It came home to me suddenly with great force as a link with a previous existence when I suddenly realized that I had referred to Tobruk in a footnote to an article which I had contributed the month before the war to the *Journal of Hellenic Studies* (Vol. LXVII, p. 68). Tobruk was originally a Greek city called Pyrgos, from which its modern name is directly derived. (The changes are normal and regular; take the accusative form, plus the definite article—Tompurgon—drop the final syllable and interchange the U and the R.) I do not think any archaeological remains were ever uncovered there, although plenty of digging was done. Its raison d'être is that it is the only natural harbour between Alexandria and Tunis, a sheltered cove running east and west behind an arm of rock, rather like Suda Bay. There were a few houses in the town, nearly all damaged, but nobody of course lived there. It had never had anything but a small population consisting solely of Italians; these had all been removed when it was first taken.

It might appear that by capturing Sidi Rezegh once more the Germans had restored the status quo. Appearances would have been deceptive. In the first place there was now no possibility of a German attack on Tobruk. That at least had been frustrated; but far more than this had in fact been effected. The German mobile and armoured forces had been so worn down that they were unlikely to be able to retain their gains. Once they were forced to withdraw the immobile Italian infantry divisions would be a liability rather than a help. General Auchinleck was plainly determined to see the thing through to the end. His policy of persistence had already paid. His tactics now were to maintain pressure from the south by the use of 30th Corps, replenished from his reserve tank stocks and re-encouraged by a number of small successes against outlying enemy parties, and at the same time to press westwards along the Trigh Capuzzo with the 5th New Zealand Brigade, which had not so far been engaged, and with columns from the 22nd Guards Brigade. This was one of the principal occasions on which the technique was used of sending out mixed columns of all arms to harrass the enemy. The reason was a perfectly simple one; since our standard anti-tank weapon, the 2-pounder, had neither the range nor the hitting power, the 25-pounder was the only weapon on which we could entirely rely to kill a tank. Each column was therefore built round one or two troops of 25-pounders or, better expressed, it was a method of carrying the 25-pounder to the enemy tank with sufficient infantry to protect it, and armoured cars or other reconnaissance elements to act as feelers. At a later period, when the Commander of the Eighth Army had under his orders far more troops than General Auchinleck ever had, and both the 6-pounder and the 17-pounder anti-tank guns were in standard supply, it was fashionable to decry the use of columns. The answer I suppose is that if circumstances had been different the employment of columns would have been wrong. One argument which may weigh with those who decry the use of columns, since they almost all subscribe to the Rommel legend, is that it was Rommel who began the practice and he carried on with it after we had given it up. He clearly thought that the method had its advantages for a General operating in the desert with comparatively small forces.

While this pressure was developing Rommel tried once more to drive back into the fortress that part of 70th Division which had forced its way out. On the 2nd December and then, after a pause, on the 4th December, heavy attacks were made on Ed Duda from the west and southwest; on the evening of the 4th the Germans did in fact climb on to the southern end of the ridge but they were driven off after nightfall. Next day it was clear that, in face of this stubborn resistance and the harrassing pressure from 30th Corps, Rommel would have to abandon his hold on Tobruk. Enemy vehicles could be seen withdrawing west along the southern face of the perimeter. On 6th December patrols from Tobruk found that the Bologna Division on the east side of the perimeter was thinning out and that evening a patrol from 70th Division stood once more in possession on the fatal height of Sidi Rezegh. We had captured it the third time and this time the enemy did not contest ownership.

I drove out myself next morning with our R.A.F. Liaison Officer to see if contact could be made with friendly forces and to make an effort at estimating the number of enemy destroyed tanks lying about on the battlefields of Sidi Rezegh and Bel Hamed. It was a pleasure to be out in the cold clean air of a winter morning and, although I had only been a week in the besieged fortress, it was a relief to come out again into the open desert. There were a number of enemy tanks knocked out and lying about, though not half as many, naturally enough, as had been claimed by our side. I noted carefully the location of a new type of Mark IV Tank with a 'long' 75 mm. gun. This was a new weapon in Libya. It meant that the heaviest German tank, instead of carrying a howitzer firing high explosive shells, now had a proper tank gun of high velocity and firing armour-piercing ammunition. There was the usual debris of a battlefield, including a fair number of dead Italians, though no Germans; but no trace of any friendly troops or indeed anything living. Suddenly, after about an hour, we noticed in the distance a line of vehicles moving our way, well spaced out. I watched them through field glasses and was surprised to see that they appeared to be advancing in oddly uncoordinated rushes. One truck would drive ahead and suddenly stop while the rest went by, then the second would pull out and stop, and so on. They looked friendly so we waited for them to come up. They turned out to be a column of Scots Guards. Their odd method of proceeding was not a tactical manoeuvre, they were merely stopping as they came to loot from destroyed enemy vehicles. They were pleased to find some people from Tobruk before pressing on to make contact with 70th Division on Ed Duda and to the west. I had an idea at the time that this was the first instance of renewed contact between Tobruk and the outside world since it had been cut off once more but I have no doubt that there are others who will contest the honour.

A day or so later I thought it might be a good idea to investigate one of the German rest camps which had been established on the coast east of Tobruk during the siege. It occurred to me that there might be useful documents to be picked up there since the place would probably have been evacuated in a fair hurry, and also no doubt other useful and acceptable objects. I set off in a 3-tonner with Donald Prater, one of the Intelligence officers, and soon found the place which had not, oddly enough, been looted by the Arabs. There were as I expected a fair amount of interesting documents; I also acquired a small Mercedes car, an accordion, three prisoners of war, a typewriter, some mixed wines and spirits, some spaghetti and a case of mineral water. The three prisoners were a miserable lot. We saw them dodging about on the edge of the wadi but when hailed they came in quite cheerfully with their hands up. I remember thinking that they did not seem surprised at being addressed by both of us in German. When the first one came in I told him to turn round with some idea of feeling to see whether he was armed; he misinterpreted this and cried out piteously "Herr Hauptmann, leave us our lives." We piled them into the back of the lorry and I drove the German car. Donald Prater added to their puzzlement by playing on the accordion very loud and with great feeling 'Denn wir fahren gegen Engeland.'

It was as well known to us as to the enemy that a defeat near Tobruk meant that the next place at which a proper stand could be made, as opposed to a mobile battle, would be in the neighbourhood of Agedabia. To abandon the siege of Tobruk, therefore, meant that Rommel must now undertake a long and not particularly easy withdrawal. Fortunately this was an art of which he was a master. His retreats from Tobruk in 1941 and from Alamein in 1942 were both admirably conducted. On this occasion the early stages were slower than after Alamein. His defeat had been scarcely less severe, but the forces at General Auchinleck's disposal for pursuit were much less numerous. The first stage therefore was a slow and contested withdrawal to Ain el Gazala. This is a place at which the coast road is crossed by a deep ravine affording an excellent defensive position. We occupied it ourselves in January 1942. The only forces fit for pursuit were the 5th New Zealand Brigade, which had come up from Bardia, and the Polish Brigade Group, both of them under Corps command. The 4th Indian Division, with two brigades only, was coming up and transferred to 13th Corps' command on the 11th December. Godwin Austen's idea was to hold the enemy frontally and to send a brigade group from 7th Armoured Division round their right flank to get astride their line of withdrawal. It was a hopeful move and fell only a little short of success; but the armoured column lost its way and took rather too long and Rommel, who had now stood long enough and got away most of the stuff he wanted to get away, was ready to go. He disengaged smartly and with great speed.

There is not much to be said about the enemy withdrawal and our pursuit. He went by road through the Gebel and also through the desert by the Trigh el Abd. I haven't mentioned this track yet though it was one of the few touches of romance in the desert. Its name means 'the track of the slaves' and that is precisely what it was, for it starts somewhere on the Niger and sweeps through Timbuctoo into the Fezzan and thence into Cyrenaica, its destination, of course, Egypt. It is a great broad track, sometimes two or three miles across, which holds its course through the most desolate parts of the desert, north of the Sand Sea. It only comes near the coast south of Tobruk and then curves away southeast again. It must have been a trail of horror for the negro slaves who followed it. We made good time down the trail, over a new and clean-looking stretch of desert and arrived opposite Agedabia to find the enemy well posted in a strong defensive position at which our own forces for the moment could only make faces, for they were very weak in the forward area. 13th Corps H.Q.

followed at good speed close behind the advance guard and on 23rd December was settled at Msus.

This seems a good opportunity, in a pause in operations, to say something about the history of Cyrenaica. It was colonized by Greeks in the 7th Century B.C., who intermarried with the Libyans. At that time and for many centuries later it was famous for its fertility. The Delphic oracle had instructed the colonists to look for a place 'where there is a hole in heaven' and they thought they had found it in Cyrene with its lavish rainfall and fertile soil. It was on its way downhill by the time it became part of the Roman Empire, and the Arab conquest brought no improvement. There had always been a strong contrast between the green mountain of the Gebel Akhdar and the desert to the south and east of it, but as the centuries went on the desert encroached more and more. At the beginning of the 19th Century there arose a prophet in the desert by the name of Mohammed el Senussi. His was one of the frequently occurring reform movements in Islam, similar to that of the Wahabis who rose about the same time in the Arabian peninsular. The Senussi in fact went one further than the Wahabis in that he forbade his followers to drink even coffee, as being too stimulating. His descendants exercised both spiritual and temporal authority in Cyrenaica until the late 1920's when Graziani's campaign against Kufra broke their power. The head of the family, the present King of Libya, took refuge in Egypt with many of his supporters. In Cyrenaica resistance was stamped out.

As a result of centuries of hard living and a decade of colonial repression, it was unusual to come across Bedouin in the desert. They were found occasionally and they seemed to live a most miserable life. They were an undersized and poverty stricken people, but so far as we were concerned they had the merit of being wholeheartedly and fanatically on our side. Sayed Idris in Egypt had sent messages to all his followers commending to them the support of the Allied cause; and their hatred of the Italians rendered this most acceptable to them. Hundreds of allied troops, escaping prisoners for instance, owed their safety to being sheltered in Arab encampments. There never was a case of one of them being betrayed to the enemy in spite of the fact that detection brought savage reprisals from the Italians. Nor was this all; a force of Libyan Arabs was raised to fight on our side. The men came partly from Libyan refugees in Egypt and partly from volunteers from members of the Italian Libyan troops captured at Sidi Barrani. The officers were a mixed lot, chosen mostly for their knowledge of

Arabic. The most famous of them was the Belgian-Russian Vladimir Peniakov, already nicknamed Popski and later to be well known as the commander of Popski's Private Army. I remember meeting him for the first time at Corps H.Q. at Acroma, just west of Tobruk. The commander was Colonel Robert Baird, a regular officer of the Irish Fusiliers who spoke Arabic with great fluency and, according to St. John Philby, an Irish accent. He also acted as head of an espionage organization. This was practically the only such organization that produced results. One reason was that Robert Baird paid his agents almost nothing—I remember being astonished when it came out in conversation that he had rewarded a man who had risked his neck half a dozen times, and had brought back some quite interesting information, with the sum of £2 10s. 0d. and a packet of tea, which both parties appeared to consider thoroughly generous. The second reason why they were some good was that their heart was well and truly in their work. They were especially useful, of course, for topographical intelligence but they could also pinpoint the location of enemy encampments in the rear areas and give some idea of what troops were in them. Apart from these humble but devoted men I only knew one other useful agent in the whole course of the war.

On Christmas Eve Benghazi was captured for the second time. The first troops to enter were the Central India Horse, the Divisional Cavalry Regiment of the 4th Indian Division. There was no enemy except for a few stragglers. Benghazi, as the capital of Cyrenaica, always made a good story for the newspapers though its fate was always decided by battles far away and it went as the unresisting prize of victory. I never entered the place myself. I was fairly busy at that time in any case because Freddie de Butts had fallen victim to—of all things—chicken pox, and I was acting as G2I. I did send some of my people there who came back with some fresh onions and lettuces. We were operating only small forces at the moment but it was fairly clear that the enemy would have to pull back from Agedabia, which was only an outpost of the real defensive position at Agheila. The Guards Brigade did attack on 27th December but lost their way and had to withdraw and next day some enemy tanks came out southeast of Agedabia and inflicted heavy losses on the 22nd Armoured Brigade. They were all the forces we could maintain at that time and we began to wonder whether we might not have to withdraw. So the old year went out leaving us in a cheerful but rather delicately poised condition.

CHAPTER VII

The Msus Stakes and the Retreat to Alamein

THE attack on Pearl Harbour happened while we were still in Tobruk. We were already quite used to the presence of Americans in the desert. The U.S. Military Attaché, Colonel Fellers, was a frequent visitor and especially to 13th Corps H.Q. There were a number of American observers who had come to watch the behaviour of such weapons as the Stuart tank. They had avoided actually taking part in the fighting but when on 10th December Italy and Germany declared war on the U.S.A. they were able to try things out for themselves. The war in the Far East was soon to have its repercussions in the desert.

The time had come for 7th Armoured Division to be relieved for a spell. Its tanks were almost all worn out, and its men had been engaged in one battle after another since June 1940. Its place could now be taken by a recent arrival from England, the 1st Armoured Division. So 7th Armoured Division went off to the Delta and not long after one of its brigades, the famous 7th Armoured Brigade, which had been in every battle since the beginning, was ordered to Burma. There could have been no more dissimilar theatre of war than the Burmese jungle to men trained in the desert, but the Brigade worthily lived up to its reputation. This was not the only toll taken of our strength by the Far Eastern campaign; indeed the reduction was more serious even than the one which had taken place the previous winter to provide an expeditionary corps for Greece. The 6th and 7th Australian and the 70th British Division were also taken away and the 18th British Division which was due to come to the Middle East was diverted to Singapore. At the same time a large part of the Middle East air forces were sent to the same theatre. While our strength was being thus depleted the enemy were reinforcing fast.

The substitution of the 1st for the 7th Armoured Division was not calculated to improve 13th Corps fighting strength. It is a fairly common experience that a division, particularly an armoured division, does not do itself justice in its first engagement. For example, the U.S. 1st Armoured Division was signally defeated in its first engagement in Tunisia, but went on to turn itself into a very fine formation. However, there were other causes at work also. The 1st Armoured Division were not merely a bunch of palefaces (as we used to call newcomers, for obvious reasons); they had a lot of wrong ideas. The divisional armoured brigade, the 2nd, was formed of three fine regular cavalry units. They had been the senior armoured formation in Britain and they had done a great deal of training in that starry-eyed, dedicated way in which training was carried out in Britain, especially in the first two years of the war. They had a most admirable self-confidence, but tended as a result to think that there was not much for them to learn. They had had numerous officers attached to them from 7th Armoured Division but appeared to have serious doubts as to whether they had anything to gain by listening to these country cousins. They were not very good at maintenance and their tanks had suffered in the thousand mile approach march from the Delta.

The Commander was General Lumsden who later had 10th Corps at Alamein. He was descended from Lumsden of the Guides and was an incisive commander. He was not, however, in command in this first battle. On his arrival in the forward area he called at Corps H.Q. and discussed various Intelligence points; I remember running through a list of enemy personalities and saying that the Africa Corps artillery commander had just been severely wounded and sent back to Germany. "Good for promotion, good for promotion," said Lumsden; an hour and a half later he was himself dive bombed and severely wounded by a bomb fragment. His place was taken by Frank Messervy from 10th Indian Division.

Maintenance was still miserably difficult, and we were still on our half battle rations at Corps H.Q.; but things were improving and part of 4th Indian Division could now operate southwards from Benghazi. The 1st Armoured Division had both its armoured brigade and its support group in the Agedabia area. The Germans accordingly decided to pull back a bit and on the night of the 6th-7th January they left Agedabia and withdrew to Agheila. We were hard put to it to follow them up. The road was thoroughly mined and booby-trapped. The desert was difficult and unknown and there were constant heavy sandstorms. Not to make too much of it, the enemy withdrew into the Agheila position without being much embarrassed by our following up. He went straight back and took up a strong prepared position behind the salt marshes. At this point the Libyan sand sea is at its nearest to the Mediterranean, leaving a gap of only some 50 miles. Almost the whole of this gap is obstructed with marshes, belts of shifting sand and small rocky escarpments. We were in no position to attack, since we only had a couple of brigades forward and that was the most that we should be able to maintain for some time.

At about the same period 30th Corps, now left far behind, were completing the mopping up of enemy positions on and near the Egyptian frontier. The main one was the fortress of Bardia and there were also a number of strong points round Halfaya. As a result we were unable to use the coast road for our supply and obliged to make wide detours into the desert. 30th Corps were using two South African brigades and had been specially instructed to avoid casualties because there was going to be some difficulty in keeping up their strength. These instructions were carefully carried out. After two days' fighting Bardia fell on the 2nd January 1942, yielding 8,000 prisoners, 2,000 of whom were Germans. The commander, who surrendered unconditionally, was a General Schmidt. We also recovered 1,100 of our own prisoners, taken in the confused fighting of the previous December. A fortnight later Halfaya also was surrendered by General de Giorgis, yielding a further 5,500 prisoners, 2,000 of whom again were German. This surrender was resisted for some time by the senior German commander, a certain Major Bach. He was a reserve officer who in peacetime was a Protestant clergyman and who had been well known for his association with the anti-Hitler movement led by Pastor Niemöller.

Meanwhile at Antelat there was nothing for us in 13th Corps to do for the moment except observe the enemy closely with a screen of light forces. The calculation was that we would not be able to organize a sound administrative base to enable us to mount an attack on the Agheila position in sufficient force until the middle of February. The view taken at G.H.Q. was that the enemy too would not be able to do anything significant before then. I remember being a bit sceptical about this at the time, nor is this one of those convenient memories, reinforced by wisdom after the event, because we were engaged at that very time in a most violent controversy on enemy strength. To put it briefly, what had happened was that G.H.Q. had failed to notice the arrival in Tripoli of that ill-omened ship, the s.s. *Ankara*. This was a merchant ship belonging to the Deutsche Levant Linie and was by now the only survivor of that Company's Mediterranean fleet. She was fast and capacious and had specially strengthened derricks capable of handling the heaviest type of German tank. She was accordingly used very frequently to bring reinforcements of armour. Whenever she was known to be sailing, determined efforts were made by our side to sink her, but the Devil appeared to be looking after his own and for all her frequent voyaging she was never touched. The Captain got quite a swollen head about his luck and would harangue the dock labourers in Naples and Tripoli on the subject. Just in January 1942 she put in one of her most timely arrivals with some 25 tanks. Another factor was that Rommel's supply position was very much easier than ours because he was so much nearer his bases. He therefore decided to make a forward move, as a reconnaissance in force in the first place, with the prospect of turning it into a serious offensive if the going looked good. The date selected was 21st January.

Just about this time he received a piece of information which acted as a considerable encouragement. By an oversight the Queen's Bays, one of the three cavalry regiments of the 2nd Armoured Brigade, put out over the air its nightly tank state in plain language, instead of in cipher. It showed the lamentable state of serviceability of the tanks of this regiment, over half of which were in workshops under repair. There was no reason to suppose that the Bays were any worse than the other two regiments and it was plain to German Intelligence that the 2nd Armoured Brigade, which should have had over 150 tanks, was very much less of a threat than it appeared. The cynic might comment that the ones that were classed as serviceable were only Crusaders, and any Crusader tank, even with the most devoted maintenance, could always be said to be only two jumps ahead of the workshops. The breach of security was, of course, spotted by Signals and an inquiry was made. The fact that the message was intercepted I learnt from Colonel Revetria, the Italian Intelligence officer to whom I have referred; he confirmed also that it was one of the deciding factors which led to the enemy's counter attack.

The operation which began on the 21st January was usually referred to afterwards by our troops as 'The Msus Stakes' or 'The Second Benghazi Handicap', from which it can be deduced that it was too shambling and scrambling an operation to admit of a detailed description. I shall not attempt to give one. Comparatively small parties of tanks and motorized infantry dashed about the desert, wheeling, skirmishing and dispersing, and most of the commanders were never too sure where they were either in relation to the enemy or to the map of Africa. Rommel's plan was to recapture Benghazi but he began with a thrust due east to secure his right flank. In the course of it he scattered or destroyed the bulk of our armour in gallant and persistent but, from our side, not very well organized battles. The 1st Armoured Division were unlucky in their first battle against such well trained troops and so dashing a commander. Their own commander, General Messervy, was quite new to them and he had never before commanded an armoured division. They determined to do better next time, a vow which was well redeemed.

An unfortunate controversy occurred at this point between General Godwin Austen, my Corps Commander, and General Ritchie, commanding Eighth Army. At the risk of being accused of bias I shall maintain that the former was plainly in the right. In any case I am biased in favour of Godwin Austen who was a shrewd and capable commander who possessed the full confidence of his troops. He took the view that, since our armour had been beaten in the open desert south of the mountains, it was necessary to withdraw out of the great bulge of Cyrenaica back to a position which was less exposed to the danger of outflanking. General Ritchie took the view that the enemy was going to make his main thrust across the desert to Mechili, following up our armoured forces. He therefore, probably influenced by the success of our policy of refusing to accept defeat in the last battle, decided to try a counter attack with infantry against the enemy's communications. Godwin Austen had ordered 4th Indian Division, which was in Benghazi, to conform to his withdrawal by falling back through the Gebel. Ritchie took the division under direct Army Command, cancelled his order and ordered them to attack southwards down the Benghazi-Agedabia road. Unfortunately this was based on a false premise. Rommel was not in fact following us up across the desert, he was already striking north on to Benghazi. He was actually moving his main forces along the top of the escarpment to the east of 4th Indian Division, at the same time as the latter was attacking down the main road. As a result he got across the road leading out of Benghazi to the east, and cut in behind the 7th Indian Brigade, which was the one designated for the southward attack. The brigade first tried to break back through the road block but, failing in this, moved off southeastwards across the desert to rejoin our lines this way. They had to make a tremendous detour right down to the south past Antelat then deeper into the desert, south of the Trigh el

Abd, then finally north again to Mechili. In this operation the Welch Regiment which had been added as a fourth battalion to the 7th Brigade, again were unfortunate. They were the troops immediately cut off when the enemy got across the road. Only a company and a half got away with the desert column. As a result the 4th Indian retreat through the Gebel was much more hasty than had been intended and the casualties were greater. This led to Godwin Austen's removal from the command of 13th Corps and his replacement by Strafer Gott.

13th Corps H.Q. from time to time found themselves once more as a rearguard to the Corps and had to do some fairly hasty moves in order to get into a more appropriate position. At least these activities distracted our minds from the weather, which was excruciatingly cold. A popular rig was the poshteen, or Hebron coat; a full length coat of lamb's fur worn with the fleece inwards. I was lucky in having one brought for me from Jerusalem. This was the first and only time that I actually saw snow in the desert. It didn't last more than about half an hour. A rather different sight was that of the destruction of the large field maintenance centre which we had just established at Msus, ready to support the next advance. Thousands of gallons of petrol were blazing in one place, in another place some German armoured cars were looking round and picking up a few things and at the other end of the enormous dump some of our own people were doing some looting. I got a case of whisky and another of chocolate. Unfortunately the chocolate had been soused with petrol either accidentally or by some R.A.S.C. man with a sense of humour. Chocolate was even rarer than whisky in the desert and we all craved for it, but the petrol flavour defeated us. I do not know whether it has been observed before in military history that retreats are often more comfortable than advances because you can plunder your own L of C; certainly there was no question now of the half battle rations that we had had to suffer from in the advance. One big advantage, compared with retreats in Greece, was that we retained air superiority. For most of the way we moved in a huge column of vehicles, not exactly nose to tail because there was plenty of room to spread out, but very thickly together and shrouded in an enormous pall of dust. I passed most of the ride in reading Sir Denis Brogan's splendid book on *The Development of Modern France*. The book would not have fetched much money second hand because it had a splinter from a stuka bomb halfway through it—fortunately I had just finished that part. Professor Brogan's admirers, which is the same as saying Professor Brogan's readers, are aware what a gripping work this is and I can testify that even when bumping about over rocky desert his wit and erudition continued to fascinate.

Mechili was an odd place consisting of nothing more than a dilapidated Italian fort. We had no idea what was going on there so I was sent ahead to see whether the Germans might not have got there first. I was glad to find it held by the Poles. After 24 hours we pushed on again to Acroma, about 10 miles southwest of Tobruk. Here there was only half a wall of a fort; but the ground was carpeted with spring flowers for there had been heavy rain. These flowers of the Libyan desert, ephemeral but freshly beautiful, only grow where the earth still holds a little water and do not last more than a fortnight, but where they are found they give for that short time a very different face to that strange and hateful landscape.

The new line was to run southwards from Gazala inlet, covering Tobruk at a distance of about 40 miles to the west. This involved giving up Derna and I was accordingly sent to take the news to the area commander. This was the first and only time I saw the Gebel Akhdar, and then only the fringes of it. Derna exemplifies once more that taste for the melodramatic which comes naturally to African scenery. As you approach from Gazala you climb gradually but steadily until, when approaching the sea, you suddenly find yourself at the top of a great cliff-like escarpment. Down below there is a little shelf sticking out into the sea and on it are the sparkling white cubical buildings of Derna. The descent is spectacular. The road zig-zags continuously and had already been blown and repaired three times. At the time of my visit and on my way down I could see our Sappers working to place demolition charges in position once more. The town is pleasant and spotlessly clean, surrounded with walls. It seemed strange to find streets full of houses, with civilians walking about. At area H.Q. the area commander and his staff all had their hats on and their bags packed. I handed over the orders, had a farewell drink and climbed back up the escarpment again.

The Germans only came forward slowly to make contact with our new position. They pushed the 4th Indian Division hard back through the Gebel but broke contact before coming up to the new line. Nearly four months passed before the next serious battle.

It was when we were at Acroma that Godwin Austen asked to be relieved of his command of 13th Corps, and Strafer Gott took over. Gott was a remarkably impressive-looking man. He was known to everyone in the desert because he had worked his way up by successive steps through each formation since the beginning of the war in Africa, from lieutenant colonel to lieutenant general. Shortly afterwards John Harding went to G.H.Q. Middle East on promotion as Director of Military Training. He was succeeded as Chief of Staff by Brigadier, later Major General Erskine, a rifleman like Gott. He was known as Tom Walls from a supposed resemblance. It was with this team that we went into action in May. I do not think it can be said that the battle around Tobruk was lost through any failing on the part of the Commander of 13th Corps, for the decisive factor was the defeat of the armour and this all came under 30th Corps.

The battle which began on 26th May was by far the biggest that had been fought in the desert up to that time and had the most dramatic fluctuations. It started off with a muddle on both sides out of which the Germans came off distinctly second best but went on with a crescendo of German successes which in less than six weeks brought them to within 60 miles of Alexandria. It was certainly Rommel's best fought battle and, though I have not felt able to agree with the judgment made of him by most of the postwar commentators, I must admit that on the showing of this battle he proved himself a better army commander than General Ritchie. (On the other hand there were some British generals who could claim the same.) Certainly he showed a superior ability in thinking and acting quickly.

Before the battle Eighth Army had been building up its strength in many ways. Divisions were brought up to strength and we had an additional British infantry division in the forward area, the 50th. We were also able to maintain forward two armoured divisions at the same time, both the 1st and 7th, and two Army Tank Brigades. One of the main reasons for this was that the desert railway had been pushed still further forward and now reached the southeastern sector of the Tobruk perimeter. Some new arms had also arrived. First of all we had a new tank, the General Grant. This was the first American effort at a medium tank; its great merit was that it mounted a 75 mm. gun, the first decent tank gun we had ever had; but its great defect was that this admirable gun was mounted in a sponson stuck out at the right hand side of the hull with only a very limited traverse. This meant that to fire the gun the whole of the tank had to expose itself— and it was much too tall anyway, like the American light tank. Another good gift was the new 6-pounder anti-tank gun, which at last put us on a level with the Germans in that department, not counting the 88 mm. gun. Finally, the whole area between the Gazala line and Tobruk, and to the south of the fortress perimeter, was sown with prepared defensive positions. Eighth Army was ready for the attack and in good spirits.

The German plan of attack showed no particular originality. It was based on the obvious idea of an outflanking move by the enemy armour round our southern flank. There was also to be a holding attack on the main front and even a diversionary landing on our right flank, but these were mere trimmings. The idea was that our armour was to be defeated on the first day, on the next day the infantry was to be destroyed between the two parts of the enemy army and two days afterwards Tobruk was to be captured. (I am not inventing this, nor was it merely something to encourage the troops; this was in sober seriousness Rommel's planned timing.) We had good information about these plans, which were in any event fairly obvious. Only two days before, an NCO from the H.Q. of one of the German armoured divisions was captured in the southern desert, and very willingly gave an outline of the plan and a list of the troops taking part. I attended the interrogation and well remember the strenuous efforts the man made to recall as many details as he could. He gave them so fully that some people thought it might be a plant. I think myself he may have been a deserter. As a matter of interest, although I had often considered the possibility of planting prisoners of war with misleading stories, I never in fact knew of a case. We were therefore well prepared.

German Intelligence, on the other hand, was less fortunate. They naturally had a very fair idea of the troops forming our front line, but they were very poorly informed indeed about the all-important reserves. In particular, they had no idea that we had created large numbers of strong points in the rear of our lines. The maps issued for the attack contained no hint of this, except for the occasional tentative indication of minefields. This made the plans in many respects wholly nugatory. For example, quite a small force was directed to seize El Adem, which was in fact defended by a permanent position surrounded by minefields and wire and garrisoned by an entire infantry battalion, plus 13th Corps H.Q. This comparison of the state of knowledge of the two sides of the front might have been expected to give us a distinct advantage, but in the opening hours of the battle at least this was not so. The enemy moved off on the evening of the 26th May and their movements were reported with great regularity and fidelity by 7th Armoured Division's armoured cars. The German armoured divisions laagered for the night southeast of Bir Hacheim, the southernmost defended point in our line, and were watched all night by the same armoured cars. Nevertheless, when the Germans got going again next morning, they swept over the H.Q. of the 7th Armoured Division, taking it completely by surprise and capturing many of the officers including the General himself. Those who were not captured were dispersed. For most of the morning command of the division was exercised by the senior uncaptured officer, the G3I. Things were made no easier by the fact that 7th Motor Brigade was also taken completely by surprise and overrun. It did not rally again until next day. We at 13th Corps, supposing ourselves to be for the moment in a back-water of the battle, which was in 30th Corps' sector, were startled at about 8 o'clock that morning, having had no news from our side, by the arrival of a number of fugitives from the 7th Armoured Division H.Q. and almost simultaneously by being taken under artillery fire from a German column. I never heard then, and I never heard since, any convincing explanation why this surprise took place. Some people say that the armoured cars' reports were not received at division H.Q., or were not plotted correctly or not believed in full; but it was a great disappointment on our side, where we thought that everyone was keenly awaiting the attack.

General Messervy the divisional Commander was not a prisoner for long. He removed his badges of rank and passed himself off as a signaller. He was interrogated with other signallers and the German Intelligence officer observed that he looked rather old to be still serving. "So I am," said Messervy, "and I think it's a bloody shame—but they won't let me go." Muttering something about England's manpower difficulties, the interrogator passed on to the next prisoner. Their captors, however, were not at all happy. They were blundering about in an area which contained numerous minefields and strong points of whose existence they had no idea, and they rapidly discovered that their orders were fantastic. They got a flat repulse from the El Adem position, and our armoured brigades, into the middle of which they had so lightheartedly driven, began to concentrate against them. By the end of the first day it was clear that the original plan had failed. This was not an uncommon circumstance with Rommel, largely because he was so badly served by his Intelligence. He was, however, like all German commanders, quick to improvise.

Rommel thus began to draw off, first of all southwards to ease the supply problem, for his replenishment convoys still had to come all the way round south of our line, and then westwards. He had now decided that his only hope was to scrap the original plan and open a corridor through the middle of our line. He had already lost a number of tanks and, in accordance with a new policy, we had sent out mobile parties of Sappers to seek out damaged German tanks and blow them up. He was therefore not able to repair many.

This was plainly the time for a strong British counter-attack, but the opportunity was missed. Our impression at 13th Corps H.Q. was that Ritchie was letting the best be the enemy of the good. He was so overcome by the opportunity offered him of a decisive defeat of Rommel that he was determined to make sure of it, and to bring together as large a force as he could possibly concentrate from all his reserves for a crushing counter blow. Rommel, on the other hand, whatever other characteristics he may have had, was always quick. Long before Ritchie's stroke could be delivered, he had turned on the centre of our line and punched a great hole in it, destroying in the process the whole of the 150th Infantry Brigade and a high proportion of the 1st Army Tank Brigade. This gave him a secure line of supply. He then assumed a defensive position and waited for the counter attack. It was not delivered until four days later, on the 5th June. It was badly organized, costly in infantry casualties, and cost us also large numbers of guns. General Auchinleck calls this failure the turning point of the battle and there can be little doubt that this is true. The most dramatic and obvious change came with the decision to withdraw from Bir Hacheim. This had for a week now been under heavy pressure and could no longer be supplied. It was never intended to resist indefinitely, but rather to serve as a firm base round which our armour could be manoeuvred. With the gradual weakening of our armour it could no longer be held. The moment we withdrew the enemy got their second wind and turned once more with vigour to the offensive. Once again the El Adem box was surrounded by the enemy and we had to man our fire trenches. They drew off later that day and General Gott moved the Corps H.Q. out of the box into Tobruk so as to obtain freedom of movement.

I was not sorry to leave the El Adem box. It was a rocky place on the edge of a small escarpment broken up by small gullies. These were indeed welcome as some protection against shellfire, and comforting at night because German bombers, which now no longer operated by day, used to cruise around dropping small bombs and occasionally machine-gunned the place. In the course of this action our office lorry caught fire and was soon totally destroyed. The loss of most of our files was less serious than might have been supposed. Many of them referred to defunct Italian divisions now vegetating in prisoner of war camps in India. In exchange we got an Armoured Command Vehicle, to our great pleasure. I do not know whether these splendid things still survive, but in case they don't I will describe ours. It looked from outside rather like a moving van, standing very high on its wheels, with a body of half-inch steel guaranteed proof against small arms and bomb fragments. Inside it had several chairs fixed to the floor, and tables and a couple of wireless sets, map boards and telephones and so on. You might have expected it to be very hot but, in fact, the steel kept out the heat quite well especially when covered with a camouflage net. It was magnificent for driving in the desert because it had four wheel drive, at that time a luxury as far as British transport was concerned. It was in this that we drove to Tobruk one night, gloomy but comfortable.

I cannot describe the battles from the 12th to the 17th June. It could only be done by a most detailed scrutiny of the records of every small unit that took part, and even then there would certainly be inconsistencies and unexplained features. It was a great whirling affair, mobile warfare in its most extreme form. There never was another such tank battle in the Western Desert in the old style of armoured squadrons manoevring like ships at sea. There were indeed more tanks at Alamein, but that was more of a stand-up fight in a restricted area. The only thing the Intelligence Branch could do was to count the score of tanks claimed destroyed and work out the balance each night of our own and the enemy tank strength. We were fairly well informed about the German tank strength from various sources and particularly through the carelessness of the officer commanding 15th Armoured Division's tank workshops. He was a Major MacLean, descended no doubt from one of the Jacobites who took service after 1745 with Frederick II of Prussia. He was proud of his Scottish descent and insisted on signing himself in official documents 'Maclean-of-Coll'. He paid less attention, however, to wireless security and we intercepted his return practically every night. It was not encouraging; for it was clear that German tank strength was holding up much better than ours.

The danger to our infantry on the Gazala position was now acute and it was obvious that they must be moved back. They were accordingly extracted on the night of 14th June and sent back to occupy positions behind the Egyptian frontier. General Ritchie's plan was to hold the western perimeter of Tobruk and a chain of posts stretching from south of the town to the frontier. He did not intend Tobruk to stand another siege, though he recognized that it might be temporarily isolated. The defence was left to 30th Corps and accordingly 13th Corps H.Q. was to move back across the frontier to coordinate the defences there. It soon became clear that we should have to leave in a hurry if we were not to find ourselves blockaded once more in Tobruk.

The day before we left Tobruk I got one of the rare letters from my past existence. I knew that George Gordon, the President of Magdalen, had died and I supposed that a successor would have to be elected. I was, however, struck with the contrast when I received in the middle of Tobruk a letter requesting me to be in my stall in the Chapel, only a week hence, to cast my vote for the election of a new President of Magdalen. It was a stirring reminder, calling up memories of the great day in 1688 when the Fellows, in spite of King James' wrath, insisted on electing Dr. Hough as President. The physical scenery could scarcely be more different. It was difficult in the heat haze and swirling dust to summon up the memory of the carved oak stalls and the sculptured reredos of the college chapel (the latter incidentally being a nineteenth century imitation of the fifteenth century). To judge from novels of University life and the gossip of Senior Common Rooms, I missed what chance I may have had of academic preferment by being out of England at this time and so unable to cast a vote. I wrote expressing my regret; but as the letter went from the Field Post Office in Tobruk which was encircled the next day, I do not think it ever reached its address.

By the time we left next morning the enemy were stretching out their tentacles towards the coast road. The wireless receiver in the ACV was tuned to our armoured car link so we could follow in that way the course of events. Otherwise everything was hidden in heat haze and a dust storm. Once more, as in the 'Msus Stakes', we were a thickly packed mass of vehicles all moving in one direction and all profoundly grateful to the R.A.F. They completely dominated the battlefield, flying continuous patrols all day long, and we never saw an enemy aircraft. Nor, as it happens, did we see any enemy ground troops. The ACV bowled steadily along and I found it the most comfortable ride in all my desert journeys. There was nothing to do except read an admirable volume in which the Oxford University

Press had combined Johnson's and Boswell's accounts of their journey to the Hebrides. We bivouacked that evening just the other side of the frontier line. It was sad to be back in Egypt once more, though there was a distinct feeling of relaxation since we were no longer directing the battle. There was also the consolation I have mentioned before; one of our Intelligence officers was sent off instantly to the great N.A.A.F.I. dump at Capuzzo, which had been railhead until recently, and still contained an enormous amount of stores. Unfortunately the 1st South African Division had got there first, about two days before, and had looted at leisure. When Mark Allen returned he only had a poor collection of trophies to show. The most conspicuous and the most puzzling were six feather dusters, and what they were supposed to be used for in the desert I cannot imagine. Besides them he had half a packing case of lavatory paper, some tinned beans and some marmalade. The drink had all gone long before.

We had moved, while he was away, to Buqbuq, down among the sand dunes on the seashore; apart from its euphonious name it was mainly renowned for its excellent supply of sweet water. While we were there the Eighth Army Commander, General Ritchie, came up to visit us. The attack on Tobruk had begun that morning. At about 8 o'clock in the evening an intercepted German message in plain language was brought in to me. It read as follows: 'Mit unbedingte Kapitulation der Garnison zufrieden.' ('I agree to unconditional surrender of the garrison') and was signed ROL, which was Rommel's ordinary telegraphic signature. It was taken at once by Freddie de Butts to Generals Gott and Ritchie. It was the first news we had that all was up at Tobruk. Strafer Gott received it with that phlegm with which, for two years of desert campaigning, he had received good news and bad.

The fall of Tobruk caused tremendous excitement throughout the Allied world, bringing in its train clouds of controversy. As I remember, it did not come to the troops in the desert with anything like the feeling of shock that it seems to have done to Mr. Churchill in Washington and the British public at home. It was known that it was not Auchinleck's intention to stand another siege in Tobruk. The Navy had made it plain that the strain would be too great. The idea was merely to use the existing defences as an anchor for one end of our line. Admittedly the centre of the line was weak, and would be so until the armoured formations could be re-equipped; and therefore he was prepared to see Tobruk temporarily isolated. It was certainly not expected that its defensive value would be nullified so quickly by its sudden capture. Still, for us it was only one position in the desert; we had lost others and were used to going backwards and forwards over ground which in itself was of no value. Everyone could see that its loss must mean a withdrawal, probably as far as Mersa Matruh; but there was no hardship in fighting the next battle 100 miles or so east rather than 100 miles the other way, and some advantage from the greater ease of communications. To the general public, however, it plainly came as a great pang. In that featureless country any name was bound to get invested with undue importance and the name of Tobruk was, of course, one which was both well known and beloved from the successful defence of the previous year.

The controversy derives largely from this same circumstance. To put it bluntly, the question which the ordinary man asked was: 'How was it that the Australians in 1941 successfully defended Tobruk for seven months whereas the South Africans lost it in two days?' It seems a fair question but in fact is entirely misconceived. In the first place, without in any way disparaging the quality of the 9th Australian Division, or of the U.K. 70th Division which relieved them, it is a fact that the successful defence of Tobruk was as much due to Rommel's mistakes as to their skill and courage. He insisted on launching his attacks at the very strongest part of the perimeter. By November of 1941 he had discovered his mistake, and if he had launched his attack of 23rd November 1941, at this point, as he planned, it is more than likely that he would have been successful in taking the fortress seven months earlier. This was the view taken at the time both in Tobruk and in G.H.Q., Middle East; it was for this reason that our 'Crusader' operation was planned to anticipate the German attack. In June 1942 he put into effect precisely the same plan, without any alteration, and captured the fortress in 48 hours just as we had done by attacking in the same place in 1940. Of course it is true to say that the defenders were at a greater disadvantage in 1942 than they would have been in 1941. The artillery defence programmes were not worked out to that degree of precision which had been possible during the previous year's siege. In the hurry and disorganization of the battle no doubt many things had been omitted which could have been done better if we had had more time at our disposal. I do not think, however, that these are the important considerations. Finally, the idea of a comparison between the two countries of South Africa and Australia is based on a misunderstanding. The 2nd South African Division had only two brigades, the 6th and 4th, and these two brigades were disposed on the western and southern sectors of Tobruk respectively. The sector on which the German attack came, and where they broke through, was held by the 11th Infantry Brigade of the 4th Indian Division and the 201st Guards Brigade. These two brigades were, in the opinion of most of the troops in the Western Desert, among the two finest in the whole Eighth Army. If the Germans were able to break through them, as they did, there is little likelihood that anyone else would have been more successful. As for the unfortunate South Africans they perforce hardly came into the picture. The enemy break-through came right into their rear areas, capturing their transport, and they had no chance either to make a fight for it or to break away. The 201st Guards Brigade were luckier in this way in that being a mobile reserve they had their transport with them, and when permission to break out was given a good number of them managed to get back in safety to the frontier wire.

The fall of Tobruk certainly marked a turning point in German strategic ideas. Rommel was elated beyond all measure. He considered that he only had to pursue the fleeing enemy to be certain of breaking into the Delta and reaching the Suez Canal. Under this conviction he persuaded his superior officer, Kesselring, and the Italian Commando Supremo, to abandon their carefully calculated strategy and to put their trust in his Rupert-like audacity in pursuit. Up to that time the intention had been that when the army in Libya had defeated Eighth Army and captured Tobruk they should drive the British back into Egypt and then stand on the defensive at the frontier while all efforts were devoted to the capture of Malta. This was a plan which had been worked out since the previous April. It was to begin with extremely heavy aerial bombardments after which a German parachute division, commanded by General Student, the victor of Crete, was to be dropped and reinforced by an Italian seaborne division. The Italians, according to Ciano, were extremely dubious about this. No doubt this was one of the reasons why Rommel found it so easy to persuade them to abandon the operation and allow him to press on into Egypt. Incidentally, according to Ciano's diary, the interception of telegrams from Colonel Fellers, the American Military Attaché in Cairo, in which he allegedly said that the British were completely prostrate and that if Rommel would continue the attack there was every chance of his reaching the Suez Canal, was an important factor in reaching the decision. Accordingly Rommel, who had been promoted a Field

Marshal after the capture of Tobruk, pressed on with enthusiasm.

It was clear that the first position on which we could hope to make a stand was the old position prepared in 1940 covering Mersa Matruh. 10th Corps H.Q., under General Holmes, was brought in from Syria to organize the defence. The New Zealand Division came round with him from Syria and he also had the 10th Indian Division. 30th Corps H.Q. went right back to El Alamein, together with the 1st South African Division. 13th Corps took command of the delaying forces falling back from the frontier. We accordingly moved once more back into our old position south of the escarpment, between Sofafi and 'Strafer's Wadi'.

The trouble about the Mersa Matruh position was that it required a strong mobile force operating in the desert to the south; otherwise Matruh would be surrounded just as Tobruk had been. Unfortunately our armoured force was no longer strong enough to be certain of preventing such an investment. Accordingly Auchinleck decided to recast his general strategy. First of all he decided to relieve General Ritchie of the command of Eighth Army and assumed command himself on 25th June. The day before, the enemy had begun an advance across the frontier at great speed. By the 25th his advance guards were only some 40 miles from Matruh. On the same day Auchinleck decided that Matruh would not be held to the last. He announced that his new strategy would consist in a mobile defence of the area between Matruh, El Alamein and the Qattara depression to the south. In no circumstances was any part of the Eighth Army to be allowed to be shut up in Matruh. This strategy was to be made known to all commanding officers, down to battalion commanders. Auchinleck believed that by taking everyone into his confidence he would give them a greater sense of participation in the battle. It was a strategy which was welcome to the Eighth Army. A mobile strategy, taking no account of the loss of definite areas, was one which made sense in the desert. It would also allow time for the Alamein line to be fairly prepared.

El Alamein was only a name to us then though a very well-known one. It had long been regarded as the best position possible for the defence of Egypt. The name itself means 'the twin cairns'. It is the dual form of the noun 'alam' (Arabic, like some other languages, has a special form for two of a kind). Alam has a number of meanings: but the root meaning is a mark or distinguishing sign and it is the ordinary word, for example, for a flag or for officers' rank badges. In the desert it means a waymark and its usual form is a pile of stones. Alam is a very common name in the desert, for example Alam Hamza, 'Cairn No. 5', which was the name of a position where the 1st Battalion of the Buffs fought a famous and disastrous action in December 1941. There are a fair number of Alameins as well. I remember one close to the frontier wire. With a very small change in the first vowel, of a sort almost impossible for European throats to manage, Alamein would mean 'the two worlds'. This seems a most appropriate name for the place that marked, at one of the crucial moments of the war, the boundary between the two worlds of the Western allies and the totalitarian powers.

El Alamein itself is nothing but a halt on the desert railway with no more than a short platform and a little hut. It marks the northern end of the shortest distance between the Mediterranean Sea and the Qattara depression. The Qattara depression is a miracle of nature as impressive as the Sollum escarpment. It is plainly the bed of a former sea, sunk below the level of the desert to the north and south. Its bottom is treacherous with quicksands and is everywhere impassable for motor transport and, at least according to our maps, even for a loaded camel. In many places it is dangerous to attempt on foot. At the north edge it is bounded by sheer cliffs which become steeper as they approach the eastern end. At this eastern end the depression is within 40 miles of the coast which, very conveniently, here bends southwards. The result is that here at last the desert offers a position, both flanks of which are secure. It is a longish position for the sort of numbers that both sides disposed of, but it is much the shortest such position anywhere between Alexandria and Agheila. This advantage had been naturally enough observed long before and Alamein was always reckoned as the last and strongest position of defence in front of the Delta. Since 1940 work had at intervals been undertaken to fortify this line. The defences were based on four strong points known in desert language as boxes. In the north was the Alamein box, southwest of the railway station. Next came Deir el Shein, based on a small square-shaped depression. The third was Qaret el Abd. This resembles nothing so much as a hill which has been hollowed out with one side removed; as its name means the hill of the slaves and it stood on the line of the track of the slaves, Trigh el Abd, it was natural to suppose that it had in the past served the purpose of a corral for holding slaves. The fourth post was on the Taqa plateau, a high flat-topped hill which reared its head immediately above the cliffs of the depression.

Other minor works were built in between these four, tracks were improved, pipelines prepared and so on. We were anything but Maginot-minded in the Western Desert but we did have a fairly cheerful confidence in the strength of the Alamein line.

While the 1st South African Division were working strenuously to improve these defences the battle of Matruh flared up. The enemy pushed on with great speed and, almost before we knew what was happening, they had broken through the long minefield south of Matruh on the evening of 26th June. The reason was that we had too few troops to guard the whole length of this field. They passed on, interposing themselves between 10th Corps in Matruh and 13th Corps on the top of the escarpment to the south. 13th Corps had a hard fight, culminating in a violent action by the New Zealand Division at Minqar Qaim. While this was going on, however, Matruh was surrounded and the 10th Indian Division and 50th Division, both of whom had already had desperately hard fighting in the Gazala battles, had to break their way out. Practically the first we knew of this was the arrival at 13th Corps H.Q. of General Holmes, 10th Corps Commander, and his Chief of Staff. The General had been wounded in the head during the breakout. General Gott was wounded next day; he exposed himself much too freely all through this battle. It was time for Corps H.Q. to move back behind the Alamein line. I was sent off to reconnoitre a suitable site with two other officers from H.Q. It was essential to avoid using the coast road since that was crowded with troops and services withdrawing, so we went straight across the desert between the escarpment and the depression. It was an extremely interesting exercise in navigation. The going was hard but rather cut up and there were no distinguishing marks on which to get a cross bearing. However, at the end of a day's run we found Qaret et Abd bearing right ahead where it should have been. It was occupied by New Zealanders cooking over open fires in disregard of enemy bombers. We pushed on for a distance behind and chose a site near the west end of the Alam Halfa Ridge. By 30th June the whole Corps was back in the Alamein line and the enemy was about to attack it.

The retreat since Matruh had been well conducted on our side. The 1st Armoured Division had particularly distinguished themselves, showing how much they had learnt since their first flighty days. The Bays moved back practically side by side with the advancing enemy and took advantage of the confusion to deal some very heavy blows. They arrived in the Alamein Line with large numbers of prisoners.

For all that we were extremely thin on the ground. All we had for infantry were the 1st South African and 50th Division in the north and the New Zealand and 5th Indian Divisions in the south. All four divisions had been heavily engaged in the battles further west and all except the South Africans had suffered disasters. We were extremely short of tanks and tank crews. On the other hand the enemy's difficulties must also never be forgotten, and they certainly were not forgotten on our side. Rommel had flogged his men along at such a pace that many of his tanks had had to drop out on the way. His German infantry had suffered very severely since the battle began on the 27th May and though he brought forward as much Italian infantry as he could maintain he did not rely on them for offensive operations. He was now at the end of the longest lines of communication that he had ever had to suffer from in Libya. For the moment, however, this was not so serious because he had captured a fair amount of our stuff which helped to keep him going.

Just as at the first sight of Tobruk, Rommel, the moment he arrived, launched a violent attack on the one point of our whole line which was not only the most strongly defended but also held by the least battle-weary troops. He attacked in fact the fortifications round Alamein itself held by the 1st South African Division. It is apparent from German accounts that he was unaware of the strength of the defences, and he certainly allowed himself no time for reconnaissance. At about the same time a second German column, which was designed to move up south of the main column and swing wide on to the coast road, blundered unawares upon the Deir el Shein box, held by the 18th Indian Infantry Brigade. This brigade had only arrived two days before from Iraq and had not had time to prepare its position fully. The defence was also hampered by heavy dust storms from noon onwards until the evening, under cover of which the enemy were able to creep up and remove the mines. Nevertheless the brigade held out all day until darkness and gained thereby a vital respite. The Alamein line had survived its first blow. It was a serious blow for all that; the loss of the Deir el Shein box meant that Qaret el Abd and the Taqa plateau could not be held and both of them were abandoned in the next two days.

The 2nd July 1942 is the day which to my mind has always been the decisive day of the first battle of Alamein. There has been some argument and discussion about this in the various historical works which have dealt with the battle but certainly the impression left on most people actually on the spot was that the 2nd marked the climax. Up to then we were on the defensive, and desperately so; from then on our thoughts and actions turned decisively to the counter offensive. The enemy continued his attacks around Alamein itself and, pressing past Deir el Shein, assaulted the western end of the Ruweisat Ridge. This ridge had always been recognized as one of the keys of the position. It is not high but high enough in that flat country to command large areas. It rises suddenly to about 200 feet above sea level 12 miles south of the coast line. At its western end it runs due east and west, then alters course to the northeast, swinging up to the road and railway. Not only does it give first class observation and fire command but also affords an avenue of good going which led directly through our position and on in the direction of Alexandria. The western end was defended by a battle group of the 5th Indian Division. It was not strong enough to prevent the enemy from climbing on to the ridge but it retreated slowly down it and restricted him to the extreme tip. Nevertheless the situation was plainly serious and there was no handy reinforcement to be thrown in. It looked as though the centre of our position would have been pierced but at this point 13th Corps turned to the counter attack. The New Zealand Division, which was extending the line southwards to the south of the Ruweisat Ridge, was ordered to wheel to the north. Close and heavy fighting took place all the afternoon of 2nd July and on the next day. The enemy was obliged to halt his attacks to the westwards and to switch forces to protect his southern flank where he appreciated there was a serious danger of outflanking which would cut his communications with the coast road.

It is from this day that there dates one of the extraordinary legends of which so many cling round the name of Alamein. At the crisis of the fighting on the afternoon of the 2nd July there was a sudden report from the 5th Indian Division that large numbers of Germans were surrendering. Six hundred was the first figure given, and this is the usual one in the story. We had tuned in the set in our ACV to the 5th Indian Division frequency and I remember hearing the report myself. Nevertheless there was no truth in it at all. It was one of those sudden battlefield rumours which are extremely common but rarely get such prevalence. There were people who said they had seen the six hundred Germans, all from the 90th Light Division, running forward to surrender with their hands up; but no one could be found who actually was present at the capture. A few months later, after the second battle of Alamein had been won, a remarkable development of this legend arose. An engineer officer who had been working on the El Alamein water pipeline claimed to be the man responsible for the surrender. According to his story these German troops were dead beat and desperately thirsty. In the course of their advance they came across a buried pipeline. Madly they threw themselves on it and drank deep. But, alas, it was salt water. The engineers had put salt water in the pipes first of all for purposes of testing before beginning the regular supply with sweet water. On the basis of this, this excellent officer claimed the credit for the defensive success of the first battle of Alamein. There seem to be some inconsistencies in this story even as it stands, for it seems hard to believe that all 600 should drink salt water simultaneously so that none of them could be warned by someone else's experience; but the brutal fact which destroys it is that the surrender never took place.

Nevertheless the enemy were now very hard pressed and from now until the end of August, Rommel had no thought of a further offensive. Auchinleck was determined to wrest the initiative from him. It was a bold and creditable decision, for both armies were very exhausted. However, we were about to receive reinforcements in the shape of the 9th Australian Division. This excellent formation began to arrive from Syria on 4th July. To begin with a brigade was put in on the Ruweisat Ridge to make sure of holding that vital feature, but soon after they were concentrated in the north allowing the South Africans to side step, thickening up the area between the Alamein box and the ridge. On the 10th July the Australians, supported by the South Africans and some British tanks, attacked westwards to capture the Tel el Eisa mounds on the railway west of Alamein. This was a dashing and successful attack which took over a thousand prisoners and gained a valuable salient threatening the whole of the enemy's line to the south. It also had a serious effect on the enemy intelligence organization. The German forces in Africa had an excellent wireless interception unit which had built up a thorough knowledge of the British forces and the habits of their wireless operators. They had followed the battle and were occupying a position on one of the mounds just in the area of the Australian attack. They turned to and helped the Italians in resisting, in fact they got so absorbed in their part of the battle that practically the whole lot were captured. This gave us some useful lessons in what to do to improve security and came as a heavy blow to Rommel. Not that he ever paid much attention to intelligence but now he was reduced to the miserable scraps produced by alleged agents. According to Colonel Anwar Sadat's book *Revolt on the Nile* there were at least two German agents in Cairo at this time; but he makes it clear that they passed back no information at all to the Germans.

Things were going quite well therefore on the northern end of the line but in the south we looked to be very much in the air. With the loss of Taqa our left had been pushed back off the depression and the Alamein line therefore no longer had its primary function. Our left rested on what was marked on all the maps as a usable track. It was one of the oldest and most regular tracks in the whole of the desert, known as the Barrel Track, because it was marked all its length with tar barrels. It led straight to Cairo, coming out beside the swimming pool at the Mena House Hotel, next to the Pyramids. In the old days, before the desert road had been built, it was the main route to the Western Desert. However, things were not as bad as they looked. I went out and made a reconnaissance of the Barrel Track myself and found that its useful life had been practically terminated by the hordes of lorries which had withdrawn to the Delta along it. The Germans in fact never tried an advance that way; when they did mount their last attack, towards Alam Halfa, they struck further north.

Our next attack was on the Ruweisat ridge on the night of the 14th July. This gained ground but left the enemy still holding the extreme west end of the ridge. Two thousand prisoners were taken. On 16th July the Australians again attacked and enlarged their salient in the north. We were on the offensive now and two more big attacks were yet to come. There was a definite feeling of optimism in the air. We knew that we had stopped the enemy and we thought that with any luck we should now be able to inflict on him a heavy defeat. These hopes were blasted. A big attack was made on the 22nd July, by a New Zealand brigade and an Indian brigade. This was to be supported by a brand new tank brigade straight out from England, the 23rd Armoured Brigade. It was 150 tanks strong and since at that time the Germans were still counting their fit tanks by tens it looked as though it might be a battle-winning reinforcement. Its performance was disillusioning. First of all it was hit by a piece of real bad luck. Its orders for the attack were to advance on a certain bearing which must have been either 270 degrees or very close to it, as the intention was for it to attack due west. By a tragic coincidence the east-west grid lines on the map at this point happened to be numbered in the 270's and instead of going on a bearing of 270 the brigade advanced along the line of that grid line. In consequence it ran into an unlifted minefield and lost a number of tanks. Being straight out from England it thought that this was all in the game and ploughed straight on with great gallantry. It then entirely disappeared from control and gave no reply to signals. The reason for this was that on the long sea voyage the batteries in the wireless sets in most of the tanks had run down and had not been recharged. Of course even if they had come to grips with the enemy they were only mounted in Valentine tanks with two pounder guns, which were quite outclassed by that stage of the war even though they were at least more reliable mechanically than the miserable Crusader tanks. The final attack on 26th July was another tragic mix-up. Here the infantry went through but the armour did not follow. General Auchinleck says, and this was the general view at the time, that the failure was due to the fact that the gaps which the infantry had made in the enemy minefields, with great difficulty, were not 'sufficiently safe and wide to be acceptable to the commander of the 1st Armoured Division.' The result was that an attack which had started extremely well and had caused the enemy something approaching panic ended in failure and with further heavy losses to the unfortunate 50th Division.

After this failure, Eighth Army went over to the defensive. We could not keep up the attacks without a complete reorganization. The enemy had been reinforcing fast; four battalions of German parachutists were brought over and a whole division of Italian parachutists. In addition a German infantry division was flown in by battalions at a time from Crete. We ourselves were also receiving reinforcements, two armoured and two infantry divisions, but it would be some time before they could receive sufficient training in desert warfare to be useful. It was more likely that the enemy would be able to resume the attack first. We were ready to receive him. The days when the possibility had to be faced of a withdrawal into the Delta and possibly even the abandonment of the Delta had long gone. Auchinleck's plan was based on holding firmly the Alamein position, the Ruweisat Ridge and the Alam Halfa Ridge. He already found it possible to await a German attack on this position with composure. Meanwhile as the defensive positions thickened up the troops could have the necessary rest. The enemy had been stopped on the threshold of Egypt, over 7,000 prisoners had been taken in the fighting in July and it was already clear that when we were ready to resume the offensive we should have greater advantages.

Very shortly after the failure of the last attack I left the Western

Desert and said goodbye to 13th Corps. I had had rather a blow in
the middle of July by receiving a belated letter from home from which
I gathered that a girl whom I thought I was going to marry had
instead married someone else. This seems natural to me now; after
all I had been away for over two years already and the standard period
for overseas service at that time was supposed to be seven years.
And nowadays I know that it was all for the best. Whether as a result
of this or some other reason I developed all the symptoms of a gastric
ulcer. Kind friends thought a change of air would be good for me
and I found myself posted to G.H.Q., Cairo.

I took the place of Bill Williams, now Brigadier E. T. Williams who
finished the war serving as B.G.S. Intelligence to Field Marshal
Montgomery at 21st Army Group H.Q. He went to Eighth Army as
G2I. A clean sweep had been made of the Intelligence staff in Eighth
Army and the new G1 was a colonel from the Indian Army called
Murphy. My immediate chief was a Scotsman called Joe Ewart.
He subsequently became a full colonel on Montgomery's Intelligence
Staff on which he served with great distinction until a week after the
German capitulation when he was killed in a car accident. His was a
severe loss, for he was a man of very great ability. He combined a
shrewd judgment with a very robust common sense. He also had a
great gift for managing people, not to say for intrigue. As his obituary
in *The Times* said, 'he was always anxious to see the right person in the
right place'. I was all the more flattered that he thought I was one of
the right persons. God rest his soul, he certainly did me a good turn.

I shared a flat with Ewart and Captain Henry Bailley-King, also in
Intelligence, in Maadi. This is, or was, a splendid garden-city suburb
of Cairo. We ran up to G.H.Q. on the little electric train like businessmen to the office. I will say that we worked longer hours than most
businessmen. The Director of Military Intelligence, Freddy de Guingand, had just gone to the Western Desert as Chief of Staff to Eighth
Army and he had been succeeded by Brigadier Airey (now Lieutenant
General Sir Terence Airey). Airey had been running one of the cloak
and dagger shows; he had been in the Middle East since the outbreak
of the war, having a good knowledge of the country and a good
knowledge of Arabic from service in the Sudan Defence Force. He
was sensible, level headed and a persuasive Director of Intelligence.
His advice weighed a lot.

The peaceful atmosphere of Maadi and the intellectual atmosphere
of G.H.Q. was a great change from the Western Desert. I still found

myself, however, feeling rather low. I went to have my gastric ulcer X-rayed and found myself flung into bed with some remarks about the state of my lungs. This came as a distinct surprise, particularly when the worst-tempered Major I ever met in the R.A.M.C. told me that I couldn't expect to last more than two months with lungs like that; the surprise came, however, at a very convenient time, when I was in a proper frame of mind to suppose such a conclusion appropriate. However, time went on and I continued to get better thanks to no medical care at all. I had been shipped off by then to another hospital in Palestine which was also rather overworked; when eventually I had a second X-ray the verdict was that I had had pneumonia, had recovered and was now fit to return to duty forthwith, with no sick leave. The ulcer, which had been playing very much a second fiddle to all this, was also deemed to have cured itself. So I only had time for one swift glance at Jerusalem and returned all the more willingly to G.H.Q. as I had just been warned by Joe Ewart that a German attack was due in a day or two. It seemed likely to be interesting.

CHAPTER VIII

A View of Alamein from G.H.Q.

A S I DROVE in the ambulance to the station on my way to hospital in Sarafand, Palestine, I bought a copy of the *Egyptian Gazette* in which was the news of the change in command in the Middle East. General Auchinleck was to be replaced as Commander-in-Chief by General Alexander and the new commander of the Eighth Army was to be General Montgomery. I do not remember being particularly struck by the news. General Auchinleck had certainly endeared himself to most people by his fighting command of the Eighth Army on the Alamein Line. His intellectual powers were always as evident as his robustness and moral courage. Indeed he seemed to have every characteristic required of a general with the possible exception of the ability to choose wisely in his subordinates and staff. In this too may be seen not so much a fault as an excess of the virtue of loyalty. I remember many years afterwards hearing Sir Winston Churchill in private speak with admiration of Auchinleck and saying how remorseful and hesitant he had felt when he informed him of the decision to supersede him. I do not know that morale in the Eighth Army itself demanded this change; perhaps opinion at home was thought to require it and it may be that the numerous reinforcements now arriving from Britain felt happier at the change. In truth these reinforcements were changing the very appearance of Eighth Army. The Army that fought at El Alamein in October was in a high proportion a paleface army.

Alexander had been in the Middle East since 6th August. Outstanding among the British commanders in the French campaign he had just returned from conducting in Burma the most difficult rearguard action in which British troops had ever taken part. His coolness and competence made an immediate impression on everyone who met him, just as much as the courtesy and quietness of his manner. But after you had known him for some time you could not fail to recognize the unmistakable flash of genius. He had a fantastically active mind which was interested in everything under the sun from the sciences to the arts but which at the same time could also focus with blinding concentration on the problem before it. I must confess at once to personal prejudice, having served him for some five years continuously, but it is a prejudice I shall not attempt to conceal and which I am quite prepared to justify.

The first step that Alexander took when he assumed command was to make it known that there would be no more withdrawals. Plans had been drawn up by Auchinleck and his staff to meet the eventuality of an enemy penetration of the Alamein front, providing for a defence of the edge of the Delta. This was in the period when the enemy were advancing on Alamein and the plans were in the nature of an insurance policy. For the whole of July it was we who were on the offensive; for the last six weeks of his command Auchinleck had been thinking more of a triumphant march westwards. Even when it became clear that Rommel would be the one to attack next Auchinleck had no doubt that we should be able to hold our desert positions. Alexander, too, was confident that in the circumstances of August we would be able to hold the enemy on the present line and he considered there was great advantage in making it known to all ranks, as he says in his Despatch, that no further withdrawal was contemplated and that we would fight the coming battle on the ground on which we stood. General Montgomery, on his arrival, fully concurred with this policy.

It was while I was in hospital that I learnt of the death of Strafer Gott; but it was not until I got back to duty that I learned that he had been designated Commander of Eighth Army, and how he had been killed. On 7th August, having been told that he was to take over when Alexander replaced Auchinleck, he decided to return to Cairo to visit G.H.Q. and to take some leave. The only aircraft available for him was a Bombay, an obsolete and very slow transport plane. The distance to fly was short, but the Bombay had scarcely taken off when it was jumped by two enemy fighters and shot down. Gott escaped unhurt from the crash, but then he went back to the wreckage to help extricate some of the other occupants. While he was doing this the two fighters returned and he was killed by machine-gun fire. I felt his death very keenly. Tall and good looking, and young for a Lieutenant General, he had an easy way with him which won him great popularity and did not conceal his intelligence and courage. During the fighting from Gazala to Alamein his only error, as it seemed to me, was that he exposed himself too recklessly for a General, as if he knew his time was short. I also felt bitterly the irony that he, who had known from the start the bad period of insufficient forces and inadequate material, was killed just at the time when at last skill and courage were to be aided by adequate resources in men and arms. A new Army Commander was to reap the benefits.

One of the greatest of Alexander's talents, exercised with that rightness and certainty of touch which is the sign of genius, was his ability to get the best out of his subordinates. In the course of the war he had a very mixed lot of subordinates on whom to exercise his gift, from Chinese generals in Burma to American, Italian, Brazilian and others in Italy. It was an advantage that he already had experience of the commander of Eighth Army who had served under him when he, Alexander, had the vital Southern Command in 1941. General Montgomery was singularly fortunate in the timing of his first important command in the field. To begin with, any British general who comes to high command halfway through a war, when the flood of munitions is at last at its height and adequate formations are in being and well trained, is luckier than his colleagues, such as Wavell, who have to take command at the beginning of a British war when the highest qualities of genius are called for to remedy the deficiencies and shortages which our unpreparedness makes inevitable. There was an additional element of good fortune in his case. He was not the first choice for command of Eighth Army; if General Gott had not been killed, Montgomery would have remained in command of First Army and landed with them at Algiers on November 8th. This would have been a very difficult command and in many ways, to judge from subsequent history, would have called for qualities rather different from those which distinguished Montgomery's conduct of operations. First Army was no sooner ashore in Algiers than it was sent off in a dash to try to seize Tunisia before the enemy could do so. This involved a rapid advance of 560 miles by two roads and an indifferent railway and the only troops at the army commander's disposal amounted to one infantry division, reinforced later with a few scraps of armour, two commandos and two parachute battalions. Try as I will, I cannot see General Montgomery taking the risks that General Anderson, the First Army Commander, took. I should have expected on the contrary a cautious advance, with careful consolidation at each stage and, before the crystal clouds, I can see a difference of opinion, which might have been a painful one, between him and General Eisenhower.

On the other hand, if Gott had not been killed I have no difficulty in seeing him as the victor of Alamein. I think it quite likely for that matter that, in spite of Rommel's mastery of the withdrawal, Gott would have caught him before he got away into Tunisia. Some people have doubted this because they say that morale in Eighth Army was in such a state that a completely new command was called for. Certainly the new arrivals would have known little of Strafer Gott, but on the other hand the old hands would have been encouraged, and for myself I think that what really improved morale was the arrival of all those new divisions from Ninth Army and from England, the great flow of new material and, above all, the coming of the Sherman tank. For the first time we had a tank which we knew to be as good as the best German tank; and then there were the new anti-tank guns and the self-propelled artillery and the air reinforcements. The whole area from the Alamein line back to the Delta seemed crammed with men and workshops and dumps of materials to a degree which made people think more of conditions in the First World War than of the to and fro skirmishing of small forces in the desert hitherto. It was certainly these things that improved my morale and I am sure that the same was true of plenty of others. In fact it must be clear by now that I am one of those who believe that General Montgomery owed his success not to wearing twice as many cap badges as General Auchinleck, but to having twice as many resources.

Heaven forbid that I should seem to depreciate any of the arts of leadership. It is a fine thing for a general to show confidence and cheerfulness and, in these days of large armies, if he is to convey his personality to the men under his orders he must paint with broad strokes. Nor can the fact that a general has a healthy superiority in numbers and equipment be used to prove that he is not a first-class general. Certainly it is easier to prove that he is if he wins a battle against odds—I think it was Moltke who said that no general should be praised who had not had to conduct a retreat—but it would be very hard to withhold praise for leadership on this score.

The fact that Eighth Army was being reinforced could not be concealed and indeed for the sake of morale it was fairly well rubbed in. The Germans were thoroughly aware of it. Their position was now like, and was worse than, the position we had been in in the two previous Januaries at the far end of Cyrenaica. We were now right up against our ports of supply, with the full resources of the Middle East base a comfortable distance behind our lines. They were at the fullest stretch to which their communications were ever extended in the whole course of the desert wars. Their two ports of entry, Tobruk and Benghazi, neither of them very well fitted for this role, were 375 and 680 miles away respectively. They were linked to them by a single road supplemented by the Tobruk railway. The whole length of these communications was under constant hammering from the air, in which element we had complete superiority. All this was a result of Rommel's over-rashness in pressing his advance. I am bound to say that I could never find it in my mind to blame him in those hectic and scrambling days when the tide of battle rolled in a wave of dust back eastwards along the Egyptian coast; but there is no doubt what the cool judgment of a military expert would be. It was clear that if Rommel was to vindicate his rash decision, and to lay hands on the glittering prizes of the Delta, so tantalizingly near, there would have to be one final fling, and it would have to come fairly soon. The coming battle was intended to be Rommel's last battle in Africa. His doctors had for some time been warning him about his health. It had now been decided that, whatever happened, he must hand over his command and leave Africa in September and his successor had already been chosen. But in fact it was all too late. It was easy to read his intentions and we had the means to frustrate them.

I got back to G.H.Q. in time for the battle of Alam el Halfa which opened on the night of 30th August. The name is that of a ridge which runs from southwest to northeast parallel to and south of the Ruweisat Ridge. It has been the cause of some controversy. In his book *From El Alamein to the River Sangro*, published in 1948, Lord Montgomery writes: 'My initial tour of the battlefield soon convinced me of the vital importance of the Alam el Halfa ridge which I found virtually undefended.' In his *Memoirs*, published in 1958, he says: 'it was undefended, because there were no troops available.' The two statements, as can be seen, are inconsistent with each other. They are still more inconsistent with what General Auchinleck says in his official despatch and also with Lord Alexander's account. Perhaps it will be enough, if Auchinleck is regarded as an interested party, to quote Alexander. He says in his Despatch: 'A strong position for a brigade had been built on the (Alam el Halfa) Ridge in July, defended by wire and minefields.' For the ordinary reader Alexander's testimony is probably sufficient, but another voice is always useful. From my personal knowledge of the area I can confirm Lord Alexander's version on the question of whether General Auchinleck had realized the importance of Alam el Halfa and had taken steps about it. My last camp in the desert was in the Deir el Agram, a depression immediately south of and below the Alam el Halfa ridge. In July, before Auchinleck handed over his command, I frequently had to pass over the knob at the end of the ridge on which the defended position stood. It was a large and elaborate stronghold similar to those in the line itself. Not only is it incorrect, it is quite implausible to suggest that General Auchinleck had overlooked the importance of the Alam el Halfa ridge. A glance at the map, still more a visit to the spot, must demonstrate to anyone with an elementary knowledge of war that this was one of the keys to the position. It commanded to its south a wide area of desert country. Should the enemy succeed in occupying it, it provided a corridor of good going which led behind all our positions, and pointed straight at Alexandria.

The enemy attack ought to have gone in on the 25th August, the night of the full moon, and this was Rommel's original intention. Shortage of fuel prevented it. Of all the difficulties with which his desperately drawn lines of communication confronted him, the most hazardous concerned fuel. Every drop had to cross the Mediterranean. This meant that the tankers had to run the gauntlet of our air forces which now, after a less confident start, had reached a high pitch of competence in their attacks on tankers. At the time of which I am speaking, and this continued until after Alamein, more enemy tankers were being sunk than arrived in Africa. On 25th August, Rommel had not got three days' supply for his attacking forces. By dint of flying petrol from Greece in transport aircraft he raised the necessary amount for an attack five days later on the 30th August. It was an attack on the pattern traditional in the Western Desert; an outflanking march round our open left wing. He even used the same divisions as at Gazala, with the addition of one extra Italian armoured division. The plan was to thrust through the screen of light forces covering our southern flank, advance eastwards to a position well behind our main line and then turn north, placing the armoured force in the rear of our main defensive positions which would then be taken between two fires. Our own strategy was also straightforward and obvious: not to oppose an immovable resistance to the opening attack, since our left flank could never be made so strong that it could not be turned, but to contest solidly the northward thrust and simultaneously to strike at the hinge of the enemy formation where their line would then be bent round to form a right-angled re-entrant. Plans were made accordingly in good time. Two infantry and two armoured divisions were allotted to 13th Corps together with a very heavy concentration of artillery.

I must mention one contribution by Intelligence to the battle. It was a fairly simple one, and could only have succeeded against the Germans. The trouble is that in trying to form an opinion about that great bogy, the British Intelligence Service, the Germans had read all the wrong books. They had studied with passionate interest, in particular, the works of Sir Compton Mackenzie about his experiences in Greece during the first war and from them had formed a false estimation of the value of agents. If instead they had read, for example, Wavell's account of Allenby's Palestine campaigns they might have taken warning by the story of a ruse which deceived the enemy before the battle of Beersheba. A staff officer, riding out apparently on reconnaissance and getting carelessly too close to the enemy's lines, was fired on by the Turks and in his flight dropped a haversack containing among other things a notebook with carefully concocted false information which was taken for gospel. It seemed too much to hope that the very same device, modified only by the mechanisation of the horse, would do the trick again 25 years later. I suppose the reason is that its very simplicity is in its favour.

The basis of the trick was that in this kind of war both sides relied very heavily, for natural reasons, on maps captured from the other. All our maps of Libya, which were excellent, were based on captured Italian maps corrected by air photographs. The Germans valued our maps highly, and for Egypt they naturally had nothing better. One particularly valuable sort of map was the 'going' map. On this different colours showed what the country was like and what sort of speed could be maintained over it. It was decided to plant a false going map on the enemy in the hope of thereby influencing his plans for the battle. Alam el Halfa was a commanding position designed by nature to hold up an enemy attempting to strike north in the rear of our defences; but there was nothing to prevent the enemy from outflanking it. If he held on past the end of the ridge and then turned in a north-easterly direction he would have a pretty clear run to the outskirts of Alexandria. The going was nowhere very good in the rear of the Alamein line but it was no worse on this northeast course than anywhere else. A map was accordingly prepared showing an area of very bad going running across the route we didn't wish the enemy to take and, by contrast, a line of good going in a northerly direction right up to the Alam el Halfa Ridge and thence along the ridge. In actual fact the approach to Alam el Halfa across the Deir el Agram was pretty bad, with numerous patches of soft sand. This map was prepared at top speed and printed secretly. A copy was given to an armoured car commander of the Royals after being creased to indicate use and a few drops of engine oil added. It was then thrown down on the floor of the car to pick up even more of a used appearance. A patrol then went out and deliberately drew enemy fire. The armoured car staggered to a halt, the other two drew up and took off the crew and made off under heavy fire.

When on the afternoon of 31st August the Afrika Korps began the encircling movement they did not attempt any wide sweep but took a course due north straight on to our strong point at the western end of Alam el Halfa Ridge. They were met there by the fire of some 300 field and medium guns and 400 anti-tank guns, and two brigades of tanks. It looked as though the ruse had succeeded but it was naturally impossible to prove this. However, about two months later I entertained at lunch General von Thoma, commander of the Afrika Korps, who had been taken prisoner in the final stages of the battle of El Alamein. He spoke freely about everything; like most Germans of all ranks he thought that British Intelligence knew everything in any case. Talking about the excellence of our equipment in the desert he mentioned in particular the 'going' maps which were so greatly sought as prizes. One of them, he said, had been of great use before the battle of Alam el Halfa because they had intended to make a wide outflanking movement but had fortunately been saved from this by the opportune capture of a map in an abandoned armoured car which showed they would have run into bad going. The plan was accordingly changed before the attack. Like Lady Bracknell, I thought it wrong to undeceive him.

For all that it formed the climax of the German operations in Libya and marked the most easterly point to which they penetrated, the battle of Alam el Halfa is simple to describe and simple in its general theme. The enemy advanced through our covering screen, suffering disproportionately from harassing fire. He attacked our positions at Alam el Halfa and was repulsed; he drew back and used all his wiles to make us attack him; when we refused to oblige him he withdrew. The results to him were a gain of ground to the extent of some four miles on the southern flank and the loss of 42 German and 11 Italian tanks. The casualties were nothing much—for that matter we lost 68 tanks ourselves—but the important thing was the failure of an effort on which much had been staked. Rommel tried to put the blame on shortage of fuel: 'Der Kesselring, der schickt mer koa schprit' he was alleged to have remarked in Swabian dialect to some tank crews—'Kesselring doesn't send me any petrol'. He was unfair to Kesselring, who was entirely in the hands of the Italians, but there was in fact some truth in the excuse. On 31st August and 1st September the air force were successful in sinking no less than three tankers. Some sort of excuse in any case was clearly necessary, for Rommel himself was about to make his departure for Germany, leaving his troops in the most exposed position in which they had ever been. Shortly after the battle he handed over his command, and though the reason for his departure was given out as sick leave, it was intended to be his farewell to Africa. He was not to know that in under two months' time he would be hastily flying back to take over command and responsibility in a battle already half lost. His successor was General Stumme, who had come from the command of an armoured Corps on the Russian front.

The Russian front was very much in our minds at the moment. We had stopped one arm of the two-pronged movement towards the Middle East sources of oil, but the northern arm was still advancing. In fact just as the tide began to ebb back from the approaches to Alexandria the flood of German armoured strength was swirling over the southern steppe and along the northern foothills of the Caucasus. Those who like to speculate on what might have happened have frequently asked themselves whether it would not have been the proper strategy for Germany to strengthen the southern arm of the pincers to make sure of getting to the oil. My friend Colonel Fellers, the American Military Attaché, was always of the opinion that the Germans had only to add another couple of divisions to the German–Italian force to make sure of being able to thrust through the British defences and reach Iraq. I have seen other American appreciations to the same effect. It is of course true that the forces facing each other on the southern shore of the Mediterranean even so late as the end of 1942 were very small compared with the huge armies that clashed on the plains of Russia. The Axis forces in Egypt only amounted to four armoured and the equivalent of ten infantry divisions and the British to four armoured and seven infantry divisions. To have detached a force capable of doubling the enemy strength in Africa would have meant very little diminution of the Axis forces in Russia. I am not very enamoured of this variety of speculation myself. One of the main factors in the situation was that Hitler had no concept of overseas operations. His eyes were fixed solidly on the great continental land masses and the great continental mass armies. The African campaign was always a mere diversion to him. If Hitler's character had been different a great many other things would have been different and not merely the conduct of the African campaign. And finally it is worth remembering that Axis logistic resources were stretched to their limit and rather beyond by the task of maintaining the forces they had in Africa. Any addition might have caused the collapse of the whole machine.

Our own position both in respect of supply and communications and in respect of men and material was so much better that we could now plan with confidence the counter stroke. General Montgomery well indicates in his *Memoirs* how great were the advantages for such planning of which he disposed. He writes 'I came to the conclusion that Eighth Army must have its own Panzer Army—a corps strong in armour, well equipped and well trained. It must never hold static fronts; it would be the spearhead of our offensives. Because of the lack of such a corps we had never done any lasting good. The formation of this corps of three or four divisions must be a priority task.' (The reference to 'its own Panzer Army' is based on an error by General Montgomery; he supposes that 'Panzer Army' was the name of Rommel's armoured forces only, but in fact it was the title of all the forces of all arms of both nations under his command, in full 'German–Italian Panzer Army Africa.') The general is indeed fortunate who can make such a decision and be able to carry it into effect. General Wavell or General Auchinleck might have decided that what was needed was a reserve corps of three or four divisions; they might for that matter have decided that what was required, for the purposes of camouflage and protection, was to cover all their tanks with a half-inch layer of 18 carat gold. Either decision would have been equally impracticable of achievement. It was easy now, however, to provide just such a reserve. We had in fact four armoured divisions, and although one of them, the 8th, was disbanded to strengthen the other three, its armoured brigade remained. The result was that the reserve Corps or *Corps de Chasse* contained the 1st Armoured Division, the 10th Armoured Division (including two armoured brigades) and the 2nd New Zealand Division, with an armoured brigade under command and there was still the 7th Armoured Division left over to provide an armoured component for the left flank of the line.

All that was now necessary was to pick a suitable time for the battle to begin. There was a lot to be done and above all there was a good deal of training required. Three of the divisions to be used were new and there were very large numbers of new drafts in the existing divisions; Lord Alexander records that between 1st August and 23rd October 41,000 men joined units at the front, not counting those in the new formations and units. This was a very high proportion of the forces involved on our side, about 140,000. It can be taken therefore that over half the men engaged were new to the desert and probably much the same proportion had no previous experience of battle. Training was essential. The lapse of time necessary, however, before this programme could be carried out was, as always, unwelcome to the Prime Minister. With that quickness of intellect and keenness for action which made him so inspiring a wartime leader, he was always leaping ahead to the next stage, impatient of any delay. Almost the first thing he asked Alexander was when he would be ready to attack. This was about mid-August, and the best that Alexander could guess was the end of September. Later this estimate had to be revised because the battle of Alam el Halfa had occurred in the interval, which had inevitably set back the programme. Accordingly, at the beginning of September, a decision was taken to launch the attack on 23rd October, the day before the full moon. This produced an instant reaction from the Prime Minister. Alexander felt himself obliged to call an old-fashioned council of war of the Commanders-in-Chief in the Middle East of the three services together with the Minister Resident Mr. Casey (now Lord Casey). Fortified by the full agreement of this council he firmly stood by the decision. It must be said that the Prime Minister gave way as he always did in the end, when convinced that his military advisers could not be overborne. It looks as though he regarded generals as persons who needed the spur. I doubt if this was always true; in the case of El Alamein anyone could see that the longer we waited the more formidable the enemy defences would become and by the 23rd October they were extremely formidable. I do not think therefore that either Alexander or Montgomery really needed a spur; but in saying this I do not intend any criticism of Sir Winston Churchill. It might sometimes, however, have done him good to be reminded that when the best known signal in British naval history was fluttering to the masthead of the *Victory* on the morning of Trafalgar, Admiral Collingwood, commanding the leeward line, observed impatiently 'I do wish Nelson would stop signalling—he knows we all know what we have to do.'

During this time of training and preparation a great deal of thought was being given to the attack on the enemy's supply system. The Air Force and the Navy continued on the lines in which they had had such success already, but plans were also made for more direct action on land.

The two most important places on the enemy's supply line were the ports of Tobruk and Benghazi. Two separate irregular organizations had plans to attack them. The plan for the Tobruk attack was set on foot by a regular officer of the Indian army who had been for a short time in enemy hands during the retreat from Gazala. He spoke fluent German and had discovered as a result of his experiences how easy it was to move about behind the enemy lines. His idea was to bring a party of troops overland in German transport and disguised as Germans to seize a beachhead west of the harbour where more troops could be landed from two destroyers. A combined party was then to seize the harbour and hold it for a period during which they would destroy all the fuel dumps they could find and carry out such hasty demolition of the port installations as was found possible. It was a daring and well thought out plan though the risks were heavy; the land party in fact was fairly successful but the sea party was detected and very few of them managed to get ashore. Both the destroyers detailed for the operation were lost and very few men got back across the desert to tell the tale.

The attack on Benghazi was to be carried out by a party under the command of Major David Stirling of the Scots Guards. His story has been written by Miss Virginia Cowles in a most entertaining book called *The Phantom Major*. The mention of one of the most spectacular of the irregulars of the Middle East prompts me to consider the general value of irregulars, raiding forces, private armies and all that.

The Second World War saw a truly remarkable proliferation of these growths. The first and most famous were, of course, the Commandos, who from small origins grew to maturity and now, under the aegis of that solid Corps, the Royal Marines, are quite respectable. They had their ups and downs in the beginning. In the Middle East they started off under a very heavy cloud because of two spectacular failures against the Italians. In the winter of 1940–41 attacks were made on the islands of Casos and Castelorizo in the Dodecanese. Neither of these islands was really strongly garrisoned but in spite of that both attacks were completely abortive. When I was on General Freyberg's H.Q. in Crete I read, and hastily burnt, copies of the Court of Enquiry which sat on these two disasters. The President of the Court, who may be held to have been quite out of sympathy with the Commando Spirit, was rather caustic in his references to the long list of missing arms, especially as most of them were of a rather exotic nature. He also expressed the view that if an ordinary infantry battalion had been given the task of capturing and holding Castelorizo it would have been done easily. As this island is a long way from the rest of the Dodecanese, not far from Cyprus and conveniently small, this judgment is probably justified.

It is not, however, of the Commandos that I propose to write, for after the first year we had none in the Middle East. For that matter I have no doubt that in the particular circumstances of the U.K. where the army was not in contact with the enemy, the Commandos filled a genuine need, not only by providing something to put in the papers but also by giving certain people experience of most vigorous forms of active service and by building up a great mass of useful facts and doctrine concerning amphibious warfare. In the Middle East, by way of comparison, we had a number of small special units. It may appear surprising that in a theatre where manpower was never in lavish supply authority should have been prepared to remove from their units officers and men who undoubtedly were of the highest quality for special but infrequently occurring tasks. Certain it is that regular officers, and in particular general officers, smiled benignly on the birth of many small units. As midwives stood the strongly contrasting figures of Colonel Lawrence and Colonel Blimp—'Hope and Fear' a classical allegorist would have called them. It could not be denied that Lawrence's highly irregular exploits in the First War had been of great military value and each time there was always the hope that the new-born unit might emulate him. Fear, I think, was the more potent emotion, the fear of being considered old-fashioned, hidebound and conservative. It was known that the Prime Minister himself took a deep personal interest in the Commandos and might be expected to view with favour these little sisters. Whatever the motives may have been for the official blessing on the activity of raiding forces, their multiplication soon began to mean that various bodies of keen young officers were looking about in competition for something really worth while to do. Their search was not always successful. Things naturally got worse when the main tide of war moved away from the Middle East. A well-known tale may perhaps illustrate this.

After the occupation of Crete at the end of May 1941 there was a period of struggle between the German invaders and the Cretans which was marred by many sanguinary incidents on both sides. When a couple of years had gone by, however, a certain calm descended on the island. The German and Italian troops were not of a very high quality and were prepared to take things easy; the Cretans, though maintaining their proud and independent attitude, were prepared to live and let live for a while. Early in 1943 the German Divisional Commander on Crete was promoted and in his place was sent a General Kreipe. He had come from a tough command on the Russian southern front which had seriously affected his health, particularly his stomach. His posting was in the nature of convalescence; the warmer climate in Crete, it was thought, would assist his recovery. One evening as he was driving alone to play bridge with some of his staff officers, he was kidnapped by two British officers who forced him out of his car and made him tramp across the mountains to the south coast where they were met by a submarine which took all three to Egypt.

It is not easy to cast up a balance sheet for this feat of arms. On the one hand General Kreipe had been removed to a still warmer climate. No doubt this meant that some Colonel somewhere got promotion a little earlier than he would have done otherwise; but the German Army at that time had well over a thousand major generals and could quite easily spare one. On the credit side of the British account there was quite a good story for the press and one more enemy general to feed (unfortunately he proved of little value to the Intelligence Branch, having been out of things for so long). It seems so far not a very impressive balance to weigh against the extra-regimental employment of his vigorous, intelligent and courageous captors. There is, however, another item in the reckoning which fell on the Cretans. The German Higher Command, who also paid great attention to what appeared in the press, were furious at the indignity to German arms. Hitler himself, or so the story ran, took particular care to select a perfectly beastly general to send in place of the kind-hearted Kreipe. Like a new broom, he determined to make a change from the laxity of his predecessor. Repression and resistance alternated in Crete. The Cretans, though not averse to a fight, regretted that they had exchanged King Log for King Stork.

Popski's Private Army was a more serious organization, at any rate in its early days. While it was small it was good. It had the simple and excellent idea of walking on to enemy airfields at night and destroying parked aircraft on the ground. This involved a very difficult task in getting to the chosen airfield across the desert without being spotted. Thereafter the actual task of destruction was less difficult. Popski himself had a personal record of aircraft destroyed outnumbering any air ace on either side of the war. The later stages in Tunisia and Italy were less impressive. By the time it got itself fully equipped Popski's Private Army became muscle bound. As his book shows, they would set off with their specially fitted jeeps with the aim of destroying enemy transport behind his lines and more often than not end up by having to destroy their own transport and make their way back on foot. The fact is that by the time we got to Italy the great days of raiding were over.

Looking back it seems to me that the reader may conclude that I am biassed against these small forces. To refute the charge I need only refer to the Long Range Desert Group, the earliest of the lot, set up under Wavell's personal patronage. This magnificent organization had all the virtues and none of the faults of the private armies. It had a useful job to do, it knew how to do it perfectly and it did it quietly. The members were geniuses at navigation and were expert at crossing all types of desert surfaces. Their aim was to be unspectacular both on active service and between times. One of their most remarkable feats, of a usefulness which greatly exceeds anything I have mentioned so far, was to establish and maintain an observation post on the borders of Tripolitania and Cyrenaica near 'Marble Arch'. At this post, day after day, they watched all the traffic that went along the main road, counting it by types and reporting it faithfully back to G.H.Q. I know of no comparable feat in the Mediterranean theatre during the war. Certainly all the agents' reports ever received through all the cumbrous and many-branched organizations set up for the purposes of espionage put together, never amounted to enough to be weighed in the balance against the information which the Long Range Desert Group supplied.

I return to the raid on Benghazi and the Special Air Service (its name was misleading, it never normally travelled by air). The purpose here was to break into Benghazi unobtrusively from the open country to the east, make for the harbour and see what could be done to sabotage oil storage and port installations. The party travelled in a small motorized column which set out from Kufra. It reached the outskirts of Benghazi unobserved and lay up concealed in the desert to await its opportunity. What followed is described in Miss Cowles' book, but not so fully as in the report which was given to me by Captain Fitzroy Maclean, as he then was, immediately after his return to Cairo.

Arrangements had been made for a friendly Arab, one of Baird's men, to come out from Benghazi, make contact with the party at their lying up place and give an up to date report on the state of things. When I say arrangements had been made I ought to add that, in the typical fashion of all raiding forces, the Intelligence branch at G.H.Q. had not been taken into their confidence. The story the agent told was certainly striking but not, to my mind, very convincing. 'Oh, sir, oh, sir,' said this tremulous Arab, '10,000 Germans arrived in Benghazi yesterday coming from the eastwards. Moreover an anti-tank ditch, protected by mines and wire, has been dug round the whole city.' As I remember the story he only just failed to add 'All is discovered, fly at once'; plainly he hoped to persuade them to call off the operation. I never found out whether the party believed the bit about the 10,000 Germans, the least plausible part of the story; but the rest they obviously took very seriously. That night they signalled to G.H.Q. repeating what they had been told and asking whether it could be confirmed. Now it so happened that only three days before there had been a complete photographic air cover of Benghazi; there was no trace of an anti-tank ditch, minefields or wiring. This was conclusive. For that matter the enemy were far too stretched to be able to spare either the labour or the materials for that kind of thing so far behind their lines. Accordingly a signal was sent in reply to reassure the party that the anti-tank ditch and its appurtenances were a figment and so were the 10,000 Germans. From Miss Cowles' book I learn that the reply included the advice to disregard bazaar rumour. I did not draft the signal myself, it was Joe Ewart; but the comment seems justified.

Unfortunately the wonders of science, if I may so describe Photographic Reconnaissance, made less impression on David Stirling's party than the supposed evidence of an eye witness. They did not believe there were no perimeter defences. Captain Maclean explained to me with great seriousness that they decided that it would be necessary to recast the whole plan of attack. 'We could not go in unobtrusively from the east,' he said, 'because we could not get across the anti-tank ditch, so we decided we should have to attack up the main road to the south.' The trouble about this of course was that, whether or not there were any defences elsewhere, there were bound to be some on the main road. 'And when we came up to the edge of the town,' he said, 'there was a road block with wire on either side of the road and a whole minefield running along the wire.' I did not ask him what else he expected. In addition there was a reasonably alert Italian guard detachment in prepared positions. After a brief fire fight the party withdrew. When we occupied Benghazi in November for the last time, there was still no perimeter defence round the town and it was simple for anyone to enter unobtrusively from the east.

It was a bad characteristic of the various private armies to try to collect their own intelligence. They were particularly fond of asking odd questions of the Intelligence Branch without revealing the purpose for which the information was wanted. This often led to a serious waste of effort. For example, one of the most famous raids of the war, that on Rommel's H.Q. at Apollonia in November 1941, which resulted in the award of a richly deserved posthumous V.C. to the commander, Colonel Keyes, was impaired by a similar failing. If Intelligence had been properly taken into the confidence of the persons organizing the raid they could have been told that Rommel would not be at his H.Q. that day.

The rest of September and October were uneventful on land. To the Intelligence Staffs at Eighth Army H.Q. and at G.H.Q. the picture of the enemy's build-up was of great fascination. Men were coming in at the rate of some 5,000 or 6,000 a week and the *Ankara* was ferrying over many new tanks. Defences were being constructed on a scale never before seen in the Western Desert. We had a very fine and detailed knowledge of these from the frequent photographs taken by the Air Force. The whole face of the desert was being covered with mines and weapon pits and thickets of barbed wire. It was odd in some ways to feel that we had said goodbye to Erwin Rommel, though this was a secret known only to a few. A difference soon appeared in dispositions, particularly of the armour. Rommel on the whole believed in keeping his armour concentrated, or at any rate not divided into more than two groups. He did have the two Panzer Divisions separate in November 1941, but then he had a difficult problem in that he had to watch both Tobruk and the frontier simultaneously. General Stumme went over to quite different ideas which, I gathered from General von Thoma, were based on the normal practice on the Russian front when fighting a defensive battle. The theory was that every part of the line should have some armour within easy reach. This was also a Russian practice. In consequence the two German and two Italian armoured divisions were broken up into six mixed battle groups and disposed at equal distances all the way behind the front. I do not know whether these tactics were successful in Russia. At Alamein they were probably more of a help than a hindrance to us.

Our principal attack was on a fairly narrow front, but the Germans nevertheless retained this schematic dispersion of their armour for the first three days—until in fact Rommel returned and immediately ordered a concentration on his northern flank.

My admiration for Rommel is a good deal less than that shown either by the press in 1942 or by the bulk of writers since the war; but I think it is a little unfair to speak of Alamein as a battle where Rommel was defeated by Montgomery. This is certainly the line taken by the latter who, in his account, never mentions the name of Stumme; but all the preliminary dispositions were Stumme's, the plan on which the battle was fought in the first three critical days was also Stumme's and Rommel only returned on the 26th to find the battle already lost.

There is one factor which I have rarely seen mentioned in accounts of Alamein (it is referred to in Lord Alexander's despatches) and that is the extremely high rate of sickness among the enemy forces in the preceding months. We were able to get a pretty good picture of this both from prisoners and subsequently from captured documents. There were units where the proportion of men absent sick was as high as 25 per cent. Dysentery and infective jaundice were the main causes of absence. We had a certain amount of the latter on our side too; I remember on one occasion being told there were as many as 600 cases in the New Zealand Division alone; but in general our sickness rate was just about average for the season, something less than five in a thousand. There was of course a much greater congestion of troops on both sides of the line than anywhere else in the previous desert campaigns. Italian medical organization was poor and certainly they paid less attention to the sanitary measures which are vital to preservation of health in the field. It was an extraordinary experience after the battle to enter the area where they had been and be almost overwhelmed by the clouds of flies. Italian troops themselves were not affected to quite the same extent as the Germans alongside them. In the German units the medical services were greatly superior, but on the other hand the troops were more careless. By and large our troops knew that they should drink sparingly by day and not over-eat (there was not all that chance of doing so anyway) and were better at looking after themselves generally. The Germans were liable to vary periods of privation with bouts of excessive eating and drinking. Their uniform also was much less well adapted to the climate than ours. Prisoners of all ranks would freely admit that they felt out of their depth anywhere outside Europe whereas the British, they supposed, were fully at home in the tropics.

We made the usual attempt to deceive the enemy about our intentions. Naturally there was no hope of getting anything but tactical surprise; strategically it was obvious that we should have to attack, and before very long. The story which we tried to lead the enemy into believing was that the main attack would be on the southern front. This was a plausible story, since the classical tactic in the desert was to strike at the enemy's southern flank. In fact Alexander had long decided that the north was the place. We should have much better communications ourselves and if we were successful in penetrating the enemy's line there we could hope to push him off his communications; and then, if we could drive up along the road, all the enemy to the south would have a difficult job withdrawing. The plan of deception involved the construction of a dummy fuel pipe line running down to the southern flank. Imitation supply dumps were also set up at proper places. All this was intended to help also in suggesting to the enemy a later date than the 23rd October. The work on the dummy pipe line was carefully timed to suggest that it would not be ready until about the 5th November.

The attempt appears to have been reasonably successful; at any rate the enemy continued to show strength over the whole front without any concentration at a particular point. This incidentally contradicts the rather elaborate story put about shortly after the battle in which the enemy (naturally described as Rommel) was supposed to have set a trap for us by deliberately weakening his centre and strengthening the left and right. The centre of the line must, I suppose, be the Ruweisat Ridge and this area had in fact the best German infantry, three battalions of parachutists. The enemy had also to guard against landings from the sea behind their lines; the raids of September probably made them cautious. The 90th Light Division was behind the northern part of the line, watching the coast in the neighbourhood of Ghazal and the best of the Italian mobile divisions, Trieste, was at Daba.

The battle of El Alamein started at 10 o'clock on the night of the 23rd October with the heaviest bombardment ever seen in Africa. A thousand field and medium guns opened fire together. There was another unusual feature. It is still, I think, rare in war for a Commander-in-Chief to perish in battle and it must be rarer still for it to happen at the very opening of the critical engagement. General Stumme was on a visit to the front line when the attack began. So far as I can gather this was not because of any particular apprehension about that night or about the northern part of his front. He was accompanied by his chief signals officer and as they stood peering into the night from an advanced observation post suddenly, out of the darkness, came a burst of long range medium machine-gun fire which struck down Stumme's companion right at his side. The shock was so severe that Stumme himself collapsed, suffered a stroke and died on the spot. It is a strange story and hard to believe; but it was told to me in full detail only a few days later by Stumme's successor and it might be supposed that he had taken care to get the exact truth. We had had, oddly enough, a hint of it, if it had been possible to interpret it, very shortly after it happened. Some German wireless station which we could not identify was heard reporting in clear that the body of a German general was lying out in front of their wire. The station addressed came back unbelievingly to ask if it was certain that it was a general. It was indeed quite a time before the enemy discovered what had happened to the Army Commander and his body was not brought in until the next day. I gathered that his death was not unexpected by the German doctors; he had been seriously overexerting himself and feeling the effect of the climate. Command was taken over, later next morning, by General von Thoma, commander of the German Afrika Korps.

The aim of the Eighth Army plan was to drive a clear path through the enemy's defences between the two ridges of Tell el Eisa and Miteiriya. A strong armoured corps, fully concentrated, was to be passed down these corridors and there invite counter attack. While this was going on our infantry would gradually clear the enemy from the area on both sides of this corridor. It was a battle of attrition on the lines of many fought in the First World War. Both the infantry and the armour knew that it would be a long and serious fight. We were bringing a considerable superiority in men and tanks against the enemy and diversions in the south by 13th Corps and a naval demonstration off Daba were successful in preventing the enemy from reinforcing the point of main penetration.

On the 24th October when the attack was still at a critical stage, and much hampered by the stubbornness of the surviving defenders who had been by-passed by the night attack, the enemy's counter attacks in the north were few and minor in scale. He took much more seriously the southern attacks. Evidently the tin cans of the dummy pipeline had done their work well. Even on the 25th he was plainly in two minds. Although 10th Corps had fought itself into a strong position, the armoured battle groups from Littorio and the 15th Panzer Division counter-attacked individually in strengths of only some forty tanks each.

When Stumme was killed and it was clear that a great and decisive battle had begun, there could be no question in the minds of the German Higher Command that Rommel must be sent back. He arrived at Army H.Q. on the 26th October. By that time the defensive positions had been pierced on a broad front and a great deal of the armoured strength had been frittered away by his predecessor's faulty tactics. The position was desperate. Although Stumme's heart attack meant that the enemy retreat from Alamein would be conducted with outstanding skill, and that the battles in southern and central Tunisia would be enlivened by some dashing displays of command in the field, it was already too late to change defeat into victory at Alamein. Never for a moment, however, did Rommel give up the struggle. Like Hitler, he believed in his luck and in keeping up the pressure till the last moment and beyond. There was a fine old-fashioned armoured attack out of the setting sun on the 2nd November at Tel el Aqqaqir but, a sign of the times, it was broken up not only by heavy shellfire but also by violent air bombardment.

On our side the theme of the battle was to keep up pressure relentlessly while preparing to drive through at any weak point. Late on the 26th General Montgomery decided to make a pause and regroup. The original plan had been changed. It now seemed that better results might be obtained northwestwards from the Tell el Eisa salient; the new plan 'Supercharge' was designed to clear up this area, break out along the line of the coast road and then to send the New Zealand Division through to capture Sidi Abd el Rahman, behind the enemy's north flank. At the last minute General Montgomery changed the axis of the main attack and decided instead to make the northwest attack a diversion and to put in the main attack due westwards. The circumstances of this change have been dramatically described by his Chief of Staff, General de Guingand. It was he himself who in large measure inspired it. It was a master stroke. It took the enemy by surprise, split his armoured forces in two and brought our tanks to the very edge of his prepared positions and beyond.

It took a little time to mount 'Supercharge' because an extensive regrouping was required. This is perhaps a good point to mention another legend of Alamein which is enshrined in the opening chapter of General Montgomery's book *From El Alamein to the River Sangro*: 'I ordered that divisions should be concentrated and fought as such; this ended the employment of brigade groups, Jock columns and the tactical methods which caused divisions to be split up.' It is generally supposed that this policy was adopted at Alamein; but it would be truer to say that after the first 48 hours, and with the exception of the 9th Australian Division, no division fought as a division at all. Brigades were taken from one and attached to another at random. For example, two infantry brigades, the 131st and the 133rd, were taken from the 44th Division and handed over to the 7th Armoured and 10th Armoured Division respectively. In the former case this association, originating in the heat of the battle, became permanent. The Desert Rats lost their original Motor Brigade, the 7th, which was taken over by the 1st Armoured Division with whom they remained to the end of the war. In its place they acquired three battalions of the Queen's regiment from the 44th Division (which was disbanded shortly after Alamein) and took them with them through the rest of the fighting in North Africa, to Sicily and Italy and Normandy and on to Berlin. The infantry were even more mixed up. 'Supercharge' was fought by one brigade each from the 44th, 50th and 51st Divisions (133, 151, 152 Brigades), the independent 23rd Armoured Brigade, the 9th Armoured Brigade (which belonged originally to the New Zealand Division) plus the two New Zealand infantry brigades (in reserve). This whole force of five infantry and two armoured brigades was supposed to be under command of New Zealand Divisional H.Q., which was itself under the command of 30th Corps. It is quite evident that no divisional H.Q. could command so great a number of formations whether they had or not a Corps H.Q. sitting on top of them. The brigade groups must have to a great extent operated individually. The final blow in the battle of Alamein, on the night of the 3rd/4th November, was a typical example of the emergency use of an independent brigade group. A brigade of the 4th Indian Division was picked up from its position on Ruweisat Ridge, dragged by difficult and devious tracks over the battlefield in a night march, and flung hastily into the battle just before dawn. When I studied the Order of Battle of Alamein I was unable to discover under whose command 5th Indian Brigade was supposed to be; anyway I am sure that in fact it operated quite independently.

'Supercharge' went in on the night of 1st November. It was an attack that was as violent as, though on a slightly smaller scale than, the original attack on Alamein. It began with an infantry attack, as on the night of the 23rd October, but with brigades taking the part of divisions, followed by the armour of 10th Corps. The infantry were to strike through the remaining enemy defences to a depth of 6,000 yards on a front of 4,000 yards. The defences were not so strong or so extensive as they had been, nevertheless they were stronger than expected. The first of our armoured brigades to emerge, the 9th, was so delayed that instead of penetrating the enemy's anti-tank screen in the night, as was the intention, it found itself at dawn right on the muzzles of the anti-tank guns. In spite of this, and in spite of losing well over half their tanks, they managed to hold open the end of the corridor to allow the rest of the armour to come out. Here was fought the battle called Tell el Aqqaqir, or the Mound of the Acacias. It was the last clash of armour in the battle. The enemy were at a disadvantage not merely in numbers but because, as we had planned, the direction of our thrust had separated his two armoured divisions. Our own armour was all concentrated and it was supported by a heavy force of artillery. Nevertheless the battle was extremely fierce. The German commanders were well aware that this was the crisis of the battle. At one point the 21st Panzer Division, in a desperate and concentrated thrust, broke right into our position from the north. But slowly they were forced back in spite of all their efforts and as the day wore on it became clear that the Afrika Korps had fought their last battle in the Western Desert.

Already, while the battle of Tell el Aqqaqir was going on, an armoured car regiment, the Royals, had broken away into the enemy's rear areas and was shooting up his communications. On the night of the 2nd Rommel decided it was time to go. He still hoped to make an orderly retreat of it and all day on the 3rd November he held firm on a front facing southeast. It was on the night of the 3rd that the 5th Indian brigade was produced out of the hat for the attack which finally loosened the log jam. In a brilliantly successful attack, mounted after a confusing night march, they turned the flank of the enemy's new position forcing it back so that it covered only the coast road. As though pouring through a swing door the armoured divisions of the 10th Corps, followed by the New Zealand Division to the south, pressed forward. 10th Corps had all three armoured divisions, and the New Zealanders had two armoured brigades under command, having annexed the 4th Brigade from 7th Armoured Division. This was the greatest concentration of armoured force that had ever been seen in the desert and it spelt the end of any attempt by the enemy at an orderly withdrawal from Alamein. Rommel had lost touch with the situation. He was with his own escort force a little way south of the road discussing with the commander of the Afrika Korps, General von Thoma, the best method of disposing his armour to allow the extrication of the infantry. While they were talking, on the southern horizon there were to be seen large masses of motor vehicles interspersed with tanks moving westward. According to von Thoma's armoured cars they were the British but Rommel refused to believe it. Convinced that Eighth Army's advance was still being held up by his anti-tank gun line, he maintained that it was the Trieste Division making their escape. The argument grew embittered and von Thoma went off in his command tank to investigate the matter himself. He was fired on as he came within range and his tank was hit and caught fire. It was little satisfaction to prove at this cost that he had been right. The fate of von Thoma, before his very eyes, was sufficient warning to Rommel. There was not much point now in trying to make provision for the Italian infantry divisions cut off to the south. The chief thought he devoted to them was that they would not now be able to make any use of their third-echelon transport which would be extremely valuable in transporting away the troops cut off to the north of the British penetration. These were preponderantly German. He accordingly forthwith ordered a rapid retreat.

I had the odd experience next day, 5th November, of entertaining General von Thoma to luncheon together with one or two other members of the Intelligence Branch at G.H.Q. He was a regular soldier, a Bavarian, no Nazi and a well-educated man. He had not been long in Africa, having been posted there from the Russian front to take the place of General Cruewell, captured in the May battles. He spoke fairly freely, and rather despondently, which was natural enough in his situation, for he thought the Eastern front was likely to go no better than the southern. There was not very much he could tell us about the German forces in Africa, for most of it was known already. He was amusing about the Spanish Civil War in which he had commanded a force of German tanks sent to help General Franco and to gain some experience. These were of course all of the old Mark I variety. He was present at the battle of Guadalajara but was well off to the flank and was accordingly not directly involved in General Nuvoloni's misfortune.

General von Thoma was the senior enemy general captured but we had eight others also. Prisoners came to 30,000 altogether, 10,000 of them Germans. The Italians for the most part were left to their fate. They had not been heavily engaged during the battle, except in the early diversionary attacks by 13th Corps, and so suffered few battle casualties. They thought the battle was going quite well; in fact one officer, a staff officer at divisional H.Q., noted in his diary on the day Eighth Army changed from 'Lightfoot' to 'Supercharge' that the battle was over and the British had accepted defeat. They had little or no motor transport in any case, and none within easy reach, and therefore were unable to follow their rapidly withdrawing allies. The armoured divisions were more fortunate. Littorio had been to all intents and purposes destroyed in the battle, but Ariete, which had been less heavily engaged, and still had some 70-odd tanks left, tried to get away. Unfortunately for them there was very little spare diesel fuel and their tanks all either ran dry or broke down before they reached Fuka. All in all Rommel got away with only about 30 per cent of his original force. This was the greatest defeat he ever suffered in the desert, even more serious than his defeat of the previous November and December.

The rounding up of the prisoners after the battle was a tremendous task. To make easier the handling of the Italians, and to help the Intelligence staff to plan their interrogation, the prisoners were ordered to divide themselves up by divisions. Bill Nolan, who later served with me in Tunisia, was one of the people concerned and told me that this sorting-out process left six prisoners standing rather self-consciously in a group by themselves, separate from the huge clusters where whole divisions were grouped. 'Why haven't you fallen in with your division?' he asked. The senior of the six, a corporal, coughed apologetically and said 'Siamo lupi, noi'— 'We're wolves, we are.' They were indeed a small draft, not yet attached to any of the other divisions, from the division named *Lupi di Toscana*, 'The Wolves of Tuscany'. This was for some reason considered a good division though it had failed very badly in Albania as I well remember and as Ciano admits with exasperation in his diary. Its members had a right to feel selfconscious about this absurd name.

What happened after Alamein must always come as an anti climax. On the morning of the 4th November, 8th Army had 600 tanks and the Germans only 80. By the next evening the German tank strength was down to about 30. The discrepancy in infantry would be very similar. In spite of this the enemy were able to withdraw some 800 miles to El Aghcila without being seriously brought to battle. It almost seemed as though we were escorting them westwards like a policeman showing home some drunk and disorderly whom he does not wish to arrest. It was indeed an anticlimax, but the fault was not all with the Eighth Army Command. In the first place Rommel had now reduced his forces to about the size which he was really good at handling and he had already shown that he was a master of retreat. In the second place a retreat and pursuit in the desert poses problems different from anywhere else. The desert has been described by a German general as 'the tactician's paradise and the quartermaster's hell'. A retreat is a matter of tactics and Rommel was at least a magnificent tactician if he was no strategist. So he had the paradise and we had the hell; for whereas he was falling back on his supplies and had nothing to worry about, beyond making sure that he destroyed what he didn't need so as not to leave anything for us, we had to organize the pursuit and carry everything with us, even water, over distances continually growing greater. These two considerations would account sufficiently for the tameness of the pursuit; but it is only fair to add that there was an element of bad luck too. On the 5th and 6th November the 10th and 7th Armoured Divisions both got in among the German rearguards with great effect, destroying some 30 tanks and capturing over 4,000 prisoners. The South African Armoured Car Regiment was shooting up the main road right to the west of Matruh. The 1st Armoured Division was actually level with Matruh to the south, and expected to cut the road to the west on the 7th. If they had done so, with the New Zealand Division to back them up, a very large part of Rommel's forces must have been irretrievably caught. On the evening of the 6th, however, it started to rain and the rain continued all day on the 7th. Rain at this season of the year is not abnormal in the desert but this downpour was certainly much heavier than usual. The New Zealand Division, and all the wheeled vehicles of the 1st Armoured Division, were firmly stuck in a morass. The enemy continued their retreat unimpeded along the main road. There was nothing else to do but follow him up along it. It was a long road for the Eighth Army, ending 1,800 miles later just short of Cape Bon.

CHAPTER IX

First Steps in Algeria and Tunisia

ON THE morning of 8th November, Eighth Army entered
Mersa Matruh after a stubborn German rearguard had kept
them out overnight. At the same time the forces under the
command of General Eisenhower were landing in French North
Africa. In G.H.Q. Middle East we had for some time been aware of the
imminence of this operation and also of the date. I was told of it, if
I remember, before Alamein began. It seemed an inevitable complement. Viewed from Cairo the North African coastline seemed to
stretch out to the crack of doom. Now that Eighth Army had doubled
in size it looked quite possible to push on past El Agheila and even
get to Tripoli, a goal which for long had dazzled our eyes in the distance. But we had always assumed that the enemy, if driven out of
Tripolitania, would withdraw without any fuss to Tunisia, and what
the French attitude would be was dubious. They had already allowed
the enemy to use Tunisian ports and roads for supply, and though they
might not be prepared to fight on the side of the Germans the attitude
of the French Mediterranean Fleet, occupying inactively large areas
of Alexandria Harbour, seemed to show that they would not give us
any co-operation. It seemed obvious therefore that a force from somewhere must start at the other end and work its way to meet us. It
also seemed a natural method of deploying American strength, and I
knew that this strategy was being strenuously recommended from
Cairo by the U.S. Military Attaché.

The date of Alamein was of course selected with the date of 'Torch',
the North African landings, in mind. A resounding defeat of the only
enemy forces in the continent could be expected to make the French
authorities less apprehensive of German reaction. The effect on the
mind of General Franco was also carefully calculated. A great deal of
the strategy of 'Torch' hinged on the undisturbed use of Gibraltar. Interference from the mainland could certainly make the airfield there un-
usable and also at the least hamper the use of the harbour. It was a good

144

thing therefore that our victory was clear and undisputed four days before D-Day for Torch. We took care to trumpet it a bit for the benefit of the French and the Spaniards, in fact for the only time in my knowledge we rather rounded upwards our claims of prisoners taken, and tanks and guns destroyed.

G.H.Q. Middle East received copies of all the telegrams sent by General Eisenhower's H.Q. so that we could follow the course of events in what was after all our continent. There were not so very many of these telegrams. For the first few days at any rate it soon became evident that things were going pretty well but very much less evident what exactly it was that was going well. General Eisenhower's H.Q., though composed in almost equal numbers of American and British staff officers, was organized on the American system. As a result, though we had their cyphers and could read their telegrams, it was very difficult to understand them. Not only were the language and the turns of phrase new but it seemed to us that, as was natural with a new H.Q. without experience of operations, the full significance of what was happening was not always grasped. So far as news about the enemy went, we in Intelligence found ourselves in even worse case. First Army was producing a little Intelligence but, try as we could, we could not make head or tail of what they were trying to communicate. The obvious thing to do was to send a liaison officer to see for himself. For some reason or another I was selected for this job. I was quite pleased to be leaving Cairo for a little to look at the picture from the west for a bit instead of always from the east. My instructions were fairly simple. I was to go to Algiers in the first place and thereafter anywhere else I thought useful, to find out what was happening and to telegraph back as full an account as the local signals would stand. I was also to act as liaison for the Operations Branch so I was carefully briefed by General McCreery, the Chief of Staff. He was ill at the time and received me in bed. He sat up in it very straight, very tall and very thin and gave a lucid and meticulous account of the present situation and future intentions. I saw a lot more of him in the next year or so and was soon to discover that the voice was misleading. When displeased about anything he would curse in the same slightly quavering rather refined voice, never raised above a murmur, but mixing complaints and threats with curiously old-fashioned but signally pungent blasphemies and obscenities. On this occasion, without departing from an exquisite courtesy, he gave a forecast of the date of the capture of Tripoli which turned out to be very accurate and a less accurate forecast of the time when Eighth Army would feel able to bring pressure to bear in southern Tunisia. This was my main news for General Eisenhower, but for the rest my duty was to observe.

On the day on which I was to leave for Algiers the enemy were back over the border in Cyrenaica, their rearguards being somewhere in the neighbourhood of Gazala and Derna. I had hoped for a trip in a Liberator or something equally big which would do the trip at a comfortably high altitude and preferably by night. I was less pleased when I found that what was provided was one of the aircraft to which I have already referred as being good for promotion. However, I reflected that, assuming it survived take-off, it would be fast and comfortable and should get us there easily under cover of night. I found that three other officers were on the plane, two of whom were going as far as Malta, while the third, a signals officer, was going on like me to Algiers. In addition the whole of the inside of the plane was packed with urgent supplies of one sort or another for Malta. Up the middle was a telescopic wireless mast. Everywhere else were boxes and boxes on which we had to perch somewhere fairly close to the roof. I have travelled on many crowded aircraft, but never on one as full as that. We flew first of all to El Adem and got there, as far as I remember, at 3 o'clock. We were at a reasonable height and it was a great pleasure to retrace the scenes of previous wanderings as if in some speeded up cinema film. The Alamein line, which we crossed in the southern half between Himeimat and Ruweisat, was plain to see, with many wrecked tanks and burnt-out vehicles on either side and the shadowy shapes of the wire and the minefields. On the left the Depression stretched away westwards in a line of steep cliffs. Matruh and its pearly lagoon was the next landmark, then Buqbuq with its white sands and the great Sollum Escarpment. We circled over El Adem before landing and I could see down below the trench where I had sat only six months before with my bombs and grenades and an assortment of automatic weapons waiting for the enemy to attack. Tea on the aerodrome was made with Wadi Auda water whose unmistakable taste was immensely evocative. The walls of the huts bore a new lot of inscriptions making a peculiar palimpsest of Italian, English and German.

I was glad we had stopped at El Adem; I expected that we would wait there until the sun went down before setting out for Malta. I was rather startled therefore when we were ordered aboard and took off shortly after four o'clock. It was a beautiful day, the sky was clear, there was a light breeze from the north and the sun shone equally but

I should have preferred fog or even a sandstorm. I suppose it is natural to feel concern when one is out of one's element. All I knew was that German fighters were still operating from airfields round Benghazi, past which we would have to go, and not too far off either, and that our plane was wholly unarmed. I was very glad when after three hours or so over the sea the shape of Malta began to come up ahead. A providential piece of land I thought it as we circled over the rich brown fields with their neat little stone walls. As we got out of the plane it was raining and I loved it.

Malta was then in the last days of the Great Siege. The first relieving convoy had not in fact yet arrived. Food was short and destruction was everywhere. For all that I was filled once more with the same feeling as on my brief visit when passing through over two years before, that the island was a credit to a hundred and fifty years of British/Maltese association. I had seen many islands in the Mediterranean; nearly all of them had much greater natural resources than Malta and yet none of them were so obviously prosperous or so obviously well ordered. The land was cultivated to the last degree, the roads were good, the houses were solidly built and handsome. There was a great feeling of hope in the air, or rather of confidence, and yet the privations of the past were still fairly obvious in people's faces. I went to Fortress H.Q. where the G2I was an old friend of mine, Alban Coventry, who had shared a dugout with me at Maaten Baqqush in the summer of 1941. He took me to see the G.O.C. General Scobie, who seemed to be making a speciality of beleaguered fortresses, since the last time I had seen him was in Tobruk. Nor was Malta his last experience. In December 1944, as commander in Greece, he found himself beleaguered in the Hotel Grande Bretagne in Athens at the centre of a fortress hardly more than half a mile square in extent. He was glad of a visitor and pleased with the forecast of Eighth Army's progress.

I was a bit ashamed to be given that night what was called 'an operational meal'. This was the ration for pilots of the R.A.F. actually engaged in operations and included an egg. The Maltese waiters looked wistfully on, as well they might, since they knew that I came from Cairo and must therefore have been living in the lap of luxury. Our pilot had at least the grace not to try to penetrate the Sicilian straits by daylight; we took off after midnight and in an almost empty plane the two passengers for Algiers could sleep stretched out at length. It was a stormy and a rainy night and dawn found us somewhere off the Algerian coast in the neighbourhood of Bone. It might have been in another continent from the eastern half of the coastline which I knew so well. The sea was murky and lashed with rain and a great, dark-green, heavily forested mountain rose almost straight out of the water, wreathed in mists. It was cold and gloomy but rather impressive. At any rate it was different and I began to look forward to the very different kind of people I should be meeting.

The landing at Algiers was the usual anticlimax. The airport at Maison Blanche is some miles outside the city. Not only was there no-one there to meet us, there did not appear to be anyone there at all. Large pools of water stood about, there were the usual wrecked aero-planes and bombed buildings, but though I splashed about in the mud from one place to another there was no sign of life. Admittedly it was only 7.30 in the morning but even so I should have expected some-one to be about, if only the cleaners. Eventually I found a building with a roof, apparently at one time a restaurant, where some French airmen were glumly drinking coffee. In one corner of the room was a field telephone. This looked hopeful and I was better pleased still when on twirling the handle I was answered by an American voice. A brief period of confusion followed, because after I had explained that I wanted to talk to someone at General Eisenhower's H.Q. the voice asked 'Do you want freedom?' It was a bit early in the morning for me to work out at once what the answer to that should be, but while I was thinking there was a click and another voice said 'This is Free-dom.' I was glad I had not made a fool of myself and reflected that it was indeed a charming name for the telephone exchange of Allied Force H.Q. Some further awkward explanations got me put in touch with the duty officer in the Intelligence Branch or G2. This was not yet, however, the happy ending. I explained that I had just arrived from Cairo, doing my best to say it modestly but with the quiet pride appropriate to a pioneer. The voice, however, an English one this time, was not merely unimpressed but uninterested. 'You will have to come here,' it said. 'Well, as a matter of fact,' I said, 'that was really the idea why I left Cairo in the first place. Can you send me a car?' This request was evidently startling; the speaker explained that he had no car himself and did not know anyone who had one. There might, he said, be a car going to Maison Blanche later in the day sometime, but it would be rash to rely on it. I forget which of us rang off, but I returned thoroughly deflated to the canteen for some more spurious coffee. Half an hour later, however, my companion, the signals officer, who had been working the opposite direction round the airport, came up cheerfully to say that he had found a British officer with a truck who knew where G.H.Q. was and would give us a lift.

Much has been written about Allied Force H.Q. in its early days in Algiers. A whole mythology has grown up round it. First of all it was in an obviously unsuitable place, the Hotel Saint George. This gave it a pleasant old-world air to me; my grandfather used to spend his winters there some twenty years before and I had been there once myself. It was a show place in the mock Arabian style but far from well adapted as a military H.Q. It was heavily guarded by the first American Military Police I had ever seen and I was properly impressed. The staff inside struck me as more of a mixture. General Eisenhower himself very civilly saw me for a few minutes and I passed on my various messages to the Ops Branch. They had a fantastic job from the purely logistic point of view passing inadequate supplies over a mountain road and an indifferent railway. The Intelligence Branch, which was where I finished up, was less impressive. It was almost entirely British with one American lieutenant colonel, a genial cavalry officer who had little experience of the game and honestly made no attempt to claim it. The British staff were plainly the cream which had been produced by the Intelligence training installations over the past three years. The trouble was that not only did they not know what they ought to be doing, they had learnt a whole lot of wrong things which they ought not to be doing. The only one who obviously knew what to do and was doing it well and with gusto was the G1 in charge of Security. He was a splendid lieutenant colonel of the Royal Ulster Rifles who was carrying on his shoulders the weight of one of the most complicated security situations of the whole war. He had not merely the ordinary problems of the safeguarding of an army serving abroad but he had also to deal with the dangers presented by the three French factions of de Gaulle, Giraud and Darlan. Security was not my pigeon, but I found Colonel Hill-Dillon much the most amusing and interesting of my new confrères.

A few days convinced me that I should never learn anything about the enemy situation, and very little about the position of our own troops, by staying in Algiers. The Intelligence Staff were occupied in pasting up in albums unimportant geographical information and collating and commenting on imaginative reports from unreliable espionage agents. In any case the signal system was so overworked that I was only able to get off two very brief telegrams to Cairo.

However, the result of my fruitless pestering was that they were only too glad to give me a beautiful staff car with a splendid American driver and a haversack ration. With this I set off to drive some 350 miles to Constantine. I have tried to avoid the cliché but it springs, as Mr. Belloc would say, unbidden to my lips. I felt liberated. Even the rain had stopped. I drove rejoicing eastwards out of the frustrating town of Algiers with a car of my own and no superior officer. The road runs through mountains and gorges. After 200 miles I had a splendid lunch in a mountainous small village at an uninviting café kept by a first-class cook. I had to do that drive again in subsequent months and never failed to lunch at the same place. It was just about aperitif time that I drove into the spectacular town of Constantine. Before it was given its name by the first Christian Emperor it was famous as Cirta, the rocky citadel of Numidia. It has the most extraordinary position of any town of its size, on a huge table of rock cut out from a mountain spur by a precipitous gorge. The very bridge over the gorge shakes as you cross and a good deal of shaking was being done under the treads of six-wheeled lorries trundling through the mud to the front. First Army H.Q. was, in accordance with tradition, in an elementary school and madly uncomfortable. But they did have some idea of what they were supposed to be doing.

The Ops Branch seemed to know where their troops were on the ground, at any rate they had a map which gave some plausible dispositions. They may have been a few hours out of date, for this was just the time of the last scrambling attempt to force our way into Tunis before the German reinforcement became too strong. The Army Commander was actually forward at the time. It was an uneasy set up from the operations point of view; the fighting troops consisted, in effect, of only one division and over them was the one Corps H.Q. and over that one Army H.Q. It was the supreme example of the one over one convention which, however valuable at Bridge, is wasteful and confusing in war. The local wits were busy with versions of Churchill's epigram about the R.A.F. which played on the contrast between so few being commanded by so many. The G.O.C. was increasingly peppery as the rain and the mud frustrated his plan of attack and his staff were correspondingly depressed. For all that there was a feeling of hope and achievement in the air. The Intelligence Branch, with one exception, was much the same calibre as that I had left behind in Algiers. They were not only gloomy like the rest of the H.Q., they were occupied in time-wasting jobs which even they were beginning to see were useless. Fortunately the one exception was an outstanding one, and was the G1, Lieutenant Colonel Christopher Dawnay. To begin with, he was the only Intelligence officer I had come across in Algeria who took a proper interest in what our own troops were doing and had some conception of the general plan of campaign. In the second place, in spite of the rottenness of his sources, he had by some means or other put together quite a sound picture of the enemy. Finally I discovered that Army H.Q. had a signals link to Malta, which was not much used and which I was welcome to use to transmit as much stuff as I liked. It immediately occurred to me that I could by this means get in touch with Alban Coventry and he could pass on the messages to Cairo by cable. At last I would be in a position, free from the restrictions put on me in Algiers, to report back to Middle East H.Q. as fully as I wanted.

It seemed to me, however, that first of all I ought to go a bit further forward to see what I could pick up there. I drove accordingly to H.Q. of the 5th Corps. If Allied H.Q. in Algiers had been frustrating, the Intelligence Branch of 5th Corps was high comedy. Here was a collection of carefully selected and lengthily trained staff officers, physically in bounding health and radiating enthusiasm and quiet self confidence. Two projects were occupying their minds to the exclusion of almost anything else. One was the production of a map of a portion of the Corps front on a scale so enormous that I am ashamed to write it down. Was it 1: 10,000? I cannot be sure, but I know that a football field would have been about the size of a sheet of writing paper. It was so big that it was even too big for the artillery who were having to produce a rival series on a more convenient scale. I dutifully expressed surprised admiration of the three printed sheets which were all that was completed of the project. Not long after my visit a very small-scale German offensive pushed us right off all three sheets and broke the heart of G.S.I., 5th Corps. The series was then discontinued.

The second activity was given by its exponents the name of psychological warfare 'because,' as Housman says (Lucan, p. xiii), 'that is a longer and nobler name than fudge'. Once more it struck me that to a large number of palefaces the latest thing in wars was the Spanish Civil War. Just as they had been urged by persons who had served on the Republican side to stick crowbars into the tracks of enemy tanks (a suicidal procedure except against the Italian light tank) so they had been led to believe in the value of battlefield propaganda. For all I know, the showering of leaflets and the bellowing of slogans through

loudspeakers may be valuable adjuncts to the tactics of a civil war—
though I am bound to say that in the Spanish case the side which made
most use of them lost. In this particular war their value seemed a good
deal less. Undeterred by these considerations the G2 and G3 of 5th
Corps plunged cheerfully into the new and exciting task of composing
telling propaganda material. They were hampered a little by the fact
that their only means of delivering pamphlets was to replace with them
the smoke cartridge of a 25-pounder, base-ejection smoke shell. This
meant that the inspiring and carefully chosen words had to be squashed
on to a round piece of paper just a little over three inches in diameter
and with a circular hole in the middle. So far as I remember the most
that space allowed was something like this: 'Dear Germans—why not
stop fighting? We will really treat you quite well.' To add to the
hopeless feeling with which it was impossible to help regarding these
efforts, was the fact that I knew the German troops for whom they
were designed. How true it is that the success of art lies not with the
artist but with the audience. The troops at the receiving end were a
collection of the toughest and most unsympathetic German parachutists in the entire German army. They were in fact the demonstration troops from two airborne training establishments who had
been picked up hastily and flown into Tunisia in the very first days of
the campaign. I do not, of course, suggest that any German troops
were ever in the slightest degree receptive to our propaganda, right
up to the last minute of the war; but this particular lot were the most
hopeless ever tackled. Moreover, they happened to be winning at the
moment, which is a period in which even the susceptible are resistant
to propaganda.

In the intervals of examining the curiously shaped pamphlets, and
being invited to cast an eye over a German script which the G3 proposed to shout over an extemporized loudspeaker system later that
night, I put a few questions about the enemy's dispositions and intentions. This was a subject on which less enthusiasm was shown and it
occurred to me that I should not get much help with my main interest.
The Corps Commander was away and the Ops Branch not really in
the picture. I accordingly worked my way back to 1st Army H.Q.
and tackled the G1 once more.

Kit Dawnay had a clear head and a fund of common sense. Between
what he told me and what I had been able to pick up for myself it was
possible to produce a description of the enemy's dispositions and an
appreciation of the likely course of events. I telegraphed this to Malta

at some length and it was sent on by cable to G.H.Q. The effect, I am told, was gratifying. At last there was something from North Africa which was at any rate written in the kind of language with which people in G.H.Q. were familiar. So far as the Cairo Intelligence staff were concerned it gave the first connected picture of the enemy's order of battle. On the operations side it set out what we hoped to be able to do. I followed it up a couple of days later, after a dash down south to visit the French who were defending the extreme right flank, with another signal almost as long.

The stroke of luck which had led to my being sent to North Africa and had put me in the position of acquiring a reputation, however slenderly based, as an authority on the campaign there, determined the future course of my army career. It was because of this that I was chosen to return to North Africa when General Alexander came over to take command of the armies in the field in Tunisia. All this, however, was in the future and in the meantime I was enjoying my visit to the southern front where a scratch collection of French troops plus an American parachute battalion was operating spasmodically from the romantically named villages of Youks les Bains and Gafsa. Their opponents were part of the Italian Centauro Division and the Aosta Lancers, the latter mounted in armoured cars which were sickeningly unreliable. As the French were equipped in a style more suited to the First World War and were under instructions not to get too involved, such rare encounters as took place were bright but inconclusive.

After despatching my final message from Army H.Q. I returned to Algiers thinking it was about time to get back to Cairo. I arrived in the late afternoon of Christmas Eve to scenes of disorganization and affright. The Hotel St. George was ringed with new barbed wire. A complete heavy weapons company was disposed all round it with heavy mortars and machine guns prominent in the front garden. I ran into Hill-Dillon looking pugnacious and interested. From him I learned that Darlan had been assassinated that afternoon. Great events were expected but none in fact happened. The murder fell like a stone into a small pond and the ripples were only brief. After the assassin had been hastily, indeed precipitately, tried and executed, it was as if Darlan had never been.

It was not until later that I discovered what tremendous excitement had been aroused in England by General Eisenhowers' acceptance of the collaboration of Darlan. Neither at the time nor since did it seem to me to deserve quite such an expense of righteous indignation. I

could never forget that in the original appreciation which I saw before
the invasion it was calculated that we might be engaged in fighting
the French for anything up to three months. As a result of doing a deal
with Darlan that period was reduced to two days. In all the discussions
on the subject, which were principally conducted in the more high-
minded weeklies, I never saw it stated precisely how many allied
casualties would have been considered acceptable in exchange for not
doing a deal. It would, of course, have been very much nicer if it had
not been necessary. The trouble is that Darlan happened to be the only
man with authority in North Africa. When he did decide to collaborate he did so whole-heartedly. He secured a cease-fire in Algeria
and Morocco, he procured the adhesion of French West Africa and he
did at least try to get the French fleet to come over to North Africa
from Toulon. I only met him once. He was not a prepossessing character but he served his turn.

General Giraud, whom the Americans had produced hopefully from
unoccupied France in a British submarine in the expectation that he
would be accepted as leader in North Africa, was a failure in that role
because no one would agree to follow him; fortunately when the
Germans, in violation of the Armistice, entered the unoccupied zone,
a compromise was reached and he agreed to serve under Darlan's
authority as a figurehead Commander-in-Chief. He asked especially
to see me. I found him a charming if somewhat archaic figure, who
thrust one hand into his tunic in the Napoleonic style and addressed
me as 'jeune homme'. He treated me to an appreciation of the likely
future course of the war which involved a most complicated series of
amphibious invasions, a thrust by two armies through Italy and the
Balkans joining up on the banks of the Danube, then the decisive battle
of the war fought somewhere in the Danube valley. On second
thoughts he altered the venue to the plains of Hanover. He had, I am
afraid, only very elementary ideas of the difficulties of amphibious
warfare. The Italians, as we were to find at the time of the Armistice,
were no better, nor were the Germans. Giraud had demonstrated this
fact even more strikingly in his famous set-to with Eisenhower at
Gibraltar on November 7th. When he was told that he had been
brought there in the hope that he would take command of the French
Forces in Algeria, Morocco and Tunisia (mainly because the American
State Department could not bear the idea of de Gaulle) he protested
that this was not what was required at all. He had plans, he said, for a
rising against the Germans in France itself. He would collaborate with

the Allies on condition that he should take Eisenhower's place as Commander-in-Chief, and he very civilly warned the General that in that event he would at once issue instructions to the convoys which at that time were moving along the coast of North Africa to turn sharp left and proceed to invade southern France. When this offer was tactfully declined he refused to play at all, and it was not until Darlan, brandishing the magical authority of Marshal Pétain, had assumed responsibility for North Africa that he agreed to take up the command of the French forces in the field.

Christmas 1942 was noteworthy to me for one other thing. As I went into the dining room for dinner one of the more reliable members of the Intelligence staff hailed me and whispered in my ear that the *Ankara* had been sunk. I do not remember any more cheering news. At that moment I had the sudden conviction that the war in Africa was lost for the Germans. Mere superstition; but I could not help remembering how often that ill-omened ship had frustrated us by bringing just the tanks that were needed to swing the balance against us and how many times the navy and air force had made a dead set at her without success.

I flew back to Cairo shortly after Christmas, again via Malta. This time the pilot did not bother to go round by the Sicilian Channel—he flew straight across Tunisia. As a matter of fact he flew a bit lower than he intended over Sousse and came under fairly strenuous anti-aircraft fire. So many writers have described how beautiful anti-aircraft fire looks from the point of view of the target that I shall refrain and say that a far more beautiful sight to me was the first appearance of Malta. It did indeed look splendid. Four large searchlights at the four corners of the island were pointing upwards and large numbers of our own fighters, showing navigation lights, were circling round like moths round a candle on their way to land. The siege was over, the relieving convoys had arrived and Malta was preparing to support the offensive.

On my return to G.H.Q. I was able to explain at greater length my telegrams which I was amused to find were being regarded as gospel even in the highest quarters. The general attitude was that things were being mismanaged over there in a pretty big way but no worse than might have been expected of a bunch of palefaces. Bill Williams, who was now GI1 at Eighth Army, Spud Murphy having gone off to a regimental command in India, said "It sounds like where I came in—all battle groups and Crusader tanks." There was general agreement that nothing much could be done before Eighth Army got round the corner into Tunisia. The hope with which we started, that First Army would come and take Tripoli behind Rommel's back, was now long faded.

At the moment I got back Eighth Army was stationary, squaring up for an attack on the enemy in the Buerat position. There had not been much of serious interest since rain stopped play at Daba back on the 7th November. Eighth Army had followed up in a not particularly enterprising way. The same could not by any means be said of the Air Force, who put on a special effort on this occasion, often establishing themselves on temporary airfields in advance of the army, moving themselves in transport aircraft and providing for their own defence on the ground.

There had been one chance of Eighth Army doing something more decisive; but it had been allowed to pass. When 10th Corps was approaching Gazala General Lumsden had strongly urged on the Army Commander that he should take his Corps across the desert through Mechili and Msus to cut off the enemy in the old style somewhere near Agedabia. General Montgomery did not agree to this. The view he expressed at the time was that it was undesirable to risk a setback; he preferred to commit his troops to operations in which there would be greater certainty of success. This decision was unwelcome to General Lumsden who had on other occasions also had differences of opinion with his Army Commander. Unfortunately shortly afterwards things were made still worse. Eighth Army H.Q. obtained absolutely reliable information that the whole of the enemy mechanical transport was immobilized on the coast road through the Gebel by the total failure of their fuel supply. Rommel's army was in fact brought to a complete standstill. On being convinced of this, General Montgomery sent Bill Williams to General Lumsden, who was then somewhere near Tmimi at the eastern edge of the Gebel, to say that, if he possibly could, he should take the whole of his corps across the desert route to cut the road south of Benghazi. Such an order would have been welcome to General Lumsden a few days before; but at this late date it was impossible for him to carry them out because no administrative preparations had been made. All he could produce was two armoured car regiments with a few supporting arms who took the short road to Sceleidima and Antelat.

This incident is described more tactfully than I have put it, in General Alexander's despatch as follows: 'The enemy was withdrawing through the Gebel, and it was a great temptation to imitate our previous strategy by pushing a force across the desert to cut him off at or near Agedabia. General Montgomery was determined, however, not to take any chances, especially in view of the difficulties of the maintenance situation, and 10 Corps were instructed to despatch only armoured cars by this route. Later, when it appeared that the enemy's retreat had actually been brought to a temporary standstill by lack of fuel, 10 Corps was ordered to strengthen if possible the outflanking force; this proved impracticable in the then existing situation.'

Petrol was flown to Rommel from Greece, the 11th Hussars and the Royals were delayed once more by violent rain, and the enemy passed peacefully down the coast road to Agedabia. By this time, the 22nd November, 10th Corps had been able to organize sufficient supplies to send the 22nd Armoured Brigade at full speed across 260 miles of desert. The moment he felt them on his flank Rommel withdrew into his old hole at Agheila behind the salt marshes which were better protection than ever after so rainy a winter. But the old days were gone forever. Although it would take another three weeks before Eighth Army could bring up enough troops and supplies to turn him out, events in Tunisia were having their effect. Well before anything serious could be attempted from our side the Commando Supremo had decided to abandon Agheila. The Italian infantry were sent off straight away and the mobile Germans only waited until they knew we were about to attack. They almost left it too late, because the New Zealand Division made a remarkable flank march and succeeded in getting in behind the rear guard. However, the Germans by this time were good at withdrawals. The bulk of them broke through and got away.

The battle of Buerat, the next place where the Germans paused, should have been interesting. It was a tremendous feat on our side to mount any attack at all because the Buerat Line was about 600 miles from our nearest base at Benghazi and that was no great shakes as a base either. There could be no stopping after breaking through the Buerat Line until we could get possession of the port of Tripoli, because, without it, it would be really impossible to maintain any significant forces. Bad luck also began to take a hand; on the 4th and 5th January Benghazi was struck by heavy gales which smashed up the harbour, sank four ships, one of which had 2,000 tons of ammunition on board, and left the place in such a mess that it could only handle a third as much supplies as it had previously. The result was that all we could maintain forward was three divisions, one to attack up the road and two to outflank through the desert. These were kept well back too, to make their maintenance easier, so that the plan was that they should attack straight from the advance march in the fine old-fashioned style of what theorists call 'the encounter battle'. All this, as I say, should have made an interesting battle, and it has been written up in Lord Montgomery's memoirs in a pretty stirring style. Unfortunately for the military historian, though fortunately for the troops at the time, the enemy had decided a fortnight before, on 31st December 1942, to abandon the whole of Tripolitania and withdraw all the troops there into Tunisia. All the Italians went off in the first week in January and were followed by the German 21st Panzer Division. All that was left opposing the Eighth Army was therefore the remains of the 90th Light Division and the 15th Panzer Division, who withdrew in good order as soon as it was evident that we were about to attack.

Although the engagement at Buerat was hardly deserving of the name of a battle and the enemy withdrawal had not been particularly hustled, it was nevertheless a great day when we captured Tripoli. The 11th Hussars entered from the South early on the morning of 23rd January, three months to the day from the start of the battle of Alamein. Since 1940 Tripoli had been the name which meant most to us in the desert. It was the last remaining capital city of the Italian Empire. For us it was the end of the desert phase, almost the end of the African phase, for the surrenders at Cape Bon seemed more like a prelude to Europe.

CHAPTER X

Kasserine to Tunis

A WEEK before Tripoli fell, on the 14th January, there opened the Casablanca Conference. I suppose that the ordinary man thinks first of the formula of 'unconditional surrender' which was produced at that conference, in a manner and for motives which are variously reported. It also took a number of strategical decisions. One was that the next operation after North Africa had been cleared would be to invade and capture Sicily. In other words, Sicily was meant to be the logical conclusion and rounding off of the North African campaign, not the start of the invasion of Europe. In order to finish things off in Africa as soon as possible a reorganization of the chain of command was decided on. To put it briefly, General Alexander was given complete control of all the forces in the field actually engaged with the Germans. General Eisenhower and his H.Q. remained responsible for the planning of future operations and the organization of the lines of communication. Alexander's H.Q. was designated 18th Army Group because it consisted of First and Eighth Armies plus the 2nd U.S. Corps and the French 19th Corps. Alexander's H.Q. staff was to be drawn from G.H.Q. Middle East. It was to be an extremely small H.Q. so that only a few officers in Cairo would be lucky, especially as some room would have to be left for American officers. Dick McCreery would carry on as Chief of General Staff and Terence Airey as Brigadier General Staff, Intelligence. I was extremely pleased to be told that I had been selected as G1 Intelligence. This was my second promotion within three months: I had hardly got used to the rank of major when I found myself putting up an extra pip.

I was given a fairly free hand in selecting the staff I wanted. I insisted on having with me John Makower who had been attached to 13th Corps H.Q. all the time I had been there and was now working with Eighth Army. A prosperous and old-established silk merchant of the City of London, he had a remarkable flair for enemy intelligence and, what is perhaps even more valuable, a great deal of experience. So much of intelligence work is based on nothing more exotic than remembering what happened last time, remembering place names and knowing all the details of the various enemy units. He was awarded an M.C. by Montgomery shortly after the capture of Tripoli.

Alexander's H.Q. was to be set up in Tunisia, as close to the battle as possible. The first choice was Constantine. On arrival there, after a brief delay in Tripoli, now Eighth Army's H.Q., we found the normal crisis in full swing. A strong attack had been launched against the southern flank of First Army, at what would be the point of junction of our two armies when Eighth Army arrived.

The enemy forces had been organized into an Army Group and Rommel, naturally enough, had been given the supreme command. In the north a German H.Q., known as the 5th Panzer Army, under General von Arnim, commanded all the forces which had been brought in through Sicily to oppose the original North African landings. These were at this time two German infantry divisions, one Italian infantry division and one German armoured division plus various odds and ends. The rest of the troops in Tunisia, or approaching it from Tripolitania, i.e. the survivors of the old Panzer Army of Africa which Rommel had commanded, were now organized under an Italian H.Q. called First Army which was commanded by General Messe. He was thought of fairly highly in the Italian Army and was one of the younger generals. He was promoted to Marshal about half an hour before he surrendered on 13th May. Whatever the formal organization was, it provided little of a curb on Rommel's activities. He insisted on commanding in the field and on devoting more attention to tactics than strategy. At the moment at which, as his opposite number, General Alexander took over the Army Group Command, he was in a favourable position. Pressure from Eighth Army on his southern flank was so light, and unlikely to increase for a long time, that he was able to remove practically all the troops from that front. In the north both sides had settled down in strong defensive positions and there was no need to maintain a reserve there. As a result he was able to assemble in the centre a remarkably powerful force. He took the whole of the 21st Panzer Division, which had left Tripolitania early in January, added to it a large detachment of armour and infantry from the 15th Panzer Division and about half the 10th Panzer Division from the northern front. The flow of reinforcements on the German side was a good deal swifter and more reliable than on our side so that the divisions I have mentioned had been brought well up to strength in men and material.

In all these circumstances it was not difficult to conjecture that we were likely to see some action in the central plains of Tunisia which are so admirably adapted to armoured warfare.

The defence of this sector was entrusted to U.S. 2nd Corps and the formation in command at the point of attack was the U.S. 1st Armoured Division. This was a strong and well-equipped division but it had seen very little action so far. It had a wide area to cover and it made the not unnatural mistake of dispersing its armoured strength in a number of small detachments. They were unlucky in that some previous minor scrapping had left in the hands of the enemy a narrow and romantic pass at a village called Faid which gave an easily concealed outlet on to the plain. When on the morning of 14th February something like two divisions of German armour debouched from this pass they gave a striking demonstration of speed and aggression, as might be expected from such experienced old hands. The Americans fought with determination but neither their experience nor their deployment were equal to the task of holding the German advance. By the end of the first two days the Germans were masters of the whole of the southern plain and the French in the north had to fall back to conform. By the morning of the 17th a further enemy advance had put Rommel in a commanding position with a powerful and concentrated force under his hand, deep in our right flank. It was the kind of position which his tactical brilliance and vigour in seizing the initiative had frequently won for him.

The first task of the Intelligence Branch on arriving in Constantine was to produce an appreciation of Rommel's intentions. I did not find it difficult. His original idea, no doubt, had been merely to give a blow to 2nd Corps, who he could see were vulnerable to a sudden attack. He hoped to inflict heavy losses, to drive them at least temporarily off the plain, to raid and destroy supply dumps and generally to dislocate them to such an extent that they would not be able to mount an attack against the rear of his forces operating against Eighth Army. He had been entirely successful; but it would not be like him not to exploit his success to the utmost and beyond. With luck it might well be that he would overreach himself as he did in the winter of 1941 and the summer of 1942; but before that happened we should plainly be in for some shocks. If Rommel could break through one of the mountain passes in the south, at Kasserine or Dernaia, which were not difficult passes, he would be in a position to roll up the whole of our right flank. Fairly easy country and good roads led straight to the rear, not only of the French 19th Corps but also of the British First Army. We would have to carry out a hasty withdrawal on the north flank which might have led to a serious disaster.

The first action that Alexander took was to assume command in advance of the agreed date. In fact when he visited the Dernaia Pass he assumed the tactical command as well for the moment. There was a scratch lot of units, mainly American, withdrawing by that route off the plain and no orders had been given for the defence of the pass. After assisting in person in the siting of some stray troops of artillery he delegated the command to the senior American officer on the spot with orders to hold out to the last. Next day Rommel's attack at Dernaia was not very strong but rather stronger at Kasserine to the north and stronger still further north against the village of Sbiba. The weak spot proved to be Kasserine. A battalion attack succeeded in infiltrating into the American positions and Rommel was quick to reinforce success. Next day Sbiba and Dernaia were left alone and everything was pushed into the attack at Kasserine. This carried the pass. On getting to the other side Rommel found himself on a main road which gave him two choices. On the one hand he could go due west and mop up our main southern depots. On the other hand he could go north and push still deeper into our flank.

There never was much doubt as to which he would choose and all our efforts were devoted to reinforcing the village of Thala, through which ran the road from Kasserine to the north. The main reinforcement came from First Army, in particular the 1st Guards Brigade. They were reinforced by an armoured brigade from First Army who had just been taken out of the line in order to change their Crusader tanks for Shermans. To their misfortune the crisis came in the middle of the change and the disconsolate troopers had to get back into their Crusaders, which they had hoped to have seen the last of, and to dash off and fight one more battle in them. The 9th U.S. Division was moving up at the time and two field artillery battalions were taken from it and brought forward at great speed. This was a scratch collection of troops but they did magnificently well. The country was open and the tank battle was fierce. We were fortunate in having a fairly heavy concentration of artillery. The 21st was the critical day. At nightfall we were still holding firm though some of the German armoured thrusts had been very dangerous. Next morning at dawn a final attack was made. It penetrated as far as the field gun positions but they held firm. At 10 o'clock in the morning Rommel decided that he must break off the battle and ordered the withdrawal to start at midday. It was an extremely skilful withdrawal, as always, and the combination of mines with highly skilled rearguards inflicted heavy casualties on the forces with which we followed up. He did not withdraw from the Kasserine pass until the 25th and we were not back on the positions we had held before the offensive until the 28th.

On our side it was a successful defensive battle and not all Rommel's skill in retreat could conceal the fact that he had suffered a severe reverse. The merits of the case have, however, been obscured by a legend which is given support by Lord Montgomery. This is that it was pressure from Eighth Army which caused the Germans to break off the battle. In the version in *From El Alamein to the River Sangro* the story runs as follows:

> General Alexander sent me an urgent request for help urging me to exert all possible pressure on the enemy on my front in an effort to draw him off the Tebessa drive. Eighth Army was administratively not ready to operate major forces in southern Tunisia, but this was an occasion when risks had to be taken and I at once planned to intensify our drive towards the Mareth Line on the coast axis, and also to push Leclerc's force north from Ksar Rhilane. The enemy had weakened his Mareth front in order to strengthen the thrust through Gafsa, and there was always a chance that by forceful and energetic action I might frighten him out of his Mareth position. Though I was weak myself in front, urgent action was necessary if we were to help the Americans.
>
> On 24th February four fighter wings were operating from the Medenine–Ben Gardane area. I ordered 7th Armoured and 51st Divisions to keep up the pressure, the former in the coastal sector, the latter on the main Gabes road. This involved a considerable risk, because if the enemy broke off the Tebessa attack and could regroup quickly against the Eighth Army, I should be in an awkward situation. I had only two divisions forward, with my main administrative area under development at Ben Gardane, and the nearest reserve division (2nd New Zealand) was still back near Tripoli.
>
> My leading formations accelerated and strengthened their action against the outer defences of the Mareth Line, and in the last days of February it was clear that this had achieved the desired results. Rommel broke off his attack against the Americans and reports of regroupings of enemy forces began to reach my headquarters.

The parallel account in the *Memoirs* is shorter, but substantially the same. He says there: 'By the 26th February it was clear that our pressure had caused Rommel to break off his attack against the Americans.'

This is a coherent story but the evidence of dates alone is sufficient to overthrow it. It was at about midnight on 21st February that General Alexander ordered General Montgomery to create as powerful a threat as possible on the enemy's southern flank without becoming unbalanced himself. This order was given in virtue of the fact that Eighth Army was now directly under the command of 18th Army Group. It is an odd choice of words to describe this as 'an urgent request for help' (or, in the *Memoirs*, 'a very real cry for help') from General Alexander. The phrase gives the impression that Alexander was not Montgomery's superior officer but a coordinate commander in another part of the field. Be that as it may, Montgomery can only claim that it was in 'the last days of February' or 'by the 26th February' that his pressure began to have an effect. Now Rommel's decision to call off the battle, as I mentioned above, was taken on the morning of the 22nd. This fact was firmly established from captured orders which were received by the German forward units before ten o'clock that morning; in other words at the time Rommel took his decision Alexander's order to Montgomery can only just have been deciphered. It was a good four days before Eighth Army could have exerted any pressure on Rommel, even according to Montgomery's version. What Montgomery omits, moreover, is that on the 23rd Alexander telegraphed to cancel his order of the 21st. He informed Montgomery that the situation was now improved—it was clear that the enemy were withdrawing—and ordered Eighth Army, while keeping up a display of force, not to prejudice the future by undue risks. All these facts are documented in Alexander's Despatch on the campaign.

There is another point in the account of these events where General Montgomery's later reflections are at variance with his thought at the time. He says in his earlier book that he took great risks in moving forward and that during the period 28th February to 3rd March, which he describes as a period of great anxiety, the Eighth Army was unbalanced. If this was the case it was of course contrary to the orders which he had received from Alexander. It is, however, an anxiety of which he gave no signs at the time. In a letter written in his own hand to General Alexander on the 27th February he claimed that 'I was never unbalanced and am now sitting pretty'. He added that he was only afraid that Rommel would not attack him.

It was good news to hear that Eighth Army was ready for anything the Germans could do because it was plain that the next blow would come on that front. Never was an enemy move more obvious. At the time I made a practice of sending every night to the two Armies a summary of the most significant information received during the day, including an appreciation of what the enemy was likely to do. The collection runs without a break from the Kasserine battle to the eve of the final surrender. Glancing through, I see that every night something further had been added to the picture of the enemy's moves. Radio direction-finding actually came in useful for once, though mainly as a confirmation. It was not normally much used because the margin of error was much too great. It could even be seen with certainty from what position the attack would be made.

By now, the first week of March, Tripoli port was working well enough and Eighth Army was able to maintain a proper strength forward. They had in fact three divisions facing the enemy, the 51st, the New Zealand and the 7th Armoured Divisions. All these three were between the coastal plain and the Matmata mountains. The gap was defended by the famous Mareth Line of which I shall be speaking later. Strategically the chain of events was rather like that of the previous late summer and autumn. Eighth Army was preparing to attack the enemy positions, but it was obvious that the enemy were able to make, and were going to make, one final attack before it was ready. It was indeed a final attack, and it was Rommel's last battle in Africa, just as Alam Halfa would have been, but for Stumme's death. He planned it, like the battle of Alam Halfa, as a flank attack. His thrust was designed to come in, as there, on our left flank, while the front was held statically by the infantry with only a small diversionary frontal attack. On our left flank rose a sharp line of mountains from which a good road debouched from the pass known as Ksar el Hallouf. The German forces collected in the mountains consisted of the 10th Panzer Division, weakened by its losses at Thala, the 21st Panzer Division and half the 15th Panzer Division. It was proper that the 21st should have fought in this, Rommel's last battle in Africa, for it was the direct descendant of the first German division that came to Africa when he arrived in the first flush of his promotion to command of a Corps. He was himself well aware of the decisive character of the battle about to be fought. Not long afterwards I spoke to a prisoner from the 104th Panzer Grenadier Regiment, one of the two motorized infantry regiments of the 21st Division. He was an old soldier from the early days who had taken part in the first attack on Tobruk, been wounded at Gazala, made the advance to Alamein and the whole of the retreat. He said as they were moving off down the pass just beyond the village of Ksar el Hallouf, where the plains came into sight, they saw the Army Group Commander standing up in an open car at the side of the road. He had frequently seen Rommel in battle before. This time he looked a thoroughly sick man. His face, normally chubby, was thin and pale and he wore a dirty neck bandage over his desert sores. There was one of the halts inevitable in any operation, during which Rommel came over and spoke to them. He made the usual remarks, but the one the prisoner remembered best was that unless they won this battle their last hope in Africa was gone.

The diagnosis was correct and the battle was not long in losing. All surprise, as I have explained, had been lost. This was a disappointment to the Germans who thought that their moves had been well camouflaged and that the diversionary frontal attacks had achieved their object. They did not realize that we had three whole divisions forward although, by some unfortunate mischance, a B.B.C. news report on the eve of the attack revealed the fact that the New Zealand Division was moving into the front line. This move had been done with the greatest secrecy and with commendable speed and I remember the shock with which I listened to a news commentator babbling cheerfully the standard stories about happy New Zealanders taking up their new positions. However, it seems that the Germans omitted their usual listening that night. The result was that the German attack came in against infantry well dug in, with large numbers of anti-tank guns and with armour in reserve. It was as if he was determined to repeat some of the errors which we made in the early armoured battles in Africa, whereas we had learnt from him the strength of the anti-tank gun in a prepared position against the tank. Four times he attacked the centre of our position and each time without any success at all. He did not even draw our own tanks into the battle; the infantry were strong enough to resist alone. He drew off that same evening back to the mountains. His retreat was so fast that he was unable to take away his damaged tanks. Fifty-two were counted lying destroyed on the battlefield, the record bag in a day's battle in Africa. It was about half the total number with which he attacked and on the whole southern front he had only about one hundred and fifty. Kasserine had been bad enough but there he could say that, although he had over-exploited his initial success, he had at any rate made a good withdrawal and taken most of his damaged tanks with him. The battle of Medenine was an unrelieved defeat.

It was very shortly after the battle of the 6th March that Rommel left for Germany, handing over to von Arnim. Von Arnim's army was taken over by General von Vaerst, a former commander of the 15th Panzer Division. We did not discover the change-over till rather later. General Montgomery did not seem to have discovered it even in 1945 when his book on the African campaign was written. He refers to Rommel as his opponent both at the battle of the Mareth Line and at the battle of Wadi Akarit (6th April). At the time of those battles he spoke freely of how he was anticipating Rommel's likely reactions and criticized him both to the press and to his staff. This casts some doubt on the practice of concentrating on the personality of the opposing general. It is naturally, I suppose, flattering to the ego of one commander to imagine that the enemy's actions and movements are determined by the genius of one great individual just as, he hopes, are the reactions of his own army. Many correspondents have recorded how the Eighth Army commander took care to have a large coloured photograph of Rommel hanging in his caravan and how he would gaze on it from time to time as though seeking inspiration. It is disillusioning to think that during the last two battles in Africa, when Montgomery was seeking inspiration from those hard teutonic lineaments he should in fact have been trying to read the mind of the smooth-faced General Messe. Perhaps, however, there is something in the theory, because I can bear witness that during the early stages of the Mareth Line battle General Alexander observed to me that it did not seem characteristic of Rommel. Here perhaps was a case of genuine rapport.

It may be interesting to record how the first definite confirmation of Rommel's relief was obtained. It bears out the fact that one of the greatest requirements for an intelligence officer, after common sense, is continuity. A week or so after he had gone we picked up some idle chat in clear language between a troop of German armoured cars and the squadron H.Q. H.Q. was saying:

"Are you going to Sfax tonight, there's a big party?"

"What's the party for?"

"To celebrate the Army Group Commander's birthday."

This artless exchange must have taken place about the 24th March. Now anyone who had been concerned with intelligence since the time of the relief of Tobruk was bound to associate Rommel's birthday with November. It was clear that someone else had taken over and although I had no means of proving that von Arnim was born in March (but I did ask him when I met him after the surrender) it was easy to conjecture that he was Rommel's successor. Not long afterwards a document was captured which he had signed in the capacity of Army Group Commander.

The question arises why Rommel was removed from Africa. His illness was no doubt a good excuse. He had been ill many times in Africa, whose climate the Germans found thoroughly unhealthy, and he had after all already been relieved once on that score, in September 1942. He now went on long sick leave and had no active command until July. Perhaps also the Supreme Command wished to preserve Rommel to fight another battle. The Rommel legend had been mainly built up by English writers and the Germans were strangely slow to climb on the bandwagon. For that matter what I might call the posthumous Rommel industry is also almost exclusively 'Made in Britain'. Nevertheless the Germans plainly had no aversion to making use of a reputation so firmly established among their enemies.

Simultaneously with the attack at Medenine the enemy launched an offensive in the north against First Army. This took advantage of the thorough disorganization into which our line had been thrown by Rommel's attempt to roll it up from the south, but in spite of that it resulted in few gains. Almost simultaneously in the south he lashed out west of the Matmata mountains at the Free French detachment there under General Leclerc. It was plainly the enemy's plan to attack at all points to keep us on the stretch. In our nightly appreciation on the 12th March, I made this point by borrowing for the first time a tip from naval signals technique. I concluded by saying 'For Rommel's general intentions see Revelations xii, 12'. The reference was 'The devil is come down unto you having great wrath because he knoweth that he hath but a short time.' Rommel's time indeed was very short. He must have left that day or the next but the whole time left for the enemy was only two months to the day.

One of the problems with which Alexander was faced was that of restoring the morale of the Americans, which had been shaken. I used to cheer up my American friends by telling them that their 1st Armoured Division had done no worse in its first battle than ours had done. They were, however, rather on the gloomy side. But all these doubts were rapidly dispersed by the appointment of General Patton to command the 2nd Corps.

General Patton had the misfortune to get across the press at an early stage in his career, in fact during the famous Louisiana manoeuvres of 1941, and the vendetta never ceased except for a short period during the campaign in the west. It reached an acute phase in Sicily, and immediately after the end of the war in Germany. On the latter occasion it led to his demotion from command of the Army he had led with such brilliance and must have embittered his last days before his tragic death in a car accident. This vendetta, together with his studiedly exuberant manner, has tended to obscure his real ability. Of all the American generals who held high command in Europe only Patton and Eisenhower, as it seems to me, can lay claim to greatness. Eisenhower cannot be denied the title because he was the man in supreme command, the man who took the responsibility, in the greatest of all invasions. To anyone who contests his title he could reply as Joffre did when told that it was not he but Gallieni who had won the battle of the Marne—'They can say what they like about who won it, but if it had been lost I know who would have been blamed.' Patton combined the merits of an inspiring leader of men, both on the training ground and in battle, with very great intellectual resources. He was a real thinking General. His first campaign as a Corps Commander indeed did not call for much thought but for a great deal of inspiration. The idea was to start 2nd Corps off on a fairly mild operation in which the chances of success were high. In principle the idea was for them to capture Gafsa and to be ready to supply Eighth Army from a dump there when they had broken through the Mareth Line and were at their furthest point from their supply port of Tripoli. There are a number of stories told about Patton's first battle. I remember an American liaison officer who swore that he had seen the famous order in connection with the attack on one hill position which ended 'I expect to see such casualties among officers, particularly staff officers, as will convince me that a serious effort has been made to capture this objective.' This was the occasion on which the divisional commander, accompanied by his A.D.C., arrived alone on the top of the hill and withdrew, honourably wounded, to demote the company commander whom he met halfway up.

These were mere diversions, but they caused General Messe to send to the Gafsa road the whole of the 10th Panzer Division which was thus kept out of the decisive battle against the Eighth Army. The latter were faced with a pretty problem. The best efforts of French military science, on the lines of the Maginot Line but more modern, had been devoted to the fortification of the gap between the sea and the mountains in southern Tunisia facing the Libyan border. It was a formidable proposition for a frontal attack. The fortifications themselves used the natural advantages of the ground, and in front of them was another natural advantage which was expected to be of some importance. All the water sources between the line and the Libyan border were strongly impregnated with magnesium, in fact with concentrated Epsom salts. This was expected to have a depressing effect on an army facing the line for any length of time. On the other side of the mountains the desert was believed by the French to be impassable. It certainly was extremely difficult but the Long Range Desert Group had by now acquired great experience in reconnoitring routes over difficult going and were pretty certain that they could prove the French wrong. Nevertheless, in the first plan the main emphasis lay on the frontal attack, as might perhaps be deduced from its code name 'Pugilist'. Two Corps were to assault frontally, 30th Corps with three infantry divisions and a brigade and 10th Corps with two armoured divisions. On the desert flank was the New Zealand Division, with an armoured brigade, and General Leclerc's force.

The battle of the Mareth Line started on 20th March in heavy rain. After two days it was clear that the original plan for 'Pugilist' would have to be abandoned. We did manage to break into the line, but the enemy defence was so strong and the difficulties of the ground so great that the assaulting forces had to be completely withdrawn with heavy losses. This was on the night of the 23rd and at the same time a change in plan was made and with pious memories of Alamein was given the code name 'Supercharge'. 10th Corps H.Q. with one armoured division was sent off to join the New Zealand Division on the desert flank. This meant an enormous detour, and in order to shorten it the 4th Indian Division was sent into the mountains to open a shorter way through the Ksar el Hallouf pass. It was one of the finest efforts of that famous division. Meanwhile the New Zealanders and 1st Armoured Division were making steady but difficult progress through the desert. This left time for General Messe, who was fighting his battle with a gaze fixed firmly over his shoulder, to withdraw from the Mareth Line. The Italians went off first and the Germans did the rearguard. In fact, like other left hooks on the road from Alamein, this one caught very few of the enemy. It was a fine feat, however, and culminated in a spectacular moonlight advance by 1st Armoured Division. On the 29th March the New Zealanders entered Gabes at the culmination of their flanking move and, not long afterwards, the advanced elements of the 51st Division, which had advanced up the main road, came in.

The 51st Highland Division, though the latest arrived and most palefaced of all Eighth Army, had a strong divisional sense and a keen appreciation of the value of publicity. It was their habit wherever they went to blazon the divisional sign, an 'HD' in a circle, on every wall they found standing. The suggestion was made that a good title for a divisional history would be 'From Alamein to Tripoli with paintpot and brush'. When the New Zealanders entered Gabes ahead of the Highlanders a party of them hastily went round painting up 'HD' all over the town and when the advance party of the 51st Division entered they were taken round the place by New Zealand guides who told them kindly, 'You see we've written it up for you already.'

The block between our two armies was now at its very last stage. Messe had withdrawn to the line of the Wadi Akarit, a steep-sided obstacle which had been artificially scarped. Immediately in its rear were two high hills from which the roads to Gafsa and Sfax to the north were completely commanded. It was an immensely strong position, stronger by nature than the Mareth Line itself, and there was no way round. In fact, it would have to be an infantry battle. General Alexander now had a chance to make a coordinated show of the attack on Messe's 1st Army. His plan was to press hard down the Gafsa road with the American 2nd Corps, drawing off sufficient enemy forces to allow Eighth Army to break through by a frontal attack; and at the same time he organized another force under 9th Corps to strike in, well at the rear. There is a pass towards the northern end of the coastal plain, at a place called Fondouk, which leads straight on to the holy city of Kairouan on the route by which Messe was withdrawing. 9th Corps had a brigade of the British 46th Division and the whole of the American 34th Division with the British 6th Armoured Division in reserve. The plan was for the two infantry formations to attack the north and south sides of the pass respectively; when this attack had succeeded in clearing the way the armoured division was to go through. Of this ambitious plan only the part entrusted to Eighth Army was successful. General Patton's attack was pressed with great vigour; but Messe was thoroughly alarmed for his right flank and disposed both the 21st as well as the 10th Panzer Division on the Gafsa road against him. This meant, rather to our surprise, that he was ready to leave only the 15th Panzer Division in support of the

Wadi Akarit line. Against two such experienced divisions, though now considerably under strength, the Americans could make no headway. Eighth Army's infantry battle was violent but short. Three divisions attacked suddenly in the dark before dawn; the 4th Indian, 50th and 51st. The latter two made no progress but the 7th and 5th Indian brigade, led by the Sussex and the 2nd Gurkhas, captured all their objectives and made a great hole for the armour of 10th Corps to exploit. It was only the brilliant work of the 15th Panzer Division and the 90th Light Division which saved Messe from a disaster. As it was he lost over 6,000 prisoners.

This was the time at which 9th Corps should have broken through into the enemy's rear and completed the disaster. Unfortunately the fight for the Fondouk pass proved too much for them. The 128th Brigade captured the northern heights but 34th Division was unable to make any progress to the south. After two days it was clear that the original plan would never do, and Alexander, who was on the spot, ordered 9th Corps to disregard the 34th Division's failure and to launch the 6th Armoured Division straight at the pass. This was one of the more dashing armoured actions of the war. The floor of the pass is quite flat but the mouth is very narrow and commanded on each side by steep though not high cliffs. There were plenty of minefields on the bottom and from the cliffs anti-tank guns in enfilade could cover the whole area at very close range. The motor battalion went in first, to make a gap in the minefield and were followed by two armoured regiments. As often happens with hazardous ventures, dash and impudence carried them through with fewer losses than had been feared. They emerged into the coastal plain in time enough to accelerate the enemy's withdrawal and cut off some of his rearguards; but the great opportunity was missed. And yet it was possible to be philosophical. After all, the enemy forces were being driven into a cul-de-sac with their backs to the sea, with never a chance to escape.

While this was going on, our 1st Army were also pressing hard in the northern sector. It was thoroughly disagreeable country, mountainous and wooded and at the same time boggy and muddy from the continuous rain. The North African spring was a serious disappointment to troops with views about the sunny Mediterranean, but it was all good preparation for the Italian climate. The enemy were not disposed to be so stubborn in this area, and in any event most of the defending troops were Italians, many of whom were now demoralized. The Germans involved in this defensive battle were of sterner stuff, though some of them were of rather unusual origin. It was in the second half of March that we first came up against a new German formation called the 999th African Division. This was recruited almost entirely, as far as other ranks were concerned, from inmates of concentration camps, nearly all Germans but with some *volksdeutsche*. A good many of them, of course, were ordinary criminals but a high proportion were political offenders, particularly members of the Communist party. A very few of them—certainly not more than six all told—took the opportunity to desert, which was not difficult under the circumstances of the front in northern Tunisia; but the bulk of them fought with great steadfastness. More than one Communist prisoner said that he and the people who thought like him were determined to do as well as they could 'in order to show them that a Communist makes as good a soldier as any damned Nazi'.

Since the second half of February, Alexander's H.Q. had moved out of Constantine and taken to its tents. We worked in various places, starting down south not far from Kasserine and gradually moving north until we were on the Tunis road. At one time we were just outside the village of Driana which derives its name from the Emperor Hadrian and has the most magnificent Roman remains. But the whole of that part of Tunisia is thickly strewn with whole townfuls of Roman ruins. These are cities that no-one but the specialist in Roman Imperial history has heard of but they demonstrate very clearly how rich this part of Africa was in the first few centuries of our era. The air is clear and dry and the stones of temple and aqueduct remain clean and sharp. The enormous amphitheatre of El Djem has been used as a quarry for centuries and yet still dominates the plain for 10 miles around.

This was, I thought, the most efficient and certainly the smallest H.Q. that I ever served on in the whole of the war. It was much smaller than either Eighth Army or First Army H.Q. We nearly all knew each other because the bulk of the senior officers had come from the Middle East. All my staff were handpicked by me from the whole of the Middle East and all personal friends. The spring was coming with violent speed after the snow and mud of the winter. We lived in soft-leaved woods with green grass springing up full of flowers. On top of all this there was the exhilarating feeling that things were working up to a victorious climax.

By 12th April the enemy had been driven back into their final redoubt which covered the extreme north-eastern tip of Tunisia. At this point a solid wall of mountains runs east and west down to the sea at a place called Enfidaville and blocked Eighth Army's further advance. The rest of the front also was all mountainous except where we still held our gate at Medjez el Bab. Von Arnim still disposed of over 200,000 troops with which he had to cover an easily defensible front of 120 miles. A fairly high proportion of them were Italians, but it was noticeable that they were putting up a much better performance than they had ever done so far in Africa. Our theory was that by this time all the Italians who had no interest in the fight had taken advantage of the numerous opportunities available since Alamein of being taken prisoner, and only the tough ones remained. Morale in general was high, and so was the level of supplies. Reinforcement was now more difficult because the air forces were able to interfere more easily; indeed on 19th April the Air Force shot down over fifty transport aircraft approaching Tunisia. However, we were faced with the difficulty that until we could clear the enemy from northern Tunisia we could hardly go on to invade Sicily and we were anxious to get on to that by early July at the very latest. Alexander had given a guess two months before that we could finish the job in Africa by 15th May and it was on that basis that plans for future operations in the Mediterranean were proceeding. Speed and certainty were therefore vital.

The final battle for Tunisia was undoubtedly one of Alexander's greatest achievements and it is not surprising that he chose to add the name of Tunis to his title. The problem admitted of only one neat and artistic solution: the only thrust that would be deadly, decisive and quick must follow the direct route down the Medjerda River straight from Medjez to Tunis and then turn right to cut across the base of the Cape Bon Peninsula. This would give us Tunis and almost inevitably Bizerta in consequence and break up any chance of a last ditch defence in an inner redoubt. As with all perfect solutions, however, what is obvious to one side is equally obvious to the other side. The skill, in fact, lies not so much in seeing what has to be done as in seeing how to do it. Unless we could baffle and deceive the enemy he must inevitably prepare to fight a desperate and decisive battle along our chosen route. However, we had some advantage on our side. Our technique for deceiving the enemy was now well tried in practice and enemy intelligence was no better at seeing through it. Moreover it was only natural for the enemy to expect our main effort to be made on the right by Eighth Army, since General Montgomery's forces were the more experienced, and their commander had the greatest reputation of Alexander's subordinates. We could hope therefore that a diversionary attack on that flank would fulfil its object of pinning down a fair number of forces. Apart, however, from this fairly obvious manœuvre, main reliance had to be placed on a fairly delicately executed form of the familiar double bluff. Strength was shown on the chosen axis; but strength was also half shown and half concealed at a point further south, a plausible point just north of some impassable salt marshes from where a network of minor roads led into the plain around Tunis. The plan was therefore to make an attack at this point in some force with strong armoured support and thereafter to move the armour back to the Medjez–Tunis road, replacing it with dummy tanks. The hope was that when our main attack went in the enemy strength would be by-passed and left behind on its right wing.

Besides its military merits the plan for the final attack had some political virtues as well. The American 2nd Corps had been squeezed out by Eighth Army's advance across their front. Alexander now planned to transfer them from the extreme right to the extreme left of his line and to use them in an attack on Bizerta. This would give the Americans, who hitherto had played an essentially minor rôle in the campaign, a definite and noteworthy objective. The transfer was a major feat of good staff work; First Army's line of communication, which ran at right angles across the path of General Patton's move, were tenuous and congested enough and with less skilful handling on his part there might have been a deadly congestion. The fact is that in the military field whether of operations or logistics Patton touched nothing that he did not adorn. He positioned his three infantry divisions and one armoured division at the left flank of First Army and proceeded to work out a plan for a methodical advance through the difficult country next to the coast which was to have strikingly successful results. At the same time Eighth Army was ordered to send an armoured division across to come under command of First Army. This was to be the first of a series of transfers which, for the sake of inconspicuousness, were to take place by degrees.

The battle opened on the night of 19th April with Eighth Army's attack in the south. Even the 4th Indian Division, with its memories of Keren, found the mountain country difficult. General Montgomery disliked the prospects too and on the 21st proposed instead to concentrate on forcing the defile between the coast and sea. For this he proposed to use the newly arrived 56th Division, so that he could rest the two divisions, 50th and 51st, which he proposed to use in Sicily.

However, when the 56th Division arrived and was first put in he found fault with their lack of training and telegraphed to Alexander saying that he felt unhappy about the possibilities of success. Alexander's plan did not require Eighth Army actually to break through the mountain barrier at this point, so he was prepared to authorize a damping-down of operations. It was, besides, time for the next detachment from Eighth Army to be transferred to the vital point.

There was rather a sad and stale air at Eighth Army in these last days of April. I remember visiting them in a beautiful meadow of spring flowers near Sousse, and reflecting that both the Army Commander and his staff appeared to have lost interest. They never liked mountains as compared with the desert and saw little prospect of another striking victory. After being so long on their own it was less agreeable to be part of a large team and rather galling that the credit for bringing the war in Africa to an end would go to First Army. Tunisia was for them an anticlimax. After all they had come a very long way, a distance further than from London to Moscow. Tripoli had been the real goal that had glittered in their eyes. The Mareth Line and the Wadi Akarit were rather in the way of extras, like the encores given by a popular performer on being recalled for two curtain calls.

There was a more cheerful spirit in the formations which left Eighth Army and came to take part in the final attack. They were singularly well chosen. They consisted of the 7th Armoured Division, 4th Indian Division and 201st Guards Brigade. Back in 1940 the 7th Armoured Division and the Guards (then the 22nd Brigade) were the only forces —plus the Welch—in the Western Desert and for the battle of Sidi Barrani they were joined by the 4th Indian Division. They were all at the top of their form. It was amusing to see the Eighth Army and First Army troops mingle. Eighth Army vehicles still had the startling yellow-and-beige desert camouflage as opposed to the dark-green and earth-coloured camouflage used by First Army, and in addition to that their vehicles could be told by their obviously advanced state of decrepitude. The troops were equally dashing in their unconventional style of uniform. The officers of the 7th Armoured Division, for example, made many eyes open with their thick-soled desert boots, corduroy trousers, loose pullovers and sheepskin coats. Like their tanks, they had a sand-blasted air, to which in many cases was added a tendency to grow R.A.F.-style moustaches.

Meanwhile our diversionary attack in the area of the salt marshes had started on the morning of 22nd April. It had been observed by the enemy, and two nights before he had put in a sudden and violent spoiling attack. It came as a distinct surprise. However, it was not a success because it hit us at our strongest point; in fact the enemy losses were distinctly heavier than ours whereas they could less afford them. It was certainly clear that we had diverted enemy attention away from the main road to Tunis. All three German armoured divisions were now drawn into the salt marsh area. This allowed First Army to make some inconspicuous but vitally important gains in the hills on either side of the Medjerda. It also meant that no reinforcements would go to the forces opposing the American 2nd Corps in the extreme north.

The Americans were making excellent progress under Patton's inspiration. Attached to his H.Q. was General Omar K. Bradley who had been sent to the front to pick up some experience of command in battle before being tried out as a corps commander in Sicily. He was at that time junior to Patton. Things were going so well that Eisenhower decided, and Alexander agreed, to remove Patton and send him back to take command of Seventh Army which was planning hard for the Sicilian invasion. It happened therefore that 2nd Corps was under Bradley's command for the last ten days of the fighting during which Bizerta was captured; but the spirit of the troops, which was excellent, and the plan of attack, which was sound and carefully worked out, both owed their origin to Patton. General Bradley went on to higher command and overtook Patton, largely owing to the results of unfortunate newspaper publicity, and there is a school of American military historians which attributes to him very superior qualities as a commander. I could never see that on the record he warranted a higher reputation than that of a good plain cook, compared with Patton, the *cordon bleu*.

The time was now approaching for the final attack, to which was assigned the code name 'Vulcan'. It was planned with very great care and, contrary to his normal practice, Alexander issued elaborate instructions for it. He gave a detailed directive to General Anderson, the First Army Commander, to make sure that he did not depart in any way from the plans of the attack as Alexander envisaged them. The first point was that a really deep penetration must be achieved on a very narrow front. Two infantry divisions were to make the hole and two armoured divisions were to pass through it and advance without paying any attention to the needs of flank protection. It was, in fact, to be an operation very similar to the German breakthrough in France in 1940. Like that too, it was to be assisted by an extra-

ordinary concentration of air power. Two thousand aircraft of all
types were to operate on the axis of the attack. Preparations had already
been made, as I have explained, to deceive the enemy about the point
of main effort. D-Day for the attack was to be 6th May at dawn and
if we could keep the main enemy armoured concentrations away until
then we could consider that enough had been done, for the distance
to be covered before the attack reached its decisive objective was less
than thirty miles.

The main method was to keep 1st Armoured Division down in the
salt marsh area and have it make a show of aggressiveness; 6th Armoured
moved away north as unobtrusively as possible while the area which its
armoured regiments had left was filled overnight with dummy tanks.
Wireless traffic appropriate to two armoured divisions and a corps
H.Q. was also kept up at a plausible intensity and with a few apparently
inadvertent breaches of security. Steps were also taken to provide
German intelligence with those agents' reports to which they attached
such value, all of which indicated a strong concentration of allied
armour in this area. It was a brilliant piece of deception worked out to
an elaborate plan and it won the success it deserved. The two strongest
of the German Panzer divisions, the 10th and 21st, remained in the
broken country well south of the main Tunis road, watching our
1st Armoured Division and its dummy tanks in the area of the salt
marshes, while only the 15th Panzer Division, which was by now very
weak in tanks, was left opposite our main point of attack—and some
of that was detached on the wrong side of the river. It was a particular
pleasure when we discovered on the day before the attack that two
batteries of 88 mm. guns had been removed from Massicault, through
which our armour was ordered to pass, and sent southwards to the
north-eastern end of the salt marshes. It seemed to me, therefore, that
there were good grounds for informing Alexander that we seemed likely
to obtain surprise next morning.

We did indeed gain surprise. Two infantry divisions, 4th British
and 4th Indian, attacked side by side at 3.30 in the morning on a front
of only 300 yards between them. They were followed up closely by
the two armoured divisions, 6th and 7th. By 11.30 the infantry had
made such progress that the armoured divisions were able to pass
through them into the lead. They laagered for the night round
Massicault, whose defence had been so conveniently weakened, about
15 miles deep in the enemy positions and half-way to Tunis. The only
German armour they had met had come, as predicted, from the 15th

Armoured Division; the other two were trying to struggle into action from the south. By this time, however, they were left too far behind. When our two armoured divisions moved forward at first light on 7th May they found little organized opposition. At 2.45 on the afternoon of the same day the 7th Armoured Division's armoured car regiment, the 11th Hussars, entered Tunis by the Bardo gate. They were closely followed by the corresponding regiment in 6th Armoured Division, the Derbyshire Yeomanry. There were indeed some ill-disposed persons in First Army who would claim that the latter were first in. I can only say that if it were so it would be a loss to the picturesqueness of history, for the 11th Hussars, the first British Cavalry Regiment to be mechanized, the eyes and ears of 7th Armoured Division during nearly three years of campaigning, had already led the way into Benghazi and Tripoli.

Tunis gave the allied troops a riotous welcome. Scenes of this kind grew common enough later but at that time it was the first example of the liberation of a great city. I attached myself for the occasion to some old friends in the 4th Royal Horse Artillery of the 7th Armoured Division, Strafer Gott's old regiment. It was pleasant to drive along the boulevards with a cheerful crowd celebrating on the pavements, but the wine was no better, in fact slightly worse, than the rather potent stuff we had been used to already and I am afraid I spent the night in a tent outside the city reminiscing in deplorable vein about early days in the desert.

The same day saw the capture of Bizerta by the Americans. They had pushed on doggedly and methodically through the mountains and at the edge of the plain the Germans opposing them broke. They had been left to fight their battle alone and the losses they had sustained had been crippling. It was a great pleasure to Alexander that the two main objectives should have fallen with such appropriate simultaneity, one to the British and one to the Americans. The campaign was not quite over, however. At Tunis the two British armoured divisions parted, the 7th going northwards towards Bizerta, where they rapidly surrounded and mopped up the German survivors of the American thrust, and the 6th turning southeast towards Cape Bon. This was as planned. It was vital to prevent the Germans from establishing themselves in the peninsula, where they would have had a good defensive position. As it was, 6th Armoured Division was held up for two days at the point where the coast turns northeast at Hamam Lif. At this point the road runs through a defile between the sea and a steep twin-peaked mountain. This is in fact the sacred mountain of the Carthaginians, then dedicated to their chief god Melkarth, and now known as Gebel bou Kournein, the Two Horns, which is a title of Alexander the Great in the Koran. At this defile the Germans had concentrated all the 88 mm. guns which they had taken from their landing grounds, and 6th Armoured Division only got through after two days by taking their tanks right through the very edge of the surf where they got some protection from the sloping beach. Thereafter the last hope of serious resistance by the enemy was gone. It was not long before 6th Armoured and 4th Infantry Division from First Army joined hands with Eighth Army north of Enfidaville.

The German Higher Command appears to have been taken by surprise by the rapidity of the end and it was not until 24 hours after the fall of Tunis and Bizerta that they announced the fact to the German public. The communiqué went on to say 'the 33,000 Germans and 30,000 Italians remaining will be withdrawn in small boats'. I see that in my nightly telegram I said I thought the R.A.F. and Navy would interfere with this programme, which must in any case depend on securing the Cape Bon bridgehead, and quoted with, I am afraid, rather obvious *schadenfreude* Churchill's 1940 phrase 'we are waiting, so are the fishes'. This question of evacuation had been occupying our minds for some time and in fact one of my people did a staff study on it. The conclusion was that in the worst case for us, and assuming that the enemy could stabilize a firm bridgehead position and showed great skill in the use of small craft, he might theoretically remove up to 70,000 men. I never thought it very likely, provided we could make the final blow sudden and sharp enough. Having been involved in two evacuations over sea, I had a certain fellow feeling for the Germans, but at the same time could see all the more clearly how completely different the situation was. To us the sea was a friendly and allied element. To be driven back to the beaches meant, for the fortunate majority, a pleasant sea voyage and a chance to fight again. To the Germans the sea was hostile; so much was this so that very few in fact even tried to get away, and the total of those who were successful was 663, all of them sailors and dockyard workers who made off in small craft for Sicily.

There were some, however, who got away by air from an airfield in the centre of Cape Bon. On 8th May we were rather startled by one of the German Reconnaissance Units striking up in plain language and passing a number of messages between N.C.O.'s from which it transpired that all the officers had left to try their luck on an aeroplane. The commanding officer was heard not long afterwards. He passed a message giving his best wishes to the battalion and expressing the hope that any survivors would visit him at his private address in Germany. This struck me as unusual. General officers, on the other hand, set a better example. We captured the commanders of all the German Divisions, the two army commanders and the Army Group Commander.

General Messe delayed his surrender until the morning of the 13th. His H.Q. was in a fairly inaccessible area which was not under attack. On the morning of the 13th he received a message from Rome informing him that he had been promoted to the rank of Marshal. The fact that his surrender followed very shortly thereafter was interpreted, no doubt unkindly, as meaning that that was what he was waiting for. General von Arnim surrendered to the commanding officer of the 2nd Gurkhas of 4th Indian Division. He was brought to Alexander's H.Q. and I interpreted for him at an interview with Alexander and McCreery. He seemed bewildered by the suddenness of the collapse. The interview, I fear, was not very productive. Alexander was courteous and civil but apart from establishing the fact that Von Arnim had served in the Imperial Army in the 4th Guard Regiment, which might be taken as the parallel to Alexander's own Irish Guards, very little of interest emerged. A couple of days later I had occasion to go to Algiers and took von Arnim with me to hand him over to General Eisenhower's H.Q. He was an unimpressive looking man with more pomposity than capacity. Messe was a bit on the pompous side too; I had to translate a long and elaborately worded protest against his treatment though, if I remember correctly, the main point was concerned with the size of his tent. The great mass of German and Italian prisoners on the roads round Tunis and Bizerta presented an extraordinary appearance, reminiscent of Derby Day. There seemed not enough troops to keep an eye on everyone so most of them were driving themselves to the prisoner of war cages, some in lorries, others in horse-drawn carts. It was a strange anticlimax after the great violence with which they had been fighting. Enemy morale in the last battle was indeed very high and there had been few cases of men failing to do their duty. The static front opposite Eighth Army had shown signs of unusual activity because the enemy decided to fire off all their spare artillery ammunition before surrendering. Incidentally, this strikes me as one of the oddities of military punctilio, and I am surprised that the recipients of this furious bombardment did not object more to such a preliminary to surrender.

The total number of prisoners came to just over a quarter of a million. This was a bit of a blow to the reputation of Intelligence, because the estimate we had given to Operations was 200,000. This turned out to be very accurate as far as fighting strength went, and we were right on the mark as regards German tank strength, but after the surrender we were severely cursed by the Q side because we were 50,000 out as regards administrative troops and in particular in Italians. The fact is that all the administrative personnel who had been running the enemy's lines of communications all the way to Alamein, plus all the Italian civil and military officials in Tripolitania, had been crowded back into the last bridgehead and, since there had been no evacuation at any time, were waiting to be picked up. None of them had anything to do or played any part in the final battle and as I explained to Sir Brian Robertson you cannot count people like that, in both senses. He was still rather scandalized; but fortunately we picked up sufficient enemy food supplies from their very well stocked dumps to enable us to feed them all without difficulty.

We also had to help with supplies for the civil population. The countryside was fairly all right but the towns were definitely short. The French were genuinely pleased at being liberated. The Arabs were prepared to cheer for either side, for the Tunisians, as other Arabs will maintain, are of an easy going and peaceful character. A story which was told me by an American war correspondent called Hal Boyle will illustrate the point. He and another correspondent spent the night of 7th May in the small town of Ferryville, on the way to Bizerta. At that time no American troops had entered though the Germans had fled. The Arabs anxiously enquired how they should greet the liberating troops on their entry, and Boyle undertook to give them advice. He drilled them in two English phrases which they got uncomprehendingly by heart. When the first American troops entered the town they were pleased to find all the population outside their houses. On one side of the street they were shouting 'Vote for Boyle, son of the soil,' and on the other side 'Honest Hal, the Ay-rabs pal.'

A coastline, if commanded by an unfriendly fleet, rules a singularly clean line across the field of battle. The battle of Tunis was thereby made into an outstanding example of the *schlacht ohne morgen*—the battle without a tomorrow—about which German theorists had dreamed since von Clausewitz was first inspired by the battle of Cannae. In a matter of a few hours an army of a quarter of a million men was deducted from the enemy side. On 13th May General Alexander sent to Mr. Churchill the following telegram:

"Sir, it is my duty to report that the Tunisian campaign is over. All enemy resistance has ceased. We are masters of the North African shores."

CHAPTER XI

The Invasion of Sicily

THE invasion of Sicily provides a good example of the thoroughly planned operation. Not so thoroughly or so lengthily planned as 'Overlord' of course, but, for various reasons, it turned out possible to devote to the study of the Sicilian operations a good deal more time than was usual. The principal reason derives from Allied Grand Strategy. The Casablanca Conference was a bit of a half-way house. It already seemed likely that the final shape of Allied strategy would be based on an invasion of northwest Europe from the United Kingdom, but in January this decision was not yet taken. Accordingly, Casablanca is now best remembered as the place where the expression 'unconditional surrender' was produced out of Roosevelt's memories of the American Civil War with particular reference to General U.S. Grant's initials. On the military side the decision was taken to carry on with the air attack on Germany, in the hope that it would produce better results than it had so far, and to put the finishing touches to the clearance of the African coastline by seizing the island of Sicily. This operation 'Husky', was a mere pendant to the African campaign, designed to open the Mediterranean as a safe passage to the Far East. This would have the same effect as if the shipping available to the Allies were suddenly increased by two million tons. What we should do thereafter with the armies assembled in the Mediterranean, whether they should advance northwards or be wafted back to the U.K. from whence to spring across the Channel at the appropriate time, was left to be settled at the next meeting in May.

Nothing could be done about Sicily until Tunisia was cleaned up and this could hardly be before May. It was possible therefore to set up a planning staff which could work away with plenty of time on its hands to evolve the perfect plan. This cloistered collection of well-trained officers assembled in early February 1943 in the calm and isolation of a commandeered school, the Ecole Normale at Bouzarea, on the hill above Algiers. It was given the code name 'Force 141' and at once immersed itself in details of port capacity and loading tables. Alexander was the designated commander and he intended to take on all the staff that he then had at 18th Army Group H.Q.; but February was the most critical month of the Tunisian battle, and March was little less active, so that neither he nor any of the rest of us were able to take much interest in Force 141. There was only a skeleton Intelligence staff; Allied Force H.Q. provided the bulk of the information. I did however take a dash down there for a look at the planning staff and to recruit some more Intelligence officers because many of those then with me in Tunisia were anxious to go back home after the campaign was over and I thought it would be a good thing for Intelligence training as a whole in England if they did so. I had no particular reason for wanting to go home myself and was looking forward to Sicily.

Bouzarea should have been a charming place, a cluster of white houses perched up above the blue Mediterranean; in fact it was bitterly cold and whenever I went there it seemed to be wrapped in fog. The fog was still going strong when we left the place for good, and with no regret, in June. However in the cheerless cells a devoted collection of staff officers were poring over admirable air photographs and calculating port capacity.

It was for Sicily that there was first studied and put into practice the spectacular art of calculating beach gradients from air photographs. It must be remembered that Sicily was the first of all the Allied large-scale amphibious operations. Everybody was determined to take all sorts of pains to make it a success but there was not much that was known yet about beach landings and in particular about how to maintain a force over beaches. It was obvious, however, that the best sort of beaches to use were those with a fairly steep gradient so that landing craft, when they ran themselves ashore, would be as near as possible to the foreshore. Now the Admiralty pilot books and the charts, not unnaturally, paid no attention to the problems involved in deliberately running a ship ashore. There was in fact really no information about beaches at all. One way of getting it was that used by the splendid organization called C.O.P.P. or Combined Operations Pilotage Parties who would be carried by submarine to the appropriate bit of coast and then paddle ashore in dinghies taking soundings as they went. They would land if they could and see what the sand was like and if possible explore the exits from the beach; but their main task lay on the water, not on the land. The second method was discovered by someone who worked out a mathematical formula whereby the slope of the beach could be ascertained from the interval between the crests of waves in certain wind conditions. This interval showed up plainly in parallel lines of white on air photographs.

Apart from these topographical studies, and the studies of the enemy's defence system from air photographs, the main Intelligence interest was naturally the enemy troops in the island and their disposition. Here we felt pretty confident that our information was sound and complete. This may seem odd in view of the fact that we had no contact whatever with the enemy troops in Sicily and therefore none of the formal means open to Intelligence. Italian wireless security was good. For that matter wireless was little used in Sicily at that time because of the existence of telephone circuits which were quicker and safer. Nevertheless we produced an order of battle that was so accurate that when our first captured Italian general saw it he said it was better than the official one he had himself. The method was simple and had been well organized in G.H.Q. Middle East for some time. Ever since the end of the first campaign against the Italians we had had in our hands several hundred thousand Italian prisoners of war. Many of them were in the Middle East, more still were in India and some were in South and East Africa; but their mail all passed through Cairo. This mail was very large and contained many letters from relatives and friends still serving in the Italian forces. These people nearly always gave as their address the unit in which they were serving. Now all these letters had passed through the Italian censorship and in view of the fact that they were going to a prisoner of war that censorship should have been very strict. In fact, however, it was marked with that cheerful inefficiency which distinguished all Italian military organization. Either the censors overlooked the service address or they merely painted a little Indian ink over it. All prisoners of war mail was examined in Cairo. Every letter from a serving man in the forces was put aside and read to see if he mentioned where his unit was. He nearly always did so and the location was recorded. The Indian ink, which had been easily removed, was carefully put back again and the letter was sent on. The organization needed was fairly large—about a dozen people in a private house in Cairo—but the result was magnificent. I am sure we knew more about the Italian Army than anyone in Rome. Pantellaria was another triumph of the Cairo team. On this tiny fortress island, with which we never came in touch until it surrendered, there was a garrison of just over 11,000 and our calculation of the size of the garrison, based solely on this one source, was only out by fifty men.

Another set of people were working away at a deception plan. It hardly seemed likely that much would come of this because we thought it must be obvious that Sicily was the next step after Tunisia. Still, there was no point in giving up without trying. I might say here that there were later stages in the war in Italy when it seemed to me, practically speaking, hopeless to attempt any sort of deception plan, but by then we had at least the knowledge that these plans had always come off so far. So we always carried on, and persistence was rewarded. Right up to the very last battle, in the spring of 1945, the Germans fell for our very last effort in this line. The deception plan for Sicily was to direct enemy attention to Sardinia on the one hand and southern Greece on the other. We had a good long time to prepare for it and it was spectacularly successful. However, the principal feature of it, which was given the official code name of 'Mincemeat', has already formed the subject of two books and a film and it is too late now to tell over again the story of the man who never was. This story of how the dead body of a courier with immensely secret papers in his pocket was planted on the Spanish authorities makes a capital one but, from my memory of what I was told at the time and later by friends in the enterprising organization responsible, I think there are one or two interesting points that have not been covered, such as why he had to be dressed as a Marine and what steps were taken to minimize the likelihood of a post-mortem and why that was so desirable. This picturesque plot was the principal part of the plan but it was also backed by innumerable other measures of a more routine nature. All in all the effect was certainly most gratifying. With feverish haste the Germans organized reinforcements for Sardinia, and the best German armoured division then available, the 1st, made a hasty journey from France to the southern Peloponnese where it took up anti-invasion positions on the beaches facing the island of Crete. Sicily received a tardier reinforcement.

Operational planning in the invasion of Sicily was, as I have said, exceptionally thorough and it is not surprising that more than one plan was put forward as it proceeded. Everyone was trying to be as safe and certain as possible and the point to which attention was in the first place overwhelmingly directed was maintenance. It is obvious that no operational plan however brilliant is worth looking at unless it is based on a sound administrative plan. At the time when planning started it was part of the gospel of amphibious warfare, as worked out at Combined Operations H.Q., that sufficient major ports for the maintenance of the total force envisaged must be captured within a very short time of the assault. It was held that the lessons of 'Torch' fully bore out this doctrine. There are only three major ports in Sicily: Messina, Catania and Palermo. An assault on Messina was out of the question because it was beyond the range of air cover and heavily defended with permanent coastal batteries. Catania was just within fighter range but, according to the planners, could only maintain four divisions in the first month and a total of six divisions thereafter—entirely insufficient for the reduction of the island. But for this, Catania would have been a good objective, because it would at once give us control of an important group of airfields from which we could cover the whole of the northeast corner of Sicily which must be our ultimate objective. Palermo had the capacity to maintain all the forces we should need in the island. It was within fighter range and not difficult of access from seaward. The disadvantage was that to begin at the extreme west of the island was to leave the enemy in possession of both Catania and Messina for his reinforcements and also of the bulk of the airfields in the island. An advance from Palermo on Messina was expected to be particularly difficult. To go for Palermo and the west would therefore be safe but rather humdrum; to go for Catania and the southeast would be strategically more sensible but apparently administratively impossible. The first plan therefore combined the two. There was to be a British landing in the southeast and an American landing in the northwest two days later. At this point the Air Force piped up and demanded a third landing in the southwest to capture a group of airfields around Castel Vetrano, alleging that otherwise the Palermo landing would be too exposed to enemy air action.

This plan never had many friends though it was, as you see, based on strictly logical considerations. Almost its only supporter was the Naval C.-in-C. Admiral Cunningham, who held the view that amphibious operations were better dispersed than concentrated. Even he thought that this degree of dispersion went a little far. When it was presented to Alexander in about the middle of February, as I well remember, he observed that it would be better to have both armies assaulting together in the southeastern corner of the island and directed that this should be investigated. The answer came back that if we were to use ten divisions for the conquest of the island we could not rely on the southeastern ports alone and must have Palermo in addition. Nevertheless this was the plan to which Alexander later reverted.

Personally I enjoyed immensely such of the planning as I saw. It was the first time that I had been associated with amphibious operations. I found the Q experts quite fascinating and I can still read with interest Alexander's despatch on the conquest of Sicily which sets out the process of planning in great detail. As he says, the actual operations are of less interest because in this case the conventional phrase is justified, that operations proceeded according to plan. I must, however, make clear one or two points which have been obscured by the account given by Field Marshal Lord Montgomery in his book *From El Alamein to the River Sangro* and in his memoirs.

In the first place it is worth making clear that the factor which was responsible for the final shape of the plan was not the Eighth Army Commander but the D.U.K.W. As I have said, before Montgomery ever saw the plan Alexander had indicated his preference for an attack side by side by Seventh and Eighth Armies on the southeast corner of the island. At that time the administrative experts were unanimous against the idea but not long after General Miller, Alexander's brilliant Major General, Administration, saw his first demonstration of the D.U.K.W. Immediately he was completely sold on this amphibious lorry and decided that with its help we could risk beach maintenance for almost the whole of Seventh Army. He proposed that we should start off with nothing more than the ports of Syracuse, Augusta and Licata. Of these, Syracuse was the only proper port, and a small one at that; however as long as the weather remained fine, and it was likely to do so in July, the D.U.K.W. would probably see us through.

General Montgomery did not study the plan until 23rd April. When he did his observations were not very helpful. He telegraphed to Alexander on 24th April 'Planning so far has been based on the assumption that the opposition will be slight and that Sicily will be captured relatively easily. Never was there a greater error. The Germans and also the Italians are fighting desperately now in Tunisia and will do so in Sicily.' There are two points to note here. In the first place his study of the plan must have been very superficial if he could come to the conclusion that it was over-optimistic. In fact, as Alexander observes in his dispatch, the Joint Planning Staff took an unduly pessimistic view. They went so far as to state 'We are doubtful of the chances of success against a garrison which includes German formations,' a serious warning in view of the fact that they estimated that there would be at least two German divisions in Sicily when the time came to invade.

The fact is that Montgomery made a curious error about the assumptions concerning the enemy on which the plan was based. In *From El Alamein to the River Sangro* he says 'To my mind this was the vital point—the proposed plan was based on the existing enemy garrison in Sicily in early 1943 and assumed that the Axis powers would not reinforce the island before our invasion.' This is a very odd statement. Not merely is it incorrect, it is in the highest degree implausible. In all my experience of planners, I never knew any who underestimated the enemy strength. The invariable complaint was that they would seek to be on the safe side by overestimating. It would have been a very unusual collection of officers who went on record in January as saying that the enemy would not have reinforced Sicily at all by six months later in spite of our having occupied the whole of the shore opposite it. Fortunately there is no need to suppose anything so peculiar. What the planners in fact appreciated was as follows. In January 1943 there were in Sicily eight Italian divisions all told. Only three of these were normal field divisions; the other five were called coastal divisions and were divisions in name only. They were wholly static, being tied to fixed sectors of the coast, were only meant as delaying formations and consisted of low quality troops with a lower scale of equipment. They totalled about 40,000 men altogether, whereas the three infantry divisions came to about 60,000. The planners judged that the probable result of the Allied occupation of French North Africa would be to cause the Axis to reinforce Sicily with between three and five new divisions, two or three of which they expected to be German divisions. In other words, they calculated, leaving the coastal divisions out of the question, that the effective mobile garrison would be doubled or more than doubled. The usual figure which we worked on was that the mobile divisions would be raised to six Italian and two German, making a total of eight. In actual fact on D-Day the mobile garrison was four Italian and two German divisions.

It is fairly easy to see how Montgomery made his mistake, though since the planners expressed themselves perfectly explicitly it can only have arisen from a very hasty reading, and it is surprising that he did not correct his misapprehension later. The confusion obviously arises from the fact that the garrison in January was put at eight divisions (three mobile and five coastal) and that the planners later speak of a garrison on D-Day of eight divisions; but the latter were of course all mobile divisions and the total counting the coastal divisions would be thirteen. The correct total figure turned out to be eleven. The planners had therefore over-estimated by two.

The second misapprehension in this message from Montgomery appears in the third sentence. His principal argument for a change of plan was based in fact on a purely temporary phenomenon, the nature of the fighting on the Enfidaville line. As I mentioned in the last chapter the Italians were at that time putting up quite a good show. From this Montgomery deduced that they would do even better on their home ground. Fortunately the exact opposite turned out to be the case. The Italian military reputation in Africa had been patchy; in Sicily it was uniformly mediocre.

The final decision about the plan was made by Alexander on 3rd May. In his *Memoirs* Montgomery claims to have inspired this, though he naturally records that the decisive word, with Eisenhower's concurrence, was spoken by the Army Group Commander. To my mind, the principal factor was not so much the Eighth Army Commander's arguments as the assurance that we could rely on maintenance over the beaches. Once this was accepted Alexander thankfully reverted to his original conception of the attack.

There was, however, one further factor to be taken into consideration which did give Alexander some thought. The Americans under George Patton had been planning for some little time their assault on Palermo. They were now to be ordered to give up all this and turn to the study of a different piece of coastline altogether, involving a very different problem: not the capture of a major port but an assault over open beaches. In their new rôle, moreover, they looked much more like a mere flank guard to Montgomery's Eighth Army, and they must have had a lively suspicion that that was, in fact, just the rôle he was casting them for in his mind. Eighth Army was going to have the kudos of the advance up the east coast, straight on the objective, and would be likely to get most of the publicity by capturing places which people had heard of such as Syracuse and Catania. The fact that Alexander and Montgomery were not only both British but also closely associated hitherto might well render the approach to General Patton more awkward. These forebodings, however, proved false. General Patton never made a murmur at being forced to change his plans. In the first place the reason was that the American Army had a great tradition of exact obedience to orders. Their theory and practice have always been based closely on Prussian ideas ever since the time of General von Steuben, and an order is something to be obeyed without question. With Montgomery it was more in the nature of a basis for discussion or, as he describes one of Alexander's orders in his memoirs, 'a cry for help'. In the second place Patton was a man with a really fine strategic insight, and the considerations which had weighed with Alexander had weighed with him too. He cheerfully agreed to accept at the start what looked like a secondary rôle, doubtless feeling confident that his genius would give him the chance to outshine his fellow Army Commander later on. His confidence was not misplaced.

The Sicilian invasion has been so much overshadowed by subsequent events, and particularly, of course, by the decisive landing in Normandy a year later, that it tends to be forgotten what a great feat it was. On D-Day each of the two Armies put ashore four divisions and an airborne brigade. On D-Day for 'Overlord' only five divisions landed from the sea and two from the air; the subsequent rate of reinforcement was, of course, very much heavier, but so far as the assault is concerned 'Husky' was on a strictly comparable scale. Moreover for 'Overlord' the invading troops only had a short sea distance to cross; the distances involved in 'Husky' were much greater. Two of the British divisions came all the way from Suez in ships, transferring to landing craft off the beaches. A third started off from Tunisia in craft, some of which staged at Malta, half-way, while the rest went direct. They suffered severely from seasickness. The fourth of Eighth Army's assault divisions, the 1st Canadian Division, came all the way from Scotland in two convoys and flung themselves straight on Sicilian soil near Cape Passero. The four divisions in Seventh Army came from Bizerta, Algiers and Oran, but one of these, the 45th Division, had come direct from the U.S.A. in ships and merely staged at Oran. All this added to the fun from the planning point of view. Alexander's H.Q. moved up from Algiers to near Carthage. Patton's was first of all in Oran and then moved to Bizerta, and Montgomery's began in Cairo and moved forward to Malta for the assault. Just before the attack Alexander moved a small tactical H.Q. to Malta, to be alongside Admiral Cunningham's H.Q.

One story about the planning at Eighth Army H.Q. deserves repetition as an awful warning, though nothing serious came of it. At a planning conference in June, about a month before D-Day, a number of officers on Montgomery's H.Q. in Cairo were given a full account of the plan, not merely the army plan but the Army Group plan, in considerable detail. One of them decided not to trust his memory but made copious notes in a loose-leaf notebook. He was wearing his best gaberdine uniform for the conference and that afternoon he decided it was time to send it to the dry cleaners. Unfortunately he forgot to take his notebook out of his pocket before doing so and, properly remorseful, informed the Security Branch. They dashed round at once to the cleaner, an Egyptian who ran a small shop in the centre of Cairo. He produced the notebook at once. It appeared on inspection, however, that practically all the pages on which the invasion plan had been written out so carefully were missing; the last two remained, with some minor administrative details about medical matters. What had happened to the rest? The cleaner was quite frank. As the officer had written on only one side of each page he had used the blank side for making out his bills. As a result, the pages with the plan on them were distributed among about twenty clients up and down Cairo.

At the same time as the final plan was adopted the date was fixed for the 10th July. Following his invariable practice, Churchill had been pressing for a date in June; but it was certain that this would be impossible because we could not organize the ports in the Tunisian tip in time. The actual date was fixed by the moon. It did however leave a few more days than strictly necessary and so we decided that it would be a good idea to capture Pantellaria for our own use instead of merely denying it to the enemy. This, as it turned out, presented no difficulty at all. There was a time when Pantellaria was written up by the Italians, and believed by some people, to be a majestic and impregnable fortress stronger than Malta. A great deal of work had indeed gone into carving defensive positions and gun emplacements from the rock and there were even underground hangars for aircraft on the airfield. The enemy garrison was 11,000 odd, including less than 100 German air force technicians. We took the view, however, that Italian morale had probably been seriously affected by the bombardment which they had been suffering and so indeed it proved to be. The bombardment from the air was intensified and towards the end of the preparatory period the Mediterranean fleet joined in the shoot as well; but it seemed to us vital at least to show the garrison an assault force in the offing ready to make a regular attack. A brigade of the 1st British Division was accordingly brought to the spot in ships. The plan was that they would transfer into craft and rush for the only possible landing place, which was right inside the harbour and likely to be strongly defended.

However, no sooner had the defenders seen the troops getting into their craft from their ships, than the white flag was hoisted. The garrison were very helpful in assisting the detachment which then landed to take over, guiding them round the numerous obstacles. A broadcast by the commander just before the surrender laid the blame on shortage of water but this fortunately proved exaggerated.

The capitulation was on 11th June and over the next two days the neighbouring islands of the Pelagian group, Lampedusa and Linosa, also surrendered. Lampedusa had a fair-sized garrison; it surrendered to the pilot of a Fleet Air Arm aircraft who had been forced to land on its airfield owing to shortage of fuel.

For the first stage of the assault on Sicily it was essential for the Army H.Q. to be close to the Naval H.Q. Admiral Cunningham insisted on setting up the latter on Malta so Alexander moved a small H.Q. there also. Malta was an exhilarating place. It was still heavily scarred by the marks of bombardment but the sight of the troops and the officers of the various H.Q.'s swaggering about on land, and the landing craft piling up in the harbour, gave promise of hitting back vigorously. Lord Gort was Governor and C.-in-C., a delightfully courteous, boyish and intrepid figure. Lord Louis Mountbatten was also on the island to observe on behalf of Combined Operations H.Q. how his various plans would work out in practice. There was a bright feeling of confidence everywhere. I remember particularly standing by the bastion of Naval H.Q. above the Grand Harbour and being told by Alexander, as a great secret, that approaches had been made by various Italian commanders in the Balkans to see whether there was any chance of their being allowed to change sides and join us. The capitulation of Italy was already in the air.

Among the interesting characters on Malta was John Gunther, the author of a number of books which I had read with admiration. He was representing, under a peculiar pooling arrangement, the whole of the American press and he was accompanied by journalist Frank Gilling who represented the whole of the British press. Gunther later on wrote a book about his experience, in which to my surprise I make a brief appearance. Nevertheless it is rather a good book. It had an inspired title—'D-Day'—because by a stroke of luck it appeared almost immediately after D-Day for 'Overlord' and everyone thought it referred to that. For a journalist's book it is extremely sensible because unpretentious. One good reason for liking it is that, writing of Alexander, he says: 'When he left I had the strong and durable feeling once more that this is one of the finest men I have ever met.' I did not come off quite so well myself. Although described as 'amazingly learned' I am said to breeze into Army Group H.Q. before lunch 'having just been briefed by the Intelligence staff'. It seemed a bit hard. I admit the briefing was usually just before lunch but I would have done at least seven hours' work already and I was the Intelligence staff, dash it.

All this time the Intelligence picture of Sicily was developing in a pretty normal way. Our deception plan was obviously going quite well. Sardinia and southern Greece were getting the major share of the reinforcements but things were moving also in Sicily in a mild way. An extra Italian field division had arrived shortly before the fall of Tunis. The Germans were slower to provide reinforcements but by late June they had the equivalent of two divisions there. We were now trying to draw their attention to the west end of Sicily as opposed to the southeast. In this we were being fairly successful, in fact at the moment we landed at the east end of the island one of the four German battle groups was moving hastily westwards in response to a fancied threat, simulated by a naval bombardment of Trapani. We calculated the enemy forces to amount to 315,000 Italians and 50,000 Germans; 40,000 more Germans arrived in the course of the campaign but no more Italians. The commander was the 66-year-old General Guzzoni who had spent the last two and a half years on the retired list on which he was placed because of failure in Albania. He had only recently taken over from General Roatta. Roatta was a much better equipped man intellectually but was distrusted, with good reason, by Mussolini.

On the afternoon of the 9th July the various convoys from all the ends of the Mediterranean began to assemble off southeastern Sicily. All in all there were nearly 3,000 ships and landing craft. By some fantastic fortune they were not spotted by enemy air reconnaissance. The weather however was bad. A sudden storm blew up. Admiral Cunningham was of the opinion that it would subside and he turned out to be right. It actually was an advantage to us in two ways. First of all it convinced the Italians that at any rate we should not try to land that night, and secondly, on the American beaches, it helped the assault craft over some of the off-lying sand bars which we had feared might hamper their access to the beaches. The gale did contribute, however, to the comparative failure of the airborne assault. On the night of the 9th I went down to Cape Delimara, the southeastern cape of Malta, which was one of the turning points on the course of the airborne formations.

Also on the same spot were Alexander and Eisenhower; the latter (I learn from Gunther) 'fingered some lucky coins he always carries, one silver dollar, one five guinea piece and one French franc and murmured Godspeed as the planes whipped overhead'. It was an impressive sight. These were all glider-borne troops of the British 1st Airborne Division whose job it was to seize a vital bridge on the approaches to Syracuse and hold it until the northernmost formation of Eighth Army, 5th Infantry Division, could come up and cross it. The gliders were towed by American pilots in Dakotas and the wind increased the difficulty. The last change of course for the towing aircraft took them due west across the coast into the teeth of the gale. It also took them into a storm of anti-aircraft fire to which the pilots of the towing aircraft were quite unaccustomed since they had no previous experience of actual operations. The result was that a great many of them, for one reason or the other, slipped the tow too soon. Out of 134 gliders nearly 50 came down in the sea, about 75 came safely to land somewhere in southeast Sicily and only 12 landed in the planned dropping zone. Out of these 12 glider loads only 8 officers and 65 men reached and seized the bridge itself. They had to hold out by themselves until 3.30 in the afternoon and were relieved by the 5th Division at the last minute when they were down to 19 men. The American parachute troops dropped ahead of Seventh Army's landing had this much better fortune in that at least all of them came down on land; but they were spread from hell to breakfast all over southeastern Sicily, hardly any of them in the right place. However, the general effect was gratifyingly demoralizing on the none too steady Italian troops, because it meant that small groups of determined men were seizing vital points and ambushing roads at hundreds of different places.

Apart from the airborne troops the rest of the operation went better than could ever have been expected. The Italian coastal divisions, who were the first troops encountered, showed little constancy, but they were lavishly equipped and they fired off all their weapons with great gusto. In spite of this 13th Corps made good its initial bridgehead to a depth sufficient to cover the coast road and then, turning to its right, advanced on and captured Syracuse. The Americans on the south coast had greater difficulty in landing because their beaches were exposed to the full force of the gale, but once ashore they had no difficulty in capturing all the objectives ordered for the first day. Next day Eighth Army continued to push up the east coast road, though more slowly; Seventh Army had to meet a violent counter attack by German troops. It lasted all day before it was beaten off, thanks in large measure to the vigorous personal part played by General Patton and assisted by heavy naval gunfire whose effect was a happy augury for future amphibious operations.

By the morning of the 13th Eighth Army had captured Augusta and Seventh Army had seized all the numerous airfields in their sector. General Montgomery was now full of an effervescent confidence which for a time took the place of his usual caution. In a message to Alexander on the evening of the 12th he said that he would capture Catania on the 16th, but he wanted plenty of elbow room to develop his manoeuvre in this direction. He accordingly asked Alexander to alter the boundary between him and Patton so that Patton's efforts should be directed off westwards and there would be no danger of his getting in the way of Montgomery's thrust. He pressed this so strongly that Alexander agreed, somewhat against his better judgment, and, as it turned out, unfortunately. It was rather a blow to the Americans to have the inter-army boundary drawn of a sudden slanting across their front. It meant that the 45th Division, which was thrusting north, had to halt in its tracks and mark time. It was out of the battle until it could be switched round behind its neighbouring division to the left. The motive for the new boundary was monumentally clear to the Americans and it required a good deal of tact on Alexander's part to smooth down their feelings. All would no doubt have been well if Eighth Army had been able to live up to their commander's optimistic forecast. Unfortunately, mainly because the Germans were now reinforcing with parachute troops brought in by air, they got held up right on the edge of the plain of Catania. These German troops were in fact my old acquaintances of the 7th Air Division who had invaded Crete. They were in France on D-Day near Tarascon, engaged in the process of splitting into two new divisions, the 1st and 2nd Parachute Divisions. Although they were transported by air to Sicily they were not dropped as parachutists but went into action as infantry on the ground; in their proper and original rôle they were never used again after Crete.

As a result of this reinforcement Eighth Army was held up from 15th July until 3rd August. Seventh Army, on the other hand, after they had recovered from the disorganization caused by the change in their axis of advance, made active and dashing progress. The Germans were hastily withdrawing all their forces to the east to resist Eighth Army's attack on Catania. The position became very like that in the second month of 'Overlord', when the British held the majority of the German forces in battle near Caen and allowed the Americans to break round one flank in a wide sweeping encirclement. This was a manoeuvre very welcome to General Patton. He formed a provisional Corps H.Q. to which he assigned the reduction of the west end of the island, and with his other corps H.Q. he pressed on to the centre of the island and thence to the north coast. Progress was so good that on 20th July Alexander ordered Patton to turn eastward on reaching the north coast and operate against the enemy on the other side of Mount Etna. In Montgomery's original plan Eighth Army was to have attacked on both sides of the mountain. In order to support this operation Patton was ordered to capture Palermo as early as possible and he seized it in fact on the evening of the 22nd July, only twelve days after the original landing. On the next day the American 2nd Corps cut the north coast road east of Termini Imeresi. There was much more marching than fighting involved in this but the marching was bad enough, for the heat of Sicily was really sweltering, far worse than anything experienced in Africa.

The capture of Palermo reminds me of an incident which illustrates American staff methods and to some extent the social life of New York. I should explain that in the American Army the responsibility for all signals lies with the Adjutant General of the respective H.Q. They are rather formidable documents to those used to the more easy-going British style, as they start with an elaborate set of reference symbols and end with the commander's signature. Every signal we received from Allied Force H.Q. ended with the words 'Signed Eisenhower', although in fact in the vast majority of cases neither he nor any senior officer of his staff had ever seen them.

Somewhere about D-Day minus 1, when we were fairly keyed up, a signal arrived 'Signed Eisenhower', in something like the following terms: 'ANXIOUS TO HAVE EARLIEST POSSIBLE NEWS OF WHEREABOUTS OF COUNTESS OF X ADDRESS PALAZZO, X PALERMO.' At the time Palermo seemed a long way away and we were worrying more about getting on shore; however Seventh Army was obviously the more likely to reach Palermo first so I had the telegram sent on, by letter mail, to their Intelligence Branch. On D plus 1 we received another signal in similar terms, which I threw into the wastepaper basket. Another a few days later was also sent by mail. I began to realise that the Countess must have some powerful friends somewhere and I began to wonder what she would turn out to be like. When operations became fluid, more signals, all professedly breathing General Eisenhower's personal anxiety, began to pour in; and when Seventh Army actually captured Palermo there was one which ran: 'UNABLE UNDERSTAND YOUR PERSISTENT REFUSAL TO INDICATE WHEREABOUTS AND WELFARE COUNTESS OF X, SEE MY SIGNALS NUMBERS . . . REPORT AT ONCE STEPS BEING TAKEN TO COMPLY. SIGNED EISENHOWER.'

I thought this was going rather far, in fact for the first time was stung into retaliation. The Countess's name had, as you may suppose, been often on our lips in the past week or so and had indeed formed the theme of a number of verses. Selecting the least offensive I composed a signal in the form of a limerick which ended (after references to a number of improbable means which had allegedly been employed in her pursuit) as follows:

'AM CONTINUING SEARCH STOP MEANWHILE WILL ANY OTHER WOMAN DO QUERY

SIGNED ALEXANDER.'

This signal, unlike the rest of the series, by some means was brought to General Eisenhower's attention. He thought it revealed a situation that might be worth investigating and I heard later what was behind it all. There was, it appears, a prominent member of New York Café Society, the Count of X; the Countess was his mother and he was very properly anxious about her. He had a friend in the Adjutant General's office of the War Department in Washington and this friend, a second lieutenant I think, had been castigating Allied Force H.Q. with a series of signals, no doubt 'signed Marshall'. The A.G.'s branch in Algiers had unimaginatively passed the signals on as a matter of routine. Eisenhower was amused; but asked the War Department to have a look at the A.G.'s branch.

Three or four days after the capture of Palermo Seventh Army eventually reported, rather resentfully, that the Palazzo X had been bombed but that it had located the Countess who was staying with Baron Y; they added that she was well and happy. This enabled us to finish the correspondence with a final telegram:

'COUNTESS OF X DISCOVERED LIVING WITH BARON Y IN GOOD SPIRITS'

By the end of July we had seized the whole of the island except the long isosceles triangle of the northeast corner, with Etna at the centre of its short side. Eighth Army had inched forward in the Catania plain and had advanced its left flank to keep level with Seventh Army on its north. On 3rd August the final advance began. General Patton kept four divisions going on the two parallel roads running eastward. His plan was to use one regiment at a time on each axis for no more than two days and then pass in turn the other two regiments into the lead, followed in turn by the three regiments of the second division. This continuous use of fresh troops must have imposed an intolerable strain on the German defenders. By this time there were four German divisions in this area; there were a few Italians still there but they were not playing a very large part. Eighth Army also had only a narrow strip of land on which to work. It broke through to Mount Etna on the 4th and captured Catania on the 5th August. Seventh Army was by now helping itself forward by small amphibious operations brilliantly planned and hastily mounted. General Montgomery tried a landing in the same style on the night of the 15th August but unfortunately it was a very short hook which landed between the German rearguards and our advanced guards and got involved in a brief fight with the latter. On the next night, 16th August, the leading troops of General Patton's Army entered Messina and the German commander, General Huber, left in the last boat to leave the island. The conquest of Sicily had taken only 38 days.

Army Group H.Q. moved over to the island soon after D-Day. We set up in a grove of almond trees at Cassibile south of Syracuse. Cassibile was the place where the Athenian expedition to Sicily met its final disaster, the turning point in the Peloponnesian war. I had ordered a copy of Thucydides in good time for our Sicilian expedition and it arrived while I was there. The dramatic and tragic tale made a good contrast with our triumphal feelings, though the ruins of the gliders of the airborne expedition lying in the sea just south of Syracuse where we went to bathe were more reminiscent of the wrecks of the Athenian galleys defeated in the great naval battle in the harbour. Sicily was not very popular with the troops. It was intolerably hot and injudicious indulgence in tomatoes brought on dysentery on a large scale. One thing that struck the troops with amusement was the fantastic number of painted slogans on the houses. I was fairly well used to this undignified Fascist habit from visits to Italy before the war; but in Sicily in 1943 it was carried to ridiculous lengths. Every single house in every village had at least one slogan in large letters. They seemed also to have got rather longer than I remembered them. Mussolini's favourite aphorism about it being better to live one day as a lion than a hundred years as a sheep was still well in evidence, but in addition there were long verbatim extracts from his speeches. All this in black letters at least a foot high gave a very bizarre effect. I remember particularly well the small town of Villosmunda, in which every house on each side of the road was decorated in this way. The last house bore the slogan: 'Poche parole—molti fatti'—few words, many deeds.

CHAPTER XII

The Purpose and Planning of the Italian Campaign

THE invasion of Sicily had been the subject of long and detailed planning for something like six months in advance. Italy was done much more off the cuff. There was indeed a whole world of difference not merely in the way in which we set about the next task, but in the very nature of that task itself. The fact was, and we soon began to realize it, that from the moment the last German soldier left Sicily we of the Allied Forces in the Mediterranean were no longer the spearhead of the war effort on land. From now on the weight was going to be transferred to northwest Europe. All this was finally decided at the Trident Conference, which met in Washington in May 1943. Here it was laid down that for the future the Mediterranean was to be a secondary theatre, its only task that of helping the main assault which was to be from the United Kingdom on to North France in the early summer of 1944.

The results of this decision were at once apparent. The Supreme Commander was ordered to prepare to transfer back to the United Kingdom eight of his best divisions, four British and four American. He was also warned that the necessary equipment for amphibious warfare, ships, landing craft and so on, would be gradually cut down in order to concentrate them in the new theatre. However, not all the forces then available in the Mediterranean would be required to come home; in fact the eight divisions earmarked, about a third of the total Allied Forces available there, represented the maximum number that could be brought back to Britain in time to take part in the operation. It was therefore necessary to find something for the remainder to do. This something must make a direct contribution to the great design for 1944. Accordingly the Supreme Allied Commander in the Mediterranean was instructed 'to plan such operations in exploitation of the conquest of Sicily as would be best calculated to eliminate

Italy from the war and to contain the maximum number of German Divisions.'

No discussion of the Italian campaign can be firmly based if it does not start from the realization that it was, from its beginning right to its end, a holding attack. Its aim was to draw German strength away from the Channel coast. Both parts of the directive from the Combined Chiefs of Staff bear on the same object. If Italy was eliminated from the war the Germans would be short of fifty-nine divisions. Admittedly they were not very good divisions, and some of their commanders were already thinking the time had come to change sides. Nevertheless they were playing a vital rôle in the German deployment because they were acting as garrisons over a large area. For example there were no less than thirty-two Italian divisions in the Balkans, and seven were guarding the southern coast of France from the Italian border to Marseilles. If all these troops were suddenly removed from the board the Germans would have to find troops of their own to take their place, for, even though fewer Germans would no doubt suffice, these important areas could not be left entirely unguarded. Then, having thus forced the Germans to lock up more troops in garrisons, the second part of the directive ordered us to bring them to battle at a place of our selection in such a way as to use up their strength as much as possible and divert as many of them as possible from the Channel coast.

The directive from the Combined Chiefs of Staff did not say where or when these diversionary battles were to be fought. It merely concluded by saying that which of the operations should be adopted and thereafter mounted would be decided by them. The fact that the ensuing operations actually had Italy for a theatre was not therefore based on the fact that our troops were by that time sitting in Messina within three miles of the Italian mainland. They might have been anywhere else in the Mediterranean area, for there was a wider gap between the campaigns in Sicily and in Italy than was represented by the narrow Messina straits. The conquest of Sicily had been part, the last part, of the campaigns in Africa. Its object was to crown the liberation of the African shores by opening a through passage through the Mediterranean to allied shipping. It was the last chapter of a volume which opened on the 10th June, 1940. A completely new volume was now being opened, in which the main theme might have been written in the Balkans or in the Italian islands or in the south of Greece.

If I have thus emphasized the nature of the strategic break between Sicily and Italy it is because many people still misunderstand the nature of the Italian campaign. 'Why,' they say, 'Italy was purely a secondary theatre.' So it was. It is the nature of diversionary attacks to operate in secondary theatres. Southern and central Italy were a long way away from the centres of German power. To pin down German troops there would therefore contribute all the more to the success of the attack in France. There were good reasons against the other possible theatres open to us in the Mediterranean. From the map it looks an easy and obvious thing to seize successively Sardinia and Corsica and to threaten from there the south of France. One war correspondent, indeed, complained that it was precisely because this course was so obvious that its advantages were overlooked by General Alexander. In fact an operation to seize Sardinia was studied at length. It was at one time rather a favourite of General Mark Clark, Commander designate of the American Fifth Army. A plan existed, given the code name 'Brimstone', and it seemed clear that we should run little risk of failure. Alexander, however, never cared for it. In the first place it seemed to have little to offer towards fulfilling our directive. The capture of Sicily would probably not remove Italy from the war and there seemed no reason why the capture of Sardinia in addition should do so. Obviously it would not hold down many German troops, because not many could be sent to the island or maintained there. The stepping-stone idea was also more apparent—on small-scale maps—than real. Each separate assault would require a large number of landing craft, of which we were going to get shorter and shorter, and of course the final step from Corsica across to the Riviera could not possibly be made until the summer of 1944. It would undoubtedly be of great assistance to the invasion of northern France to be able to threaten an invasion of southern France as well at the same time; but the threat was not required until the time of the actual operation which we already knew could not be earlier than May 1944 and would probably turn out to be in June. Up till then it would be better, if we could, to draw German troops away from France rather than to attract additional ones into it. Meanwhile for the next nearly twelve months we should be fighting very few German troops in the islands, giving the remainder a welcome respite and only putting to useful employment a small part of our troops.

Our view at Alexander's H.Q. was therefore that although the capture of Sardinia and Corsica was possible, and might be useful, it was not good enough for our main effort. We also felt fairly sure that if we landed on the mainland in Italy and made good progress

Sardinia certainly, and probably Corsica as well, would fall into our hands anyway. 'Brimstone' was therefore kept on as a planning exercise, but we hoped we would not be reduced to having to mount it. As things turned out no formal operation was called for beyond a rather hastily organized and purely French affair in Corsica which harassed, but did not notably accelerate, a German withdrawal which they had already decided to make.

The third course was to go for the Balkans. As far as I personally was concerned nothing could have given me greater pleasure than to take part in the liberation of Greece. There were certain obvious advantages. Everywhere in Greece and Jugoslavia we should have had the whole-hearted support of the local population and they had already shown that even by themselves they were capable of keeping the Germans on the stretch. We should certainly have tied down a large number of German troops, possibly even more than in Italy. For some reason Hitler attached much greater importance to retaining the Balkans than to retaining Italy. He demonstrated this right up to the end of the war when he was still making desperate efforts to retain his position in Croatia. Moreover his famous intuition had told him that we were more likely to attack the Balkans than Italy—his intuition had of course been assisted by the carefully prepared documents found on the body of the bogus marine. So all in all there is no doubt that we should have been able to tie down plenty of German troops in the Balkans, and of course they would then have been even further away from France than in Italy. Whether an invasion of the Balkans would knock Italy out of the war was much more questionable. The value of their military support would without doubt have decreased still further but, with the homeland intact and with no Allied Forces in the neighbourhood to surrender to, the Italian Government would probably have jogged along in much the same way as they had done hitherto.

As far as we were concerned the military reasons against the Balkan expedition were decisive. It would be a difficult operation and, above all, it would take too long. Amphibious power gives great opportunities, but in the year 1943 we were still tied by the range of land-based fighters. We could not invade the mainland of Greece without air cover and therefore it would first be necessary to seize air bases in the outer ring of islands from Crete to Rhodes. This would require a separate operation of its own so that at least two amphibious landings would be necessary. The second could not be mounted until an advanced date in the autumn, when the weather round the southern coasts of Greece is at its worst. The terrain of Greece is even more difficult than that of Italy, and although no doubt operations on land can be assisted by seaborne operations even more readily than in Italy, this was small consolation since our resources in landing craft were meant to dwindle away for the benefit of 'Overlord'. There was quite a chance therefore of our finding ourselves blocked somewhere in the Peloponnese. There was also one other strong reason against a Balkan campaign; the Americans were firmly opposed to it. They thought then, and many of them think to this day, that Churchill was determined to inveigle them into a Balkan campaign for some undefined but certainly dubious political purpose. This suspicion was firmly shared by Roosevelt and Eisenhower. It was not in fact justified. I have heard Sir Winston himself declare with a chuckle, and I am aware of the evidence that supports him, that he never had any intention of proposing a proper campaign either in Greece or in Jugoslavia. What he did want was for us to push on in Italy sufficiently to pass a force through the Ljubljana gap in northwestern Jugoslavia into the plains of Hungary.

So, by elimination, we returned to peninsular Italy. It had positive merits as well. Obviously the best way of fulfilling the first part of the directive, to eliminate Italy from the war, was to land in the country and see how much of it we had to occupy before the Italian Government surrendered. We thought it might not be necessary to go very far for this purpose. As far as containing the maximum number of German divisions went, Italy was certainly as good as, if not better than, the Balkans and definitely better than the islands. It was only just across the way from Sicily and we should probably have enough landing craft for one landing elsewhere so as to enable us to kick off a little further north. If so we should not have very far to go to the large complex of airfields near Foggia which the Air Force thought they could put to excellent use for bombing targets in southern Germany inaccessible from the U.K. If we got into the Po Valley we should be better off still for airfields. Italian industrial production was not on a particularly high level, but at least Italy was the most industrialized of all Germany's allies and could make a useful contribution to her war economy.

Of course there could be no doubt about the disadvantages of a campaign in Italy. First and foremost among them was the terrain. Many people who have written on the campaign appear to think that it was only after we had landed in Italy that the mountainous nature of the country was realized by the Allied Command. Why it should be supposed that people who have given their lives to the art of war are incapable of reading a map can only be attributed once more to the influence of Colonel Blimp, or perhaps of Lloyd George's views about Haig. Possibly Churchill's remark about 'the soft underbelly of the Axis' may be responsible. This vivid figure, inspired by a drawing of a crocodile which he did for Stalin's benefit, was not meant to suggest that a campaign in Italy or the Balkans would be a military promenade. Its principal meaning was that the fixed defences on the shores of the Mediterranean nowhere approached the complexity of the Western Wall constructed along the Channel and Atlantic coasts of Europe, and that there were fewer German troops, and those less concentrated, in the Mediterranean area; there was also the obvious fact that the target area was bigger and the possibility of help from local resistance forces greater.

Having decided on peninsular Italy, the next stage was fairly easy —as it usually is in planning. Take a pair of compasses, extend them to a distance representing 180 miles and then, placing one leg on the northeastern tip of Sicily, describe an arc across the Italian peninsula. Somewhere inside that area the target for your landing must be chosen, for 180 miles represented the maximum range of our standard land-based fighters. No other targets need apply. We had all had enough of fighting without air cover when it could not be helped, to want to try it again when it was not necessary. Inside this area we could put ashore, assuming the normal chances of war, two corps plus whatever we could ferry across the Straits of Messina. We could also drop one airborne division. This, it will be agreed, is not a very strong hand for an aggressive-minded general to have to play. Moreover there were, when planning started, a number of important questions to which the answer was far from plain. First of all, what shape were our forces going to be in after the battles in Sicily? Secondly, and even more important, what shape were the landing craft going to be in? Thirdly, what sort of fight would the Italians put up in defence of their home ground?

General Montgomery, after his experience in Tunisia, took a rather gloomy view and was all for caution. His idea was to use two corps just to secure Calabria, the toe of the boot, and to make it a deliberate set-piece attack of the kind for which he was most distinguished. Until we could see how things were going in Sicily this idea had to stand, though many of us at Alexander's H.Q. were afraid that it would result in our getting held up at one of the isthmuses across the toe. This plan left one, American, Corps available for other possibilities and it was natural that we should turn our eyes to them. The arc with the radius of 180 miles cuts through the island of Capri, crosses the west coast just north of Salerno and comes out in the Gulf of Taranto, short of the heel and about 15 miles short of Taranto itself. Both Naples and Taranto were most desirable objectives. Naples in particular was a port capable of maintaining any forces we could put ashore in Italy. Taranto was a great naval base. Both of them were of course heavily defended and could not possibly be attacked direct; but if we could risk a landing at the extreme limit of our range it would be worth while to get as near to them as possible and hope for the best. However, before Husky had even begun it was premature to be too sanguine. The last pre-Husky Intelligence appreciation was that the Calabrian assault must be carried out, probably as a set-piece attack, and only in the event of an Italian collapse could more optimistic possibilities be considered. The view was that Italian morale, both civilian and military, was then low and would deteriorate further if Sicily was lost but that there was no organized body of opinion which was prepared to seize power and force a surrender. This of course turned out to be, strictly speaking, incorrect, though correct enough in the sense in which it was intended. The planners at Allied Force H.Q. were considering the movements of popular feeling and came to the conclusion that the main feature was apathy. The overthrow of Mussolini and the Italian change of sides were due to a small, almost anonymous, group of conspirators, nearly all soldiers, of whose existence we had no idea. It is only fair to our planners to say that the Germans were also taken completely by surprise by the event. It all goes to prove that the only safe conspiracies are those where the secret is kept to a very small circle. However, I shall be dealing with this subject later; for the present the point is that Allied Force H.Q. did not expect the collapse of the regime. If there were a collapse, a term which they did not define, they considered that our aim should be to pass a small force as rapidly as possible across country to seize Naples. It would have to be small because of the nature of the country and the difficulties of maintenance; but after Naples had been seized it could of course be opened to seaborne reinforcement. The real conclusion was that we must wait and see what happened in Husky.

The main lesson of Husky was that the Italians could pretty well be disregarded even when fighting on their native soil. It also brought full reassurance about the validity of our amphibious technique and made it clear that we should be able to capture Sicily without suffering serious losses in men or in landing craft. These were gratifying answers to our questions and the planners picked up their pencils and slide rules again with avidity. As a matter of fact we thought at one time, about two days after the Husky landings, when Eighth Army got the idea that they would be able to dash up the east coast of Sicily in the inside of a week, of letting them carry on first bounce, as it were, into Calabria, using Catania as a base, and sending 78th Division which, on this hypothesis, would not be required in Sicily. However, cold feet followed this burst of enthusiasm when German reinforcements kept us out of Catania, and it became obvious that we would have to clear Sicily before we could land in Calabria. Nevertheless things were obviously better and the next planning conference which took place at Carthage on 17th July marked a distinct step forward. Alexander, Eisenhower, Cunningham and Tedder agreed to study a whole range of possible courses. First of all they thought that operations in Calabria could now be carried out in the form of a quick exploitation across the straits of Messina without having to resort to elaborate preparations or too great concentration of forces. Secondly, they decided to plan a large-scale operation against Taranto. This was given the code name 'Musket' and was to be carried out by Fifth Army with two corps, assuming that they had sufficient landing craft left by then. Finally, thoughts turned once more, and this time hopefully, towards Naples. An amphibious landing still seemed out of the question; but operation 'Gangway' contemplated pushing a force across country from Calabria to seize the port from the land. It would only be possible if the Italian forces were disintegrating and if the Germans withdrew to avoid getting caught too far south. Formal planning would obviously have to concentrate on Taranto.

The final deciding factor was the sudden and startling announcement of the fall of Mussolini on 25th July. I was bathing near Carthage when I heard the news, feeling full of classical allusions. True we were going to invade Italy at the opposite end from Hannibal, but it was impossible to avoid thinking of history's revenges. I went on to reflect on Silius Italicus who wrote an excruciatingly dull epic poem on the Hannibalian campaign about which the only fact I could remember was that according to him Hannibal was accompanied by a soothsayer, whose advice he always took, by the name of Bogus. The parallel with the Intelligence staff seemed too close.

The actual mechanism by which the fall of Mussolini took place has been often described. It was a small conspiracy led by Acquarone from the Palace and Badoglio and Ambrosio representing the Army; they cunningly made use of a group of discontented or frightened fascists led by Grandi with the adhesion of Ciano. The trouble about small conspiracies is that, though efficient, they allow no scope for planning to be continued beyond a given point. The follow-through is difficult. This was certainly the case here; so little active planning had been given to the more remote future that Badoglio found himself obliged to declare in his first broadcast that the war would continue. However, in spite of these brave words it did not strike us as being a very likely result. We felt fairly confident that it would not be long before some-one came forward officially from the Italian side with proposals for a capitulation. In the circumstances it was obviously reasonable to plan on a more optimistic and daring basis. The Supreme Commanders met next day, the 26th July, at Carthage. All were agreed that greater risks might now legitimately be taken. As a result an order was issued to General Clark commanding the American 5th Army to prepare plans for seizing the port of Naples 'with a view to preparing a firm base for further offensive operations'. The code name Avalanche was allotted to this assault.

General Clark was told that he must submit his plan in outline by 7th August and that the target date for the assault would be the 7th September. This turned out to be nearly a month after all enemy resistance had ceased in Sicily. This apparent delay was found in-explicable by many self-appointed military commentators at the time and a variety of explanations were concocted to explain it. The most popular theme was that we had wasted time haggling with the Italians over the precise meaning of 'unconditional surrender'. It is a dis-illusioning result of being on the inside of important events that one learns that the simple explanation is almost always the right one. Perhaps this is not quite fair; amphibious operations are not simple. The ruling facts in this case were, first of all, that we should have no troops to spare until we had finished in Sicily because every available division was committed there, including the two reserve divisions, the U.S. 9th and the British 78th. There were other divisions which could be made available in due course but they had been deliberately given second priority to the Husky divisions and were not up to strength in men or equipment. No doubt they could have been used if it was really essential to do something in a hurry, but for a second and even more vital factor: there were no craft to convey them in. All the craft we had were still working on the maintenance of the troops in Sicily. The best estimate that the Naval staff could give was that the first week in September was the earliest time by which enough of them would be available and serviceable to transport a sea-borne force of three divisions. Even this presupposed no unusual losses in the interval. This was the really decisive factor in settling the date; a subsidiary one was the fact that the moon would be at its most suitable between 7th and 10th September.

The strategic aspect was fairly clear. Avalanche would have to be an army show because it was a good way in advance of our present positions and would have to be in as great force as we could manage. Accordingly Fifth Army was to have two corps, 6th U.S. Corps organized as for the Sardinian operation and 10th British Corps organized as for the Calabrian landing. A slight complication was that it was not certain that 10th Corps would not have to do the landing at Reggio so the Corps staff had to prepare two operational plans and make sure that their loading tables and 'Q' arrangements would fit either. The purpose of Avalanche was to capture Naples in order to allow us to use it to build up as large a force as possible on the Italian mainland. This was reckoned to be, by the process of argument I have already outlined, the best method of carrying out our directive.

The tactics were laid down by the order directing that the landing should be made in the Gulf of Salerno. There has been some controversy about this choice of objective since and I think it deserves a word or two of explanation. The Gulf of Salerno provides a continuous strip of beach twenty miles long. The shore is flat and troops and vehicles can drive straight inland from practically any point on the twenty miles. The offshore approaches are excellent with underwater gradients varying from 1 : 40 to 1 : 80. This means that landing craft can run right up on to the beach and land the troops without any difficulty. In fact, from the point of view of the seaborne assault, this is the finest strip of coast in the whole of Italy, perhaps anywhere in the Mediterranean. There is always a snag somewhere, however; in this case the trouble is that the coastal plain at this point is hemmed in by mountains, and to the north there is a particular rocky and difficult spur of the Monti Picentini which cuts across the road from Salerno to Naples. It was clear that we were likely to get ashore quickly, and incidentally to seize a useful airfield which was just inland from the beaches, but that we should have some real fighting to do before we could break through into the plain of Naples. These geographical facts were naturally obvious to anyone who could read a map. Two distinguished commanders accordingly thought that a much better place for landing was north of Naples in the coastal plain of the Volturno. I refer to General Clark and Field Marshal Kesselring. This plain is one of the few places on the whole of the west coast of Italy which is not dominated by mountains. There is good level ground, excellently adapted for the use of armour, and an easy run on the flat to Naples. The beaches are not so good, in fact some of them have awkward sandbars lying off them. On the other hand, from the point of view of a Staff College exercise, the strategic advantages are obvious because it would put us in the rear of all the German forces from Naples southwards. These arguments convinced Kesselring that this is where we should land, and the first two divisions coming out of Sicily that he could lay his hands on were accordingly directed there. General Clark also began by strongly favouring this alternative. There was, however, one decisive argument against it; it was well out of range of fighter cover. This was what weighed with Alexander. There could be no doubt that he was right to let this reason prevail. Avalanche had some very tricky moments as it was, but if it had been fought with the enemy enjoying air superiority it would inevitably have failed.

Nobody considered the possibility of sailing straight into the Bay of Naples. The Navy would not hear of it. The whole area was sown with minefields, booms and net barrages and covered with fixed coastal defences. There were more than forty heavy calibre guns in permanent positions. There was indeed one war correspondent who favoured this solution; he assured me earnestly that he had visited Naples on a cruise and that it had excellent harbour facilities for discharging men and material. Our tanks, he said, would find the Marine Parade very convenient for forming up. General Montgomery, at one stage of planning, proposed that Fifth Army should land a good deal further south so as to give greater assistance to Eighth Army. As we already considered that Eighth Army's advance through Calabria was likely to be opposed only by small rearguards Alexander thought that this would be wasteful over-insuring.

General Clark duly presented his plan—at enormous length incidentally—and the final decisions on the invasion were taken at a

Commanders-in-Chief Conference at Carthage on 16th August. It was decided to go ahead with Avalanche and General Montgomery was firmly told that he would have to make do with one corps which would still give him a more than satisfactory margin of superiority over his opponents. Avalanche was to have two corps, but only three divisions in the assault plus an airborne division. It cannot be denied that the plan was a pretty bold one. To land three divisions on a hostile coast at the extreme limit of air cover and well out of touch with the rest of our forces was a courageous stroke in any event and the more so when we take into account the strength of the enemy opposing us. To begin with there were something like twenty Italian divisions. We were shortly to be able to write these off altogether as a result of the capitulation, and even before that we did not allow them to exercise an undue weight in reckoning the odds; but there were, by the time the decision for Avalanche was taken, already eighteen German divisions in Italy including five armoured divisions. It was going to take us until December before we could get eighteen divisions into the country. Finally, just to add to the risk, our air cover was not as certain as all that because the bulk of the fighters would be based on Milazzo in northeastern Sicily, where a number of airfields had been rather hastily extemporized. Heavy rain would render them unserviceable, and there is no month in Italy in which heavy rain does not occur.

At the same time as the orders were issued for Avalanche, that is on the 16th August, final orders were issued to Eighth Army for their part. This was given the code name 'Baytown'. It was a simple operation, to be carried out by a single corps, 13th Corps, with two divisions, 1st Canadian and 5th British. They were, however, to be given a fine send off by the massed artillery of the whole of Eighth Army plus four American batteries of medium guns and with two battleships, three cruisers, three monitors, two gun boats and six destroyers joining in to thicken up the barrage and as a token of the Navy's goodwill. As the Intelligence appreciation was that the defenders were not likely to contest the landing at all obstinately this might seem rather like overdoing it; but Eighth Army had always been fond of a good barrage since the opening minutes of Alamein. However, if they were to be humoured in the matter of artillery and ammunition they were to be put on strict rations as regards landing craft. As soon as possible they would all be whipped away for the benefit of Avalanche; in fact some of the vital LST's were to be ordered away on the afternoon of D-day itself.

So all was now ready for the invasion of Italy, and after retaining for two months the benefits of the flexibility which command of the sea confers we had now finally come down on the side of the most daring of the projects planned. Alexander returned to Sicily on the night of the 16th after this conference. On the 17th, in the evening, I was summoned to his caravan. Terence Airey, as I remember, was on leave. Alexander was in obvious good humour, though not over-elated, and he told me briskly that he had just been informed that the Italians had now made an official approach to negotiate a capitulation.

'It is not only a capitulation they want,' he said. 'Their idea is to change sides and fight the Germans beside us.' I don't remember what I said but I remember that he went on for some time in philosophical style about Hitler's strategic errors and the parallel with Napoleon. Hitler, he said, was a fool who considered war more important than politics and thought trickery cleverer than honest dealing. If only in 1940 he could have overcome his natural feelings of triumph and, forswearing for the present any further military glory, have behaved with even a modicum of moderation and reasonableness, he could have so united all the peoples of continental Europe contentedly under his new system as to create a block which could never be overthrown. We had seen in North Africa how the French reacted against the New Order, and now the Italians were falling away. I asked whether he thought the Italian change of front should alter our strategic plan. He did not think so, a conclusion with which I respectfully agreed; our plans largely discounted Italian resistance and there seemed no logical reason why they should be more of a menace to the Germans.

The story I was told that evening was that an Italian emissary, a General, had called on Sir Samuel Hoare, our Ambassador in Madrid, on the 15th August. He represented himself as empowered to negotiate on behalf of Marshal Badoglio and asked that Allied representatives should be sent to meet him in Lisbon whither he was bound. 'He has no written credentials,' said Alexander, 'but he seems quite genuine; it all fits in with some indications we have received through the Vatican and through Berne in the last few days. At any rate Bedell Smith and Kenneth Strong are leaving for Lisbon tomorrow to meet him.' The Italian emissary was a General Giuseppe Castellano who was chief of the Planning Department. He had close and cordial connections with General Ambrosio, Chief of General Staff. A pleasant little Sicilian, of less than average height, and rather reminiscent of

Napoleon in his general manner, he was clearly a highly trained staff officer with, in addition, distinct political adroitness. After the armistice he became liaison officer on General Eisenhower's H.Q. and in October 1945 published a book *How I Signed the Armistice of Cassibile* in which he gives a full account of his negotiations (a revised and expanded version, *La Guerra Continua*, was published in 1964). Italian historiography has not enjoyed a particularly good reputation, in particular in respect of books on the war, but Castellano's books are strikingly accurate. In what follows I have restricted myself to information from him, from Alexander's official despatch and from my own experience.

In this century many great powers have seen themselves obliged to capitulate. Their motives, however, have not always been the same. Germany capitulated in 1945 because there was literally nothing else to be done. Her armies had been beaten in the field, practically the whole of her territory had been occupied, and there was no longer any possibility of serious military resistance. It is one of the most extraordinary examples in military history of the length to which resistance can be carried. The French when they capitulated in 1940 were in almost exactly the same position except that further resistance was possible in certain of their overseas territories, as was demonstrated by General de Gaulle. The Italians were in a different case. Their overseas empire had already gone, but they were still perfectly capable of carrying on resistance at the side of their allies in the homeland. This is not a conjecture, it is demonstrable. Tens of thousands of Italians did continue to fight on at the side of the Germans for twenty months more, and large areas of Italian soil remained all that time unconquered by the Allies and under the rule of an Italian government. The Italian General Staff must have realized perfectly well that it was not a case of now or never; they could pick their time later if it seemed more convenient.

The Italians have always considered themselves, and with some justice, to be a rational and clear headed people. They do not believe in pushing things to extremes. When in difficulties they pin their hopes on the possibility of working out some acceptable compromise. These were the motives that inspired the General Staff when they found themselves, after the dismissal of Mussolini, responsible for the destinies of the nation. I do not consider them discreditable motives. They had taken over from a bankrupt system; they knew that the Italian people, though they were not expressing themselves openly, found the German alliance unpopular, had lost faith in victory and wished to be out of the war. The Italian General Staff have been accused of carrying to extremes the doctrine of 'sacro egoismo' which Salandra recommended to the Italians in 1914. General Montgomery accuses them of 'the biggest double cross in history' and others have recalled Bismarck's phrase about Italy springing to the aid of the victors. These are harsh words; the truth of the matter is that their action correctly interpreted the wishes of the vast majority of the Italians.

This mixture of motives led to considerable complications and meant that our negotiations with the Italians could not be easily or shortly concluded. If it had been a mere question of arranging the capitulation there would have been little difficulty, but Castellano was not really interested in that. At his first interview in Lisbon with General Smith, Eisenhower's Chief of Staff, and General Strong, his Chief Intelligence Officer, he was told that the only terms they could discuss were unconditional military surrender. This was, however, merely an opening gambit; after our repeated public declarations that this was our policy it would have been impossible for them to have started with anything less; but they were quite prepared, should it become necessary, to mitigate the rigour of their attitude. Castellano replied (I quote from a facsimile which he publishes of the official record) that 'he had come to discuss the question of how Italy could arrange to join the United Nations in opposition to Germany'. These were his very first words; and this remained his attitude throughout the negotiations. It was never a case, as has sometimes been thought, of our wasting precious time by struggling to impose unconditional surrender on an unwilling Italian Government. Some people have actually imagined that this struggle went on all the time from the first contacts on 17th August until the announcement of the armistice on 8th September. There is nothing in this; the date of the announcement of the armistice was chosen as D minus one of Avalanche and the date of Avalanche was fixed by the state of our landing craft and the phases of the moon.

The principal complicating factor in our negotiations was something quite different and more difficult. I have said that Castellano was a well trained staff officer and Ambrosio and his other colleagues were also well read and experienced. There was, however, one serious defect in their knowledge of the military art: they had no conception of amphibious warfare. I do not suggest that this was their fault—at that moment of time only the British, the Americans and the Japanese could have had any knowledge of the subject. Also their Intelligence Service, though much better than the German, was not very reliable and in particular had the serious fault of always overestimating our strength. The result was that, when they thought about how they were to collaborate with us in throwing the Germans out of Italy, they credited us with being capable of feats which were well beyond our powers. They knew we were planning to land a force somewhere in Italy, and their idea was that as soon as it landed they should throw off the mask, declare war on the Germans and bring their forces into line with ours. Stated like that this was a reasonable plan and our ideas coincided. The trouble was that none of the Italians realized that in our invasion the initial forces were bound to be quite small and that they were tied closely by the range of fighter aircraft. Take, for example, Marshal Badoglio; he was a man who had served in the highest staff positions in both world wars and this encouraged him to suppose that he might put his experience at our disposal. He urged us strongly, through Castellano, to land somewhere in the Leghorn area with a force of not less than fifteen divisions. He added that it would be useful to land a similar force of about the same strength on the other side of Italy near Ancona, so that the two together would make a strategic pincers. This advice was seriously given; but he might as well have been advising us to establish a bridgehead on the moon. We had landing craft for three divisions; and Leghorn was a good three hundred miles outside the range of our fighter aircraft. As for Ancona, even Castellano saw that that was going a bit far. I have mentioned this before, but it is useful as a yardstick for amphibious operations: when the United States and Britain made their greatest effort of the war, after careful and lengthy planning and concentrating every possible soldier and landing craft in the Overlord landing, the assault force was only five divisions.

The result of this fundamental misconception was that we were throughout at cross purposes with the Italians. Castellano was always demanding to know what our plans were for invading his country and we were always telling him to wait and see, while maintaining that we should of course invade in great force. Our programme, we told him, was the following. First of all someone properly accredited by Badoglio should sign the surrender terms, which would be kept secret. Then we would inform Badoglio at a certain moment that the fact of the armistice was to be announced simultaneously by us and by him, and that the day of the announcement would be D minus one for the invasion. In other words, the Italians would have to announce the capitulation before, even if only just before, we invaded. Castellano naturally objected that he was being asked to buy a pig in a poke. He began to suspect that our invasion might not be in such force as he had hoped. He also, since he had some sense, began to realize that an assault wave of fifteen divisions was rather too much to ask for, but he explained that he expected us to build up to that strength within a day or so. There were two obvious objections to entrusting him with any details of our plans. To begin with we were still enemies, and there was no knowing that he might not pass the information straight on to the Germans. Secondly we all felt very strongly, and I am sure quite rightly, that if we had told the Italians that we were proposing to land no further north than Salerno, and with a force of only three divisions, they would have decided to postpone the surrender to a more auspicious occasion. This would, after all, have enabled them to back both horses in case our invasion should be a failure. Many times in fact Castellano, who as I say had some inkling of what might happen, suggested that it would be a good idea not to announce the armistice until after we had landed and made a certain amount of progress. His idea was that if the British and Americans were established on a solid front in Italy, opposed by a German/Italian deployment, this would offer a much safer occasion for an Italian change of alliance than if it had to be made at the moment of disembarkation. I suppose that morally speaking it would be open to even graver criticisms than those which I have already mentioned. But although we considered it we could not agree to it. As was pointed out to Castellano, it would be very difficult to explain how we had allowed Italian troops to continue fighting against and killing allied soldiers when we were treating with them for an armistice. In our minds was the thought of the hazards of operation Avalanche. It was without doubt a risky operation. If the Italian armistice were announced on the night before the landing there was at least a very good chance of throwing the enemy into confusion. We were not sanguine of any actual assistance from Italian troops—there were not large numbers in the area in any case—but we were in the frame of mind where every help was welcome.

All in all it was fairly clear that each side was to some extent trying to bluff the other. Castellano eventually got back to Rome on the 27th. He had had to delay in order not to break the cover under which he had gone to Lisbon. On the 30th Marshal Badoglio and the King decided that the terms should be accepted and that Castellano should go to Sicily next day to settle matters. He flew on the 31st in an Italian aeroplane to an airport in western Sicily from where he was transferred in an American plane to Cassibile. The only subject that he would discuss, as he made plain, was the methods by which the Italian change of side was to be made most smoothly. The Italians were now getting extremely worried about the German reaction. German troops continued to pour into Italy, and they were afraid that they would not be able to defend themselves when the surrender was announced. Accordingly, in an attempt to stiffen their morale, we decided to offer them the assistance of a complete airborne division, the American 82nd, which should land on airfields under Italian control near Rome and join in the defence of the capital. This was a risky proceeding for two reasons, first because of the obvious danger that this reinforcement might not be sufficient to make head against the Germans—it seems pretty clear from after knowledge that we should in fact have lost the whole division—and secondly because it meant that there could not now be an airborne operation in support of Avalanche as was planned, because we only had enough aircraft to carry one division. However, the offer made a great effect on the Italians; it also weakened their arguments in favour of postponing the armistice until after a large-scale allied landing. Castellano accordingly flew off again back to Rome and returned to Sicily on the 2nd September.

We were expecting that the armistice terms could now be signed. The Italians, however, either because of genuine misunderstanding or because they wanted to play things out a bit longer, had not authorized Castellano to sign. This came as rather a blow. It was not clear to us whether Castellano himself was holding out or whether his Government had genuinely not authorized him. In case the former hypothesis was correct Alexander himself went formally to see Castellano, having put on his best uniform for the occasion since he normally went about in a bush shirt, and spoke sternly to him. The wretched man describes this in his memoirs as the lowest point that he reached. It was not in fact his fault but Badoglio's. The latter took twenty-four hours to reply to Castellano's signal asking for authority to sign and when he did reply he evaded the point merely saying 'the affirmative reply given with our telegram No. 5 contains implicitly the acceptance of the conditions of the armistice'. However, if this was meant to be an evasion it did not last long. Three hours later, at five o'clock in the afternoon of 3rd September, a second telegram arrived saying 'Cancel my preceding telegram. General Castellano is authorized by the Italian Government to sign the acceptance of the armistice conditions.'

At 5.15 he did sign followed by General Smith signing on behalf of General Eisenhower.

It may be asked how these communications were kept up. The fact is that in Lisbon Castellano was given one of our special wireless sets designed for spy work and housed in what Castellano calls a magnificent leather suitcase. He was also given a set of ciphers and was told to identify his messages by taking a sentence out of a book in Italian. He bought three copies of the same book in Lisbon of which one went to London, one to Algiers and a third one went to Rome. It was a book called *L'Omnibus del Corso* by Sanminiatelli, but of its merits as a work of literature I am unable to speak. He was advised when he got to Rome to obtain the release from a prisoner of war camp of a subaltern in the Parachute Regiment called Mallaby who had been captured shortly before and who knew how to work this type of set. All these instructions were faithfully carried out, though it took some time to persuade Lieutenant Mallaby that he was not being asked to take part in some crooked affair, and on that set all the messages between Badoglio and the allied commanders were passed. The other method was by aircraft. Several times an Italian aircraft took off from Rome and flew to Palermo in accordance with a flight plan arranged with the Allies. It surprises me that in spite of this no word reached the Germans. No thanks for this are due to certain allied war correspondents who at least once tried to report this to their papers. The only way that they could have hoped to get it past the censor was that the affair was so secret that there would be no specific stop on it; but what they expected to gain if the censor had passed it is obscure. Their editors, one must suppose, would have had enough sense of responibility not to print it; but once the story got on the air in clear it would be bound to get to the Germans' knowledge. Fortunately the American censor had enough common sense to bar it completely. There were of course plenty of Sicilians who saw the coming and going but none of them had any means of communicating with the mainland.

CHAPTER XIII

Salerno

SO THE armistice was signed and the Italians were out of the war. Indeed they were now approaching the status of co-belligerents. Those of us who had been engaged against the Italians since the start, in the days before the Germans came along, no doubt felt even greater satisfaction. First of all, in the peninsula itself we did hope that the German position would be made more awkward. It was not so much that we expected the aid of Italian troops but it seemed to us that if the Italians withheld their labour and refused to cooperate with the Germans it ought to make the latter's lines of communications difficult and perhaps oblige a withdrawal. We did not really hope to get much more than Naples but it looked as though we might get there fairly quickly. Looking at the Balkans one began to sigh over opportunities which would have to be foregone. The Jugoslav partisans would undoubtedly receive a considerable accession of arms and equipment if they moved quickly to take over from the Italians; but unfortunately there was nothing we could do to get in touch with them. Crete had a mainly German garrison and was too big a mouthful to take on as a sideline. The Dodecanese looked a more hopeful prospect. There the garrison was almost entirely Italian and in considerable strength. Moreover it was within reasonable range of our Middle East Forces. The trouble was that G.H.Q. Middle East had got practically no forces left and fewer means of transporting them. Unfortunately too, the Italian Commander-in-Chief in Rhodes was not a man of great resolution. When after the capitulation the Germans made an air attack on his headquarters, he broadcast in clear 'Every bomb is chipping a little piece off my heart,' and surrendered immediately. British troops were sent to Cos and Leros, but without proper air defence or proper communications they were unable to hold them. It is incidentally remarkable, and symptomatic of Hitler's preoccupation with the Balkans, that at a time when he was hastily evacuating Sardinia and Corsica and withdrawing up the leg of Italy, he turned and struck with great violence, diverting large air resources from the Russian front, at this minor British incursion. Equally forceful efforts were directed at Corfu where the Italian commander was a man of courage and resolution and his troops fought well. Without Allied aid, however, which we were powerless to give, their resistance could not be long.

Only one new possibility offered itself. We had one spare division fully ready for action, the 1st British Airborne Division. It had no transport because all this was required for the American 82nd Airborne Division in its bold descent on Rome. Alexander, however, thought that somehow or other it should be transported to Italy and the Navy came to the rescue by offering the 12th Cruiser Squadron. This was now going spare because it would not be required to guard against a possible attack by the Italian Navy. It was no use putting more troops into Calabria where Eighth Army had more than enough to beat the small number of Germans on its front and difficulty enough already in supplying them. Cruisers could not land them at Salerno nor could they be maintained there. Accordingly it was decided to send them to Taranto to seize the naval base and airfields for our use and to spread out and occupy as much country inland from Taranto as they could manage, using whatever means of transport they could lay their hands on. We were going to need ports on that side of Italy very soon and it would be an advantage to get them open as quickly as possible. Meanwhile the troops would be no drain on Eighth Army's hard-pressed maintenance organization. The operation was given the name 'Slapstick'; not so long before, the capture of Taranto was being considered as an operation worthy of the serious attention of the whole of Fifth Army.

Meanwhile planning was going on for the airborne operation against Rome. Obviously it was going to be a pretty tricky arrangement and outside the normal scope of such things, so it was decided to send a senior officer of the American airborne forces to have a look. Brigadier-General Taylor was chosen, the man who afterwards defended Bastogne in the Ardennes. As he was going to what was still technically enemy territory there was a possibility that his signals might be twisted; he was accordingly told that if he decided against the operation he should include in any telegram he sent—even if he was forced to send one recommending it—an innocuous sounding code word. If I remember rightly it was 'certainly'. Similarly, Castellano decided that he wanted some staff officers and a miscellaneous party was brought from Rome in an Italian motor boat, first of all to Ustica, a small island off the north of Sicily, and then in a British motor boat to Trapani in the west end of the island. I was asked to meet them and bring them to North Africa because our H.Q. was moving back there for the Salerno invasion. There were about half a dozen of them, mainly of the rank of lieutenant colonel and above, and they were all splendidly turned out. Two of them were Bersaglieri and two Alpini which involved cock's feathers in the hat at different angles and their uniforms were certainly a contrast to the rather casual style at any rate of British troops in the Mediterranean. It was a tiresome flight. I picked up an American Dakota whose pilot had no idea what was going on and who had been expecting to go straight back from Cassibile to Algiers to enjoy some leave. He was surprised by his passengers but seemed quite happy when I told him to go to Tunis. I was less happy when we arrived in Tunis, which was the destination which had been ordered, because the welcoming party from Allied Force H.Q. which I had been told to expect was not there. I left my fine feathered collection waiting in the plane with strict orders not to look out of the windows and went off to telephone. It took some time to get in touch but eventually I got on to a friend at Allied Force H.Q. who told me to deliver the party to Bizerta. The inside of the Dakota, which had been kept carefully shut, had now reached a fine temperature but the flight to Bizerta was only a matter of minutes. On arrival we were met by General Strong, Eisenhower's Chief Intelligence Officer, and Castellano in civilian dress. He gave his future staff officers the most furious dressing down for coming in uniform, lasting about five minutes, looking as he did so even more like the young Napoleon.

D Minus One for Avalanche was 8th September and the Commanders in Chief were all gathered at Alexander's headquarters in Bizerta at 11 o'clock. We had had to move back to Bizerta because the Navy said they could not control the battle from anywhere else; it was also convenient for the Air Force but distinctly inconvenient for the Army. The Commanders in Chief met in what had been a small school room and I had been called in to describe the latest picture of German dispositions when two telegrams were brought in which had just been received on the wireless link with Rome. Both of them went over big. The first was from General Taylor, advising firmly against the airborne operation. The code word was there as well so there was no option but to call the thing off. The second was from Badoglio himself. This said that in view of the change in the situation and the presence of German forces near Rome it would not be possible to accept an immediate armistice. In other words Badoglio clearly wanted to go back to the original plan, which the Italians had always favoured, of postponing their announcement of the armistice until they had made quite certain that we had landed in Italy in sufficient force to ensure a safe exchange of sides.

General Eisenhower was, and I believe still is, an exceptionally mild-mannered man with a perfect control of his temper. On this occasion, however he was furious and expressed himself with great violence to poor Castellano who, I am sure, had not the slightest inkling of what was going on. Obviously however the impulses of anger and of sound strategy both pointed in the same direction. If we allowed the Italians to change their minds they might well change them altogether when they saw what a comparatively meagre force we intended to use. Although we had not relied on their help for Avalanche we had at least relied on their absence from the firing line. The troops were on their way to Salerno in convoys passing along narrow swept channels through minefields and it would not be possible to turn them back. Besides, any further delay would almost certainly mean that the Italian intentions would be betrayed to the Germans and we should lose the advantage of surprise and such other avantages as might reasonably be expected. The discussion was brief. Eisenhower, still red in the face, demanded to be led to a telephone to speak to his Chief of Staff in Algiers. I took him to mine and waited while he bellowed down it, dictating on the spot a remarkably incisive telegram to be sent forthwith to Marshal Badoglio. He reminded the Marshal that his accredited representative had signed the terms of the armistice and had undertaken on his behalf that they should be carried out. Whatever happened it was his intention to make the broadcast as arranged at 6.30 that night. If Badoglio did not do likewise he would 'publish this whole affair to the world. The Italian people could be sure that no future action on the part of the Italian government could ever restore any confidence in their good faith and it would consequently involve the destruction of your Government and of your country.'

No reply came, and all we could do was to wait for 6.30 to see whether Badoglio would play his part. The signallers set up a large wireless set in my office tuned to Rome radio which was broadcasting operatic selections. Another set was tuned to Algiers radio and as 6.30 came we had the pleasure of hearing Eisenhower reading the announcement of the armistice. The other set continued with Donizetti. I am afraid there were many in the room who thought of a double-cross. It certainly could not be excluded, though if I remember I myself advanced the theory that Badoglio's watch was wrong. My kindlier theory was actually nearer the truth because an hour later he did come up on the radio. I do not think I ever saw an explanation of the delay but it was almost certainly merely another aspect of that vacillation and indecision which marked all the Italian actions connected with the surrender. The cancellation of the airborne operation was another. It was not correct, as Badoglio claimed, that the German forces in the neighbourhood of Rome had been strengthened or that they were in control of all the airfields. As a matter of fact there were five Italian divisions near Rome and only two German, neither of which were particularly close to the city; the 3rd Panzer Grenadier Division, which did most of the fighting, was at Lake Bracciano, about 30 miles to the north. General Taylor's recommendations had been based not so much on the military situation as on the fact that all the Italians he had met were obviously in a dither and he feared that his solitary division, which was only intended as a stiffener to the five Italian divisions, would not receive the military support necessary. I have no doubt he was right and certainly no-one can question his courage.

There was indeed no sign of decisive action at Rome. Immediately after his broadcast Badoglio, accompanied by the King and Crown Prince, left Rome by the road running eastwards to Pescara. There they were picked up by a cruiser which brought them to Brindisi. No one was appointed to take command in the capital. In the circumstances it is not surprising that the Italian troops, who had just been startled and delighted at the news that for them the war was over, should not have resisted seriously when the Germans ordered them to lay down their arms. The division of Sardinian Grenadiers, traditionally loyal to the House of Savoy, made some attempt at resistance, and so did some of the Carabinieri; however it did not last long and the 3rd Panzer Grenadier Division, hastily brought up, was soon able to move on again southwards to oppose Fifth Army at Salerno. At Salerno too the Italian troops, particularly those manning the coastal defence positions, either took themselves off or were disarmed by the Germans. The captured diary of a lieutenant in the Reconnaissance Regiment of the 16th Panzer Division described the scene; 'The Italians handed over their arms with goodwill, delighted that for them the war was over.' Accordingly when our troops began to land at Salerno there were none but Germans waiting to meet them.

This brings up the question which is one of the great controversies of the Italian campaign; were the Germans expecting us to land at Salerno or did we achieve surprise? To my mind there is only one answer though it differs from the one given by many of the allied writers on the campaign and all the Germans. The latter, in various accounts published since the war, have not unnaturally maintained that they were in fact expecting us to land just there. The critical point, it seems to me, is to consider not what they say afterwards but what they did then. On this the evidence is fairly clear; and we were also very well informed at the time. To begin with Castellano gave us a detailed sketch of German dispositions in Italy and told us what the German appreciation was of our likely intentions, a point on which he was naturally fully aware in view of his responsibility for planning. I have already said that the Germans were as ignorant in matters of amphibious warfare as the Italians. They did work out that we were more likely to attack the west coast of Italy than the east, which was sensible so far; but they were as ready as the Italians to ascribe to us the capability of landing anywhere on that west coast. They decided that the four most likely places were Calabria; the area from Salerno to Gaeta; the Rome area, particularly Civitavecchia; and the Genoa-Spezia area. They would not attempt to defend Calabria but they would resist strongly, on the beaches themselves, any attempt to land in the other three areas.

Their principal concern was to have a firm base in north Italy, north of the Apennines. Here Rommel was in command with eight divisions. He had a separate H.Q., known as Army Group B, and was responsible also for Slovenia and north Croatia. South of the Apennines was Kesselring's command, and he also had eight divisions. Two of them were in Calabria, with orders to withdraw as soon as attacked, one was in Apulia, three were between Salerno and Gaeta and two were in the Rome area, one of them on the coast near Ostia and the other at Viterbo. These dispositions fit in exactly with Castellano's report and clearly did not imply any foreknowledge of our intention to land at Salerno. It is quite clear in fact that when Kesselring considered the general area Salerno to Gaeta, a coastline of 150 miles, he thought it more likely that we should land north rather than south of Naples. It was to this area on either side of the Volturno River that he sent the first German troops to become available, the Hermann Goering Panzer Division and 15th Panzer Grenadier Division. These two divisions took up defensive positions on the coast from Naples all the way to Gaeta, carried out anti-invasion exercises and were kept continuously on the alert. The result was that when they were urgently needed at Salerno they first had to be concentrated from very widely dispersed positions and then brought down by road through Naples, through the defile between Vesuvius and the sea, and then through the still more difficult defile through the Monti Picentini before they could intervene in the Salerno battle. Clearly Kesselring had the same high opinion of the Volturno beaches as had General Clark. The Salerno beaches, however, all twenty miles of them, were left to the charge of only one division, the 16th Panzer Division. It only arrived a week before we landed. As an armoured division it only had four battalions of infantry plus one of engineers, one reconnaissance battalion and a battalion of tanks. This is surely a very small force with which to hold twenty miles of coast. I submit that this, particularly when contrasted with the German strength north of Naples, must lead to the conclusion that Salerno was not regarded by the Germans as the most likely point of attack.

To this those of the Allied forces who took part in the assault will indignantly object that the Germans were ready for them when they landed—indeed many people have reported that German troops actually called out 'Come on, we are waiting for you.' But this is not the point; I am not talking of tactical surprise but of strategic surprise. I cannot see how any amphibious operation could possibly gain tactical surprise (though I admit we came very near doing so at Anzio). The invasion fleet for Avalanche was well over one thousand strong, and it would be too much to hope that a force of this size could enter the Gulf of Salerno without someone on shore drawing attention to the fact. The invasion fleet had in fact been sighted 25 miles south of Capri at 4 o'clock the previous afternoon. Two and a half hours later, to their great alarm, the Germans got the additional news that the Italians had taken themselves out of the war. All the divisions in the Naples area were ordered to take over coast defence positions from the Italians, and this brought them down to the beach. Another piece of evidence has been produced by Mr. Majdalany in his book *The Battle* which is a most admirable account of the battle of Cassino. He obviously regards it as clinching the argument; 'the very day before the landing,' he says, '16th Panzer Division held an anti-invasion exercise.' And what, may I ask, with the greatest respect to Mr. Majdalany, did he expect them to hold, a whist drive? The Division had arrived at Salerno a mere week before, and the fact that it had only just got around to holding an anti-invasion exercise is rather a proof that Salerno was not regarded as the most likely place for an invasion. This is borne out also by the captured diary to which I have referred. The Germans had a system for defence of three 'States of Alarm' (Alarm-zustände); of these (1) involved general alertness (2) meant that an attack in the general area was possible and (3) meant that there was an imminent likelihood of attack on the formation or its neighbouring formations. State of Alarm 2 had been in force north of Naples for the better part of the past three weeks, but it was only ordered by the 16th Panzer Division at Salerno at 4 o'clock on D minus one, at the time when they received the news of the invasion fleet being at sea. Even as late as this, it will be seen, the Divisional Commander did not expect an imminent attack in his own sector.

For all that the 16th Panzer Division was on its own at the start of the battle, and doubtless thrown into some confusion by the necessity of taking over the posts abandoned by its former Italian colleagues, it nevertheless put up a very fine defence. The Germans had, as may be supposed, studied very carefully the Sicilian operations as an earnest of things to come. Their deduction was that they had been wrong in supposing that defending forces should be held back so as to be able to make a deliberate counter attack when the invader's hand was shown. They now took the view—and this was incidentally still the ruling theory at the time of Overlord—that troops should be ready on the beaches and counter attack at once so as to force the invaders back into the sea at the moment when they are weakest.

Inspired by this doctrine, and no doubt enraged by the news of the armistice, the 16th Panzer Division resisted the landing with the greatest vigour. It must also be admitted that the three assault divisions were not the best in the Allied forces in the Mediterranean. The British 46th Division was the only one that had had operational experience before, under First Army in Tunisia, and it had always been unlucky. The British 56th Division had only been in action once and then for a very short time; to be quite frank its poor performance in an attack on the Enfidaville Line had decided Montgomery to call off that attack. The U.S. 36th Division had never seen any action before. It had an extremely high opinion of itself, being a National Guard Division from Texas. It certainly contained some excellent material but our experience was that National Guard divisions were never so good as the divisions raised by the draft. The middle ranks of the officers were the weak point of these divisions. Not that the 36th

Division did badly in this battle, but they were no better than average. The American Corps Commander, General Dawley, was replaced by Mark Clark, in the middle of the battle, by General Lucas who in his turn suffered the same fate himself at Anzio. In both Corps the time for training had been short and there was a fair amount of confusion on the beaches. The result of all this was that the single German division was able, at the cost of very heavy casualties to itself, to delay and to some extent disorganize our attack. Once that happened it was likely that the German rate of reinforcement by land would be quicker than we could manage by sea.

The Germans had been able to put down all resistance around Rome so quickly that their troops there were able to come on rapidly to Salerno. In fact Kesselring concentrated there all his forces in southern Italy. He took away almost all the troops retreating in front of Eighth Army, reckoning that the latter's advance would be too slow, in view of the difficulty of the country, to have any effect on the crucial battle. By D plus 4, accordingly, the troops at Salerno were being attacked by forces as considerably superior in numbers as they were in experience. It was a fine backs-to-the-wall effort, with the sea uncomfortably close. It was here for the first time that the immense power of naval gunfire against troops was demonstrated—if we except the Navy's shelling of the Libyans at Meiktila in December 1940. Admiral Cunningham ordered *Warspite* and *Valiant* to the Gulf of Salerno and these fine old ships startled both sides by the violence of their 16-inch salvoes. Alexander himself went to Salerno on the 14th, which was the crucial day. On the same day there arrived the landing craft with the first part of the 7th Armoured Division. With this reinforcement it looked as though the bridgehead would now be safe. Ironically the Germans thought that the landing craft had come to take the invaders away and Berlin Radio began speaking excitedly of 'a second Dunkirk'. By the 15th the German race against time was lost. Eighth Army's leading elements were only 50 miles away, and it was clear to the Germans that they were not going to be able to push us into the sea. They were obliged therefore to fall back slowly and saw themselves committed to holding a line across the peninsula.

The Italian surrender had not turned out as well as the Italians had hoped. We on our side were not particularly disappointed because we had never expected very much. In terms of ground gained we had made an immense stride forward, with all Italy south of Naples now in our hands. We were carrying out our directive even more spectacularly than the Chiefs of Staffs could have expected. Italy was out of the war, the Germans had acquired a whole new lot of defensive commitments in the Balkans and elsewhere, and we had drawn down into Central Italy just about as large a German force as we could hold in play with the resources at our disposal. On the other hand, it could not be denied that the apparent effect of the Italian surrender had not been as spectacular as the uninstructed might have expected. The Italian Air Force, as far as it could, carried out the terms of the surrender; but it had not been playing any particular part lately so that the change of sides was of little consequence. By one of the ironies of fate the Italian aeronautical industry had just succeeded in producing their first really efficient fighter aircraft just too late to have any effect. The Italian Navy carried out the terms of the surrender punctiliously as far as it was able. Here too, however, the effect was not striking since the Italian fleet had long renounced any attempt to contest the supremacy of the Mediterranean. Nevertheless its surrender made an impression.

The main fleet, in accordance with the terms of surrender, sailed for La Maddalena, at the northernmost extremity of Sardinia, and thence down the west coast of Sardinia and past Bizerta to Malta. The German Air Force on 9th September pursued it with a not unnatural animosity and in an attack with radio-controlled bombs managed to sink the flagship, the *Roma*. When the remainder of the fleet, two battleships and four cruisers, with accompanying destroyers, was due off Bizerta, Admiral Cunningham went out in a destroyer to see them go past. Another party went out in a minesweeper and I managed to persuade our Naval Liaison Officer to take me.

I am glad to have seen it. A few miles off Bizerta harbour there appeared suddenly out of the haze the *Warspite*, leading the line. *Warspite* had been rebuilt and remodelled several times since she was first constructed in 1917. She was a remarkably lumpish looking ship with the most peculiarly shaped superstructure, known in the Mediterranean Fleet as 'Queen Anne's Mansions'. *Valiant* came next. After them came the two Italian battleships which seemed to me the most beautiful ships I have ever seen. By contrast with *Warspite* and *Valiant*, which were painted a silver grey, almost white, the Italian ships were a dark sea-green which made them stand out startlingly against the sun dazzle on the calm waters. Their bows had an extreme sheer and their masts and upper works a symmetrical rake. They reminded me in fact of the liner *Rex* which I had seen in Naples harbour in 1935 and thought the most beautiful ship in the world. Two heavy cruisers followed. On all the ships practically the whole complement were on deck, still wearing the yellow life-saving jackets which they had no doubt kept on since the last air attack. Their decks were brightly painted with the red and white diagonal stripes which all Italian warships had worn since the early days of the war when they were the favourite targets for their own side's aircraft. One of the battleships still had the signs of the German air attack, a great hole high up on the starboard side near the bows. All the ships were flying enormous black flags in sign of surrender; this was according to instructions and the Captains had evidently determined that the flag should be big enough to admit of no mistake. The ones flown by the battleships looked the size of a tennis court. So they passed on smoothly into the heat haze again, heading eastwards, and before long Admiral Cunningham was able to send to the Admiralty his famous signal: 'Be pleased to inform their Lordships that the Italian Fleet is anchored under the guns of the fortress of Malta.'

I had another excursion shortly afterwards which might have ended less agreeably. I thought it was time to see what was going on in the heel of Italy, where we had just put in the 1st Airborne Division. I accordingly arranged a lift in one of their transport aircraft which was going there with some supplies. I was comfortably placed in the co-pilot's seat and had a fine view of Pantellaria. The crew was young and fairly new to the Mediterranean. In those days I had a great respect for the R.A.F.'s accomplishments and it was only as a matter of interest that I asked the young navigator, an Australian, what his course was. He showed me the line on the map which would take us within sight of the southeast corner of Sicily. Some land was coming up to port as we were conversing and he waved his hand at it and said "There is Cape Passero at this very minute." Now, during the course of preparation for the invasion of Sicily, I had spent several hours studying photographs and models of most of the south coast; I was therefore able to identify at a glance the harbour of Licata which was just going past only 2,000 feet below us. The navigator was not in the least disturbed at finding he was 50 miles out, and so we turned to starboard and continued along the south coast until Cape Passero did turn up. As the Sicilian coast at this point turns through an extremely sharp angle it is hardly possible to mistake it. Accordingly some more work was done with parallel rulers and we set off on another course aiming straight for Taranto. It was a hazy day and I was not surprised when the heel of Italy did not immediately turn up. I was a little surprised, however, not long afterwards, to see some remarkably rocky mountains appear in front of us, and below the unmistakable outline of Corfu. I had not seen it since 1940 but it is easy to recognize and the Albanian mountains behind are a uniquely unhospitable collection. As all this coast was held by the enemy I tapped the Australian on the shoulder and suggested that we might turn through an angle of 180 degrees. He was obliging as always and we flew back westwards. Very soon afterwards the heel of Italy appeared and we followed round the instep until Taranto was in sight, with its two large land-locked harbours. I parted on friendly terms with the aircrew though resolving to make the return journey by sea.

Not long afterwards a similar error in navigation befell an aircraft that was transporting eighteen British nurses to set up a base hospital in Bari. Their plane got so lost that it was obliged to crash-land in Albania. The nurses all got out eventually by walking to the coast under the guidance of some friendly Albanians and were taken off in a boat. But all this took a bit of arranging; for example a special flight had to be laid on to drop eighteen pairs of boots for the nurses without which they would never have got to the coast.

It was odd to be walking about Taranto, which was full of Italian soldiers and sailors with just a sprinkling of British parachutists. Neither Taranto nor Bari showed many signs of war; the Italian war effort had of course been very much smaller, so far as the general mobilization of the nation's resources was concerned, than we thought of as natural in Britain. There was plenty to buy in the shops, including the most frivolous things. After calling on the Airborne Division H.Q., and on General Allfrey commanding 5th Corps, who was just arriving in Taranto with his H.Q. to take charge on the east coast, I met an old friend from Eighth Army who had come across in a small landing craft. I cadged a lift on this that night as far as Crotone and thence by road to Eighth Army H.Q. on the west coast of Calabria at Vibo Valentia. It is not surprising that Calabria is not visited much by tourists in view of its position but it is strikingly beautiful. It must be heart-breaking country to farm but it certainly contains a splendid variety of wild scenery with some handsome cities perched up on hilltops. I made my way back to Sicily in a launch and a trawler; the latter came from Grimsby and although the temperature was high in the nineties as we steamed from Messina to Syracuse we sat down to roast beef and Yorkshire pudding followed by roly-poly.

By this time the final returns were in of the effect of the Italian armistice on land northwards from our advanced spearheads. In the Rome area there had been a little resistance on the first day but it was rapidly crushed. In the extreme north the Cuneo Alpine Division refused for a time to lay down its arms. Elsewhere in Italy the Germans had little trouble in gaining complete control. In most places this was achieved by the employment of impudently small forces. An exception should be made for the extreme northeast. Here the Slovene minority, nearly half a million strong, had always resented Italian rule. Some Jugoslav partisans had already penetrated into the mountain regions of the Karst and when the surrender came there were willing hands ready to take over the weapons for which the Italian troops in the neighbourhood had no further use. In the first flush of enthusiasm the Slovenes penetrated into and took temporary control of Fiume and Trieste. It was in this direction that German Army Group B under Field Marshal Rommel directed its first and main efforts. The Slovene frontier with Italy is a vital link between Italy, Austria and the Balkans and commands the principal roads into the Balkan Peninsula. Strong forces were therefore disposed to regain control of Trieste and Fiume, the Tarvis Pass, the Ljubljana Gap and the Save Valley.

In southern France the Italian troops were already in the process of withdrawing. Those that remained were speedily disarmed without incident. In the Balkans the problem was more complicated. The Italian divisions were dispersed over a wide area and in many places there were no German divisions conveniently placed to disarm them. There were also the Partisans who were anxious to disarm them first. Tito's men got a good haul of arms and were able to come down to the coast in Dalmatia which gave them a chance of getting into touch by sea with the allies for further supplies. One Italian division actually transferred its allegiance to the partisans. There was similar confusion in Greece. In Crete, the 52nd Siena Division was speedily disarmed by the Germans who were present in force and already suspicious of their Italian colleagues' intentions. I have already mentioned the fate of the Aegean Islands and the Ionian islands.

If General Eisenhower had ever given to the world the strictures on the military results of the Italian capitulation of which he delivered himself at the time to his staff, the Italian reaction would have been much more violent than it was to the criticisms of Generals Alexander and Montgomery, which were milk and water in comparison. It may well be thought that though Eisenhower always claimed that he did not expect much from the Italians, he did, in fact, have higher hopes than his British comrades and was the more disappointed. Alexander attributes a great deal of the blame to twenty-one years of fascism. For twenty-one years the Italians had been exposed to a regime which systematically destroyed by its cynical corruption and inefficiency all the sound bases of patriotism.

CHAPTER XIV

Anzio and Cassino

O N 1ST October the Kings Dragoon Guards, the armoured car regiment of the 7th Armoured Division, entered Naples. This was the estimated date for the capture of Naples in the first plan made in July. At the time that the plan was made, however, it seemed more reasonable to suppose that that day would see us about to assault either Taranto or, in the worst case, Sardinia. At about the same time another event occurred which was to mould the future shape of the Italian campaign; Hitler suddenly decided to make a stand. Hitherto he had been content to withdraw slowly up the leg of Italy and he had already set irrevocably in motion the evacuation of Sardinia and Corsica. It was already becoming clear however that, tactically speaking, there was no real need to be in a hurry. The Italian change of side had passed off without much trouble, apart from a little wear and tear on the motor transport used in rounding up the Italian troops as prisoners of war—and the Germans had at last formed a better appreciation of the limitations of amphibious warfare. There were only about eight Allied divisions in Italy, as opposed to their own nineteen, and although they heavily overestimated, as always, the number of troops we had available in North Africa, they could see that it would be some time before we could transport to Italy any large forces. The Italian terrain was of course the most suitable for defence that could be found in the whole of Europe and it was only natural that Hitler, who regarded any withdrawal as a sign of almost criminal weakness, should decide to make a stand. He accordingly issued orders that the German troops should establish a line south of Rome and endeavour to hold it for the rest of the winter.

This decision well illustrates what is the main paradox of the Italian Campaign. Although we, as the attacking force, had the tactical initiative, strategically speaking it lay within the decision of the German High Command whether we attained our object or not. The object laid down for us was to contain the largest possible number of German divisions; but a good deal depended on whether the Germans allowed themselves to be contained. Suppose they had decided to conduct a fighting withdrawal up the whole length of the Italian peninsula through that winter of 1943-44. They could have done this, thanks to the perfect adaptation of the terrain to a defensive campaign, with the employment of only about half a dozen divisions. If we were to maintain any reasonable pressure we should have been obliged to employ at least twice as many, say twelve divisions. In those circumstances they would have been containing us. Admittedly if they had employed this strategy a time would have come when they would have run out of mountains and would have had to retreat across the open plains of the Po Valley. After this interlude, however, they would have been presented by nature with the even more formidable mountain barrier of the Alps, on the southern borders of the Reich. At this point they would naturally have had to make a serious stand; but so great are the defensive possibilities that we should certainly have required a superiority of at least three to one to have made any penetration. To have adopted such a strategy would have meant that they could have made available for the decisive campaign in the west some twenty more divisions. It is foolish to build a hypothesis on a hypothesis and I will not try to conjecture what effect this might have had on Overlord; but twenty divisions is a formidable force and it would be hard to argue that it would have had no effect. Fortunately the Germans collaborated enthusiastically with us in the attainment of our object; they insisted on piling reinforcements into what was in essence an irrelevant battle even at times when the main effort of their enemies from East and West was being directed at their very vitals.

At the time the Germans decided to stand they had in Italy nineteen divisions to our fifteen. Three of our divisions had had very heavy casualties and a further three were due to leave before the end of the year for the new Western Front. Our strength was not expected to rise to eighteen divisions until February next year. There could be no doubt therefore that we were containing more than our share of German troops. From the general strategic point of view it would be fairer to take into account the whole German force in the Mediterranean theatre from southern France to the Balkans, some fifty odd divisions, because it was essentially our potential strength in the theatre that tied down these enemy forces. I freely admit, of course, that the Jugoslav partisans would by themselves have tied down a fair number of German troops, but the strength of the German garrisons in the Balkans was necessarily greatly increased by the need to guard against an allied landing. It was an interesting calculation to make. Our sources of information were good and we were able to pinpoint with great accuracy the location of every division. We even contemplated the possibility that the Germans might take the offensive in Italy, and Alexander faced with equanimity the thought that they might even succeed in pushing us out of Naples. From the point of view of Allied Grand Strategy this might well have been an acceptable setback. The exigencies of the Italian terrain counted for them as much as for us; in other words, for them to mount an offensive on this scale would have dragged in even more of their strength and diverted it further away from the vital sector in northwestern Europe. In the event this idea did not occur to them. The German idea was to hold us on what they called their 'winter position'. This was a line across the narrowest part of the Italian peninsula, only 85 miles long. On the east coast it was based on the steep trench of the Sangro river, on the west coast it ran along the Garigliano with its key position in the strong point of Monte Cassino. The centre of the position ran through the wildest country in Italy, the Abruzzi National Park, the home of bears and wolves.

If I were to write a full history of the Italian campaign, trying to bring out its essential character, it would have to be in large measure a tactical account. It would be necessary to describe in detail stubborn and bitter fighting for one mountain ridge after another. It was as unpleasant a campaign as any in modern history. The weather was unvaryingly cruel. The mud was as devouring as anything on the Somme. The mountains were stony and bare of cover. Much of the real history consisted of small tactics, company and battalion actions. As a staff officer ensconced in the rear, my mind was directed to the strategy, the great balance of who was containing whom. It was easy enough to be present, as a spectator, at the innumerable sharp and fierce battles, for the country provided not only good defensive positions for the enemy but good points of vantage for the observer. I covered in fact a good deal of ground; but it was mainly as a relief from the steady and continuous task of working out the balance and disposition of the enemy forces in a map-covered office where we moved about symbols denoting not merely the divisions in Italy but those moving into and out of the theatre and in the Balkans.

Our first major strategic operation was the combined battles of Anzio and Cassino. Here I am treading on some of the most controversial ground in the whole history of the war. A recent American book bears the challenging title *Anzio: the Gamble that Failed*. In what did it fail? Our orders, as I have said, were to contain in Italy the largest possible numbers of Germans; the landing meant that the length of the line the Germans were holding in Italy was increased from eighty-five miles, the shortest they ever held, to a hundred and twenty miles, that they sent four extra divisions there, including one from France itself, and that, being enticed on to the offensive, they suffered heavy losses. Our object was not to capture Rome, or anywhere else, but to destroy Germans. If the landing had led to the capture of Rome in January instead of, as it did, in June, would that have been so much better? The actual date, D-2 for Overlord, gave a splendid psychological boost to the Allied cause. Militarily the timing could hardly have been better, because it meant that at the very moment of crisis in the West eight German divisions were diverted from there to Italy.

It was on 8th November that Alexander indicated in his plan of campaign that when we got near Rome the assault on the city would be helped by an amphibious landing directed on the Alban Hills. His first idea was that the landing should go in at Anzio when our advances on the main front had reached Ferentino and Priverno, about fifty miles from the city. It would be in the strength of one division only, which was all we had the craft for; the operation would be given the code name 'Shingle'.

The trouble was that all this depended on Fifth Army making good progress overland. Three months hard fighting had brought us by the first week in January face to face with the Cassino position and it was only too obvious that this was going to hold us up even longer. Monte Cassino, and the line of the Garigliano below it, had long been a favourite of the Italian General Staff as an example of an almost impregnable position. The same reasons had commended it to Saint Benedict in the sixth century as the site of a monastery. On the left the Aurunci mountains were impassable for any large forces. Only the Liri valley offered a broad and direct route to Rome. Before the valley could be entered there was a river crossing to make. The western, enemy held, bank of the river was higher than the eastern, and to this advantage was added the magnificent observation post and commanding firing position offered by the monastery hill. It was obvious, therefore, even when we first approached Cassino, that this would be a most difficult position to force. It certainly made it impossible to say with any exactness when our main thrust would be within supporting distance of a landing at Anzio.

One possible solution would have been to shift the point of landing further down the coast and nearer the present position. This, however, would have been of no value. The mountains run so close to the sea along all this coast as far as Terracina that a landing force would have been easily blocked off. They would have been faced with trackless mountains and would have had no serious possibility of being able to debouch into the Liri Valley. The next possibility was to put off the amphibious landing until we had forced our way past the Cassino position. There were two objections to this. First of all we were working to a fairly tight time schedule with regard to the return of the landing craft to the U.K. The Combined Chiefs of Staff would never have allowed us to hang on to them indefinitely. Secondly, as the difficulties of the Cassino position became clearer, we began to consider Shingle as a means of helping us to overcome this awkward part of the advance. A serious threat in the rear might well dispose the enemy to fall back.

The final solution was to mount the operation at roughly the time planned but to do so in such strength as to ensure that the landed force could hold their ground by themselves for a fairly long period, at any rate much longer than the original week. This was an idea which appealed strongly to Mr. Churchill, who was in the theatre at the time. The decision was taken at a meeting in Tunis on Christmas Day. It proved possible to rephase the programme for the return of landing craft to the U.K. and, by a stroke of luck, we picked up no less than 15 landing craft which were returning there from the Far East where an operation against the Andamans had been cancelled. The result was that it was decided to use a force of two infantry divisions plus some armour. The target date was to be on or about the 20th January. 6th Corps headquarters was out of the line at the time and seemed the obvious choice to command. It had done the Salerno landing, and General Lucas, its commander, was therefore well acquainted with the sort of problems to be faced. It was to have under command the 1st British Infantry Division, which had only recently arrived in Italy, and the U.S. 3rd Division, which had for some time been planning the operation. It was next necessary to decide on a plan to conceal the preparations for landing and to ensure, by a violent diversionary attack on the mainland, that German reserves were diverted away from the proposed beachhead.

At this period we were in the unusual position of having for a time the services of the only secret agent who, in the whole of my experience, ever produced any information worth having. He was a very exceptional man, exceptionally placed. To point the contrast it might be as well to make some remarks on the common run of secret agents or spies. To begin with, I will say that in the course of my career as a senior intelligence officer on important headquarters I read many hundreds of reports from spies, some long, some short; the bulk of them I disbelieved, a very few I suspended judgment on, but I never once based a single appreciation on information from spies and I never lived to regret not having done so. Almost the only use I ever made of them was sometimes to confirm a piece of information already known from other sources. Why should this be? The first reason is the old economic axiom, Demand Creates Supply. In war there are plenty of people ready to pay good money for information. Perhaps to begin with an agent may have a piece of information which is almost correct, and he gets paid for it. It is only sensible to expect that the next time he feels like making more money he should send something which is less firmly based, and thereafter he should use his imagination or extracts from the press. The second reason is that no-one can give more than they have got. The spy can see things and he can, sometimes, report what he sees; but because he really does not understand what he sees his report is likely to be inaccurate or misleading. In a great war where very large formations are being manoeuvred it is most unlikely that any person could be able to realize what is going on from a single vantage point, unless that vantage point should be the map room of the general directing the movement. Motor transport moving about on the ground may look purposeful but is hard to interpret. Perhaps a fully trained staff officer might, if he was very luckily placed, be able to understand something of what was afoot. But fully trained staff officers, in my experience, are not usually in a position to become spies. Suppose they were, there is always the trouble about communications. The only reliable method is by wireless in cipher; but the moment wireless sets open up they are liable to be detected by the enemy and their position tracked down by direction finding.

The use of agents was not well organized on our side. It was in the hands of various special organizations who were not under command of the Army formations to whom they supplied the information. For example I used merely to receive typed slips with the information and a cover name for the agent and a space for my comments. In Italy these comments were usually violent. The organization in question appeared to have large sums of money available and recruited widely. Results were miserable and never looked like being anything else. The trouble is that the organizers, more often than not, had no military background and did not realize what sort of rubbish they were purveying. The worst error that these naïve and useless organizations made was when they fell for a complete rogue, in the last autumn of the war in Italy, a so-called partisan leader. He claimed to be in touch with a colonel on Kesselring's staff. He invented for him the name of a Hungarian playwright whose works were published in Italy in translation; like most Italians he could see little difference between the nomenclature of the barbarous nations beyond the Alps. After providing two or three pieces of completely inaccurate information about the moves of individual German divisions this man boldly claimed to give the German plan of withdrawal from the Apennines across the Po. This so excited his British sponsors that they rewarded him with a sum in gold sovereigns so large that I am ashamed to record it. When, with all the airs of proud parenthood, they brought me the vital document, it was difficult to know whether to laugh or to cry. It was written in Italian, to begin with, and the first glance showed that it was written by someone with no military experience whatsoever. No commander could have made head or tail of it. To crown it all, as I pointed out, we happened to know the code word for the German withdrawal and the poor agent had naturally guessed it wrong. Not only was it the wrong word, it was the wrong system; whereas the Germans used code words the Italians used numbers and this bogus plan was given the name Plan 014. When, looking for a kindly word, I described the document as a whole as gibberish, it caused great offence. It was really not much worse than the average, only the unduly lavish payment singled it out. I may add that no destructive criticism was successful in disillusioning the sponsors of this fraudulent partisan. Only after the end of the war did they sadly admit that there could be some doubts about him. By that time the bulk of the organization had moved to a villa near Cannes and had passed an agreeable winter and spring directing the efforts of yet more unreliable agents in the French Alps.

From this gloomy but truthful survey of the espionage scene I turn to the one exception which I mentioned before. This is not to be put to the credit of the British organization because this agent was the agent of Colonel Revetria, the former Italian Intelligence officer whom I have mentioned already in connection with the Western Desert. He set up an espionage network before leaving Rome and when he came over to our lines in October he allowed us to use his agents. The particular one I am thinking of was a Colonel Montezemolo. He was a highly trained staff officer and I notice from one of the documents found among Mussolini's private papers that he was present at the meeting between Hitler and Mussolini at Feltre on 18th July 1943. He was therefore a man who knew the sort of information that was wanted and could interpret it properly. Next, and even more important, he was exceptionally well placed to obtain it because he was liaison officer on the staff of the German general commanding in Rome. In this position he was naturally able to find out all about the movements of German troops through Rome to the front. Finally, thanks to Revetria, he had a wireless set and ciphers whereby he could communicate with us rapidly. For some time, therefore, he passed us information a great deal of which was completely correct. He did not last long however; his use of the wireless was a bit too rash, he was tracked down and executed. I do not say that Montezemolo gave us much information that we could not have got from other sources, but he was the only man I knew in that line of business who was of any use at all.

The date for the Anzio landing was fixed for the 22nd January and the preliminary operations began on the 17th. The opening move was an attack by the British 10th Corps across the Garigliano River near its mouth in the mountains to the south of the Liri Valley. This started well and the Germans were forced to bring in two divisions to stem the thrust. One of them was brought over from opposite Eighth Army and the other, most gratifyingly, from reserve near Rome. A further contribution still was made to our main object in Italy: the Hermann Goering Division was under orders to go to France where it was to be deployed ready to meet the expected invasion of next summer; but as soon as we attacked, these orders were countermanded and this division too was put into line against 10th Corps' attack. With this reinforcement there were now four German divisions to our three, impossible odds in mountain country.

The next phase of the attack was to be a crossing of the Rapido River by the American 36th Division. This was a complete failure though it was pressed with great gallantry at the cost of heavy losses. It was also, in America, the greatest source of controversy in the entire Italian campaign. The 36th Division, as I have mentioned before, was Texas' pride and there is nothing small about the State of Texas, especially when it comes to complaints. What the grounds were for the complaint I never found out. After all, not all attacks are successful, and a contested river crossing is always a particularly delicate operation. The 36th Division, whatever its members might have thought of themselves, was neither the best nor the worst division in Italy. Their own view, however, was that their failure, since it could not possibly be their fault, must be directly due to General Clark himself. In the years immediately following the war there were constant demands from the National Guard Association of Texas for an investigation into the affair and condemnatory votes in the strongest terms were carried against General Clark. They very civilly sent a message to Lord Alexander, then Governor General of Canada (I was serving on his staff at the time) saying that of course nothing of this was to be taken as critical of him, for whose strategic genius they had the highest admiration.

The attack by 36th Division went in on the night of the 20th January and failure was accepted on the 22nd; but whether successful or not, the two attacks made by 10th Corps and 2nd Corps on the main front drew in every reserve division in von Vietinghoff's 10th Army. All of them were heavily engaged when the 6th Corps sailed from Naples in the early morning of the 21st January. At that moment the state of the opposing forces was as follows. Allied strength amounted to slightly over twenty divisions, but two of them were not yet available for employment. The Germans had between twenty and twenty-one divisions. Thirteen of these were in 10th Army, facing ten to twelve on our side. The remainder were under command of the German 14th Army under General von Mackensen. As a result of our diversionary operations all 10th Army's divisions were concentrated on the main front and most of them were fighting hard. The nearest division of 14th Army was around Leghorn. It will be seen that the Germans had entirely failed to anticipate an amphibious landing on our part. The only troops in the neighbourhood of Anzio were a very much under strength battalion from one of the motorized divisions. This had been sent for a rest by the seaside to recover from its heavy losses in the fighting around Cassino. Anzio was considered a suitable place and the C.O. was told to practice his men in demolition by starting to blow up the small harbour works at Anzio. Fortunately he had been told that there was no hurry about this so that hardly anything had been done at the moment when we landed. Not only did we thus get strategic surprise, we nearly achieved tactical surprise as well, which is a thing almost past praying for in an amphibious operation. The main credit for this goes to the air force, who made a heavy attack on the 19th January on the base for the enemy's long range reconnaissance aircraft at Perugia. The result was that the invasion convoy sailed up the coast all day of the 21st in perfect weather without being noticed by anybody. As a further help, the Navy carried out a demonstration off Civitavecchia, north of the Tiber, on the night of the 21st, so that when the Germans did get their reconnaissance aircraft off the ground on the morning of the 22nd they went straight to Civitavecchia. The first solid news that the Germans got came from a fighter pilot who happened to observe an invasion in full swing at Anzio at 8.20 a.m. This was more than six hours after the first assault troops had landed. All in all it seems to constitute some sort of a record for amphibious landings.

It may well be asked why this highly auspicious beginning did not lead to more immediate and positive results. A fair answer, I think, would be to say that our side was rather too slow and the enemy side was distinctly too quick. To start with our side: General Lucas had first risen to command a Corps at the crisis of the Salerno landings. He therefore was bound to have in mind the necessity of having a firm base and being ready to stand off the inevitable counter attacks. It seems likely, though there is nothing in writing to show it, that General Clark had given him pretty firm advice not to run too great risks. The very fact that he had got his troops ashore without any fighting, and that he had twice as many as planned in the original conception of the operation, must have persuaded him that he could proceed fairly deliberately and provide both for a firm beachhead and also for a strong thrust into the Alban Hills. There was a further, mechanical, reason. The Anzio beaches were not good, and although we soon brought the harbour into use there was a distinct delay before the guns and the motor transport and the tanks could be got ashore and into the hands of their crews. But this would have had little effect if the Corps Commander had seriously intended to press on inland with speed.

The primary credit for frustrating the intentions of Shingle in the first phase must undoubtedly go to Field Marshal Kesselring (I say in the first phase, because in the final phase in May the Anzio beachhead played a full and vital part). I do not think we ever attacked Kesselring in Italy without taking him completely by surprise. He never guessed where our blow was coming and always fell into our diversionary traps. At the crucial moment, however, when he seemed to have made a complete mess of everything, the German genius for improvisation came brilliantly to the rescue. When a commander who is heavily engaged along his whole front suddenly finds that a large enemy force has appeared in his rear and is about to attack his sole line of communication it would be normal to expect that he would prepare to pull back the troops whose communications are in danger. Kesselring did not yield an inch. First of all he scraped together odd units of his main line forces who happened to be in the rear and sent them off one at a time to take up blocking positions round the bridge-head. With that disregard of rigid subordination which was character-istic of the German Army they were formed into scratch regimental and divisional groups under whichever commander happened to be the senior officer present. The next move was to bring down as many troops as he could from his 14th Army. The Fuehrer's H.Q. also acted speedily. They hastily despatched to Italy two new divisions plus infantry, artillery and tank units totalling altogether more than another division. With these Kesselring was supposed not merely to contain but to eliminate the Anzio Bridgehead. All this was thoroughly in line with the directive under which the Allied forces in Italy were working.

This reinforcement meant that when 6th Corps did make a serious thrust forward, which was not until the 25th January, the Germans were in a position to hold it up. The next attempt on 30th January made even less progress. On the 3rd February the Germans counter-attacked and drove us out of the long, thin, salient which we had gained. It was clear that this was only a foretaste of further offensives to come.

In readiness for them Alexander sent two more reinforcing divisions to Anzio and diversionary attacks were made on the main front. The latter made no vital gains of ground and did not divert enemy troops away from Anzio. The attack by 14th Army began with some preliminary operations between 7th and 12th February which were intended to gain a firm base. The principal attack went in on the morning of 16th February. The Germans had got together the equiva-lent of about ten divisions; Allied strength was rather under five divisions. Many of the German divisions were new, and pride of place in the assault was given to the Infantry Demonstration Regiment, a picked body from the infantry school at Doberitz. Two new battalions of Panther and Tiger tanks were brought from Germany. Also a new secret weapon was employed for the first time in 1944, a year which was to be famous for secret weapons. This one had the name Goliath. It was a miniature tank about three feet long and sixteen inches high filled with explosives. It was controlled through two wires which it paid out behind it. When the controller, from a safe position in the rear, saw that it had reached a suitable place he set off the explosive by remote control. This should have been quite a good idea but it proved a fiasco at Anzio, partly because there was too little suitable cover (the bocage country of Normandy would have been ideal) and partly because the ground was so cut up with water obstacles. In addition there was a special order of the day from Hitler. In spite of all this, and in spite of great disparity in strength, the attack was unsuccessful. The defensive was a new game for us in Italy but it was well handled by the new Corps Commander. Just as Lucas himself relieved the previous commander in the middle of the battle of Salerno, so now, at the crisis of this battle, he was relieved by General Lucian D. Truscott. Truscott was undoubtedly the most gifted of the American commanders in Italy. He later showed himself a master in the attack as well.

It was a heavy German defeat. Unfortunately we also suffered a defeat at the same time in our offensive on the Cassino front. Alexander was now bringing over divisions from Eighth Army and the eastern flank to strengthen the pressure around Cassino. The Americans had tried to get in from the north but were held up just short of Monastery Hill. For the second attempt Alexander decided to use the New Zealand Division and the 4th Indian Division, both of whom were put under command of General Freyberg. Their attack was simultaneous with that of 14th Army at Anzio on 16th January. It was in connection with this that the bombardment of the monastery was ordered. There was a great deal of discussion about this at the time and since, but there is no doubt that as Alexander says in his despatch: 'It was an integral part of the German defensive system, mainly from the superb observation it afforded.' We were naturally most interested to pick up whatever confirmation there could be of the Germans being actually in the monastery at the time of the bombing. Our people were listening in on the regimental net of the German Parachute Regiment concerned to see if anything turned up. There was indeed quite a hasty exchange of messages in clear and the officer responsible came and laid on my desk, with an air of satisfaction, the following question and answer from the regiment to battalion:

'Is battalion H.Q. still in the monastery?'

'Yes.'

This appeared to be a handsome confirmation, but for the sake of greater certainty I asked to see the German original of the question. This turned out to be 'Ist Abt noch im Kloster?' ABT was the standard abbreviation for 'Abteilung' which means battalion—but not infantry battalion, which is 'bataillon'. I looked on to the next question which was 'Are the monks there?' and the truth suddenly dawned: Abt is also the German for abbot, a word which had not hitherto come to my notice in German military messages. The Abbot of Cassino was indeed in the monastery at the time of the bombardment and so were some of his monks.

Even 4th Indian Division in the mountains and even the New Zealand Division down below were unable to make any progress. In heavy snow and rain the attack was called off. We were now approaching the time when an offensive must be planned which would give direct and simultaneous assistance to the landing on the coast of France. To this end we were already making the useful contribution of holding down twenty-three divisions but we must make certain that the same number at least were held up until June. This was the object of an appreciation by General John Harding, Alexander's Chief of Staff, on the 22nd February. He defined the object of operations in Italy as 'to force the enemy to commit the maximum number of divisions in Italy at the time Overlord is launched'. There was no point, therefore, in our frittering away our strength in unsuccessful minor operations. The aim must be to build up the greatest possible force so that when we attacked in May, to take a target date a month before Overlord, we should not merely hold in Italy the German formations which were already there but should destroy as many as possible of them and thus force the Germans to replace them with divisions from elsewhere. Such reinforcement would either come direct from France or would be divisions which were being held in readiness to go to France. Before that time, however, Alexander thought we should try once more to capture Cassino, or at least as much of it as would give us a bridgehead over the Rapido for future use.

At this point in the planning the Air Force suddenly took a hand with claims both in the strategic and in the tactical field, which sounded promising but were rapidly shown to be fallacious. To take first of all the strategic field; when Alexander reported his intentions, based on John Harding's appreciation, to General Wilson, General Eisenhower's successor, it appeared that a different and much more sanguine view of the possibilities was common at Allied Force H.Q. in Algiers. General Wilson replied that, in his view, if a moderate but continuous pressure were maintained on the ground the effect of allied bombing of the enemy's communications would be so great as to compel him to withdraw at least to the Pisa/Rimini line. The idea was that as time went on the enemy would discover that he was completely running out of both food and ammunition. General Wilson was even worried that our spring offensive might prove to be a blow in the air. This cheerful, not to say starry-eyed, overestimate of the powers of the air offensive was not borne out by events.

The strategic part of the Air Force plan took some time to disclose its fallaciousness; the errors of the next tactical suggestion were shown up more quickly. As though amused at our footling efforts at Cassino the Air Force offered to get us out of our difficulties by an annihilating air bombardment. John Cannon, although as a practical man he had not quite the easy optimism of the strategic backroom boys, said that given decent weather he would 'whip out Cassino like an old tooth'. Orthodox methods had had no success so far, so it was no time to look a gift horse in the mouth. Without very much hope, but in the mood to try anything once, the Army agreed to let the Air Force show their paces. General Cannon had asked for clear weather for his attack; for the sake of the troops on the ground, particularly the tanks, the Army thought it would be as well to have three fine days. Three fine days together are of course the greatest possible rarity in Italian winters; but after two failures Alexander was determined to wait, even though it meant keeping General Freyberg's Corps waiting at 24 hours' notice. However, after three weeks, on the 14th March, it looked as though conditions were going to be just right. The greater part of General Alexander's H.Q. went forward to watch. Cassino is the most hateful name to front line troops but as a spectacle it had numerous advantages. From Monte Trocchio, a steep hill about half a mile away, the observer could get a perfect grandstand view of everything that was going on without danger to himself. Or so at any rate it seemed, since the Germans rarely wasted any artillery fire on the summit but they had strewn the whole thing with mines. I used to scramble up Monte Trocchio fairly frequently but did so with less enthusiasm after General Kippenberger had both his feet blown off while doing so. However, for the bombardment Alexander, Cannon and their staffs took their places in a fairly deep trench to the north of Monte Trocchio.

The attack was made by the whole of the Tactical Air Force in Italy, plus all the Strategic Air Force in the Mediterranean theatre. The total weight of high explosives dropped amounted to over 1,100 tons. The Flying Fortresses, who were perhaps used to working with rather larger margins of error than was available in a tactical situation of this sort, distributed their favours fairly widely. It was as well that the trench was deep, for it was nicely bracketed by one bomb load. The New Zealanders had pulled well back but they also suffered losses and one group of strategic bombers attacked with great violence the H.Q. of the French Expeditionary Corps, some 10 miles further north. However, the better aimed proportion of the 1,100 tons, plus some 2,000 rounds of artillery fire, were enough to make the buildings dance in the air. A heavy dust cloud rose to the top of Monastery Hill. When the bombing ceased the New Zealanders were very quick to follow up into the town; but to their surprise they found the Germans still resisting. It was the 1st Parachute Division and Alexander says that he doubts whether any other division in the German Army could have done it. They had of course suffered very heavy casualties and quite a number had actually been driven mad; the remainder, who had sheltered in the numerous deep cellars of the town, found when they emerged that the heaps of rubble left by the bombing offered admirable defensive positions. The whole ground was turned up into ridges and furrows as though by some great plough. Landmarks were unrecognizable and the tanks had the greatest difficulty in forcing their way in. Nevertheless the New Zealanders were successful in securing most of the town. That night the Italian climate, surely the worst that any miserable country was ever cursed with, took a decisive hand. The meteorologists had promised us fine weather, but, as they freely admitted, no forecast is of any value in Italy. The rain descended as if poured from a bucket. The bomb craters filled up like lakes, the Rapido overflowed its banks, which had of course been breached in a number of places by the bombing, and nothing on wheels or even tracks could move. The heavy rainclouds blacked out the moon and 4th Indian Division's night attack on Monastery Hill also failed of final success. At this point Alexander decided to stop. He had got a footing over the Rapido at the entrance to the Valley route and the Anzio bridgehead, which had just successfully repulsed another German counter attack, was secure. A six weeks pause would allow us to gather our strength for the decisive moment, while the German position was so stretched that they were not likely to be able to spare any men for France.

This was a hard winter both for the Italians and for the troops in the field. For the former it started out with a violent outbreak of typhus in Naples. This might be called a traditional accompaniment of any war in Italy, but this time it was stopped short with dramatic suddenness by the application of D.D.T. Every man, woman and child in the city was sprayed with it by rapidly formed teams, and the death roll came to an abrupt halt. As if by way of revenge and to show the full range of which Italy was capable, Vesuvius staged its largest eruption for 300 years. It was a splendid sight at night with great flames leaping from the crater but when I went to watch a lava flow which was destroying a village I found it much less exciting. The lava looked like a slag heap in the Black Country which could be seen to be moving simply because bits kept on tumbling down from the top to the bottom. Occasionally when a large piece fell forward the internal glow could be seen. It would lean against a wall until the wall collapsed suddenly. When it engulfed a tree the tree flamed straight up in the air like a torch.

In January, Alexander's H.Q. moved across to Naples and settled in the great Royal Palace of Caserta, about 50 miles outside the town. This is an enormous building inspired by Versailles. The gardens are on an even vaster scale with spectacular waterworks. The cascade had indeed lost much of its beauty by being bombed halfway along its length and the ornamental lawns and groves were untended. We slept in the grounds; I had my own caravan which had accompanied me from Tunisia and was camouflaged in what the designer intended as a bosky grove. In appropriate eighteenth-century style, it was loud with nightingales, so loud in fact that I had difficulty in sleeping. Everyone agrees that the nightingale's song is beautiful but I have never seen it mentioned before that it is also extremely noisy. With a dozen or so singing at once the total sound is about equivalent in volume to a small goods-yard. The eighteenth century was also with me when awake. I had been given access, through the good offices of one of my staff, to the Palace Libraries. The books had all been put away for safe keeping in one of the attics but I was allowed a key and for the five months I was there read myself steadily through the standard French eighteenth-century authors. I formed the opinion that Lytton Strachey had been wrong in writing down Voltaire's plays and Aldous Huxley right in writing up Crébillon. Another standard repertoire to which we were exposed during this period was that of opera. The Palace had a small jewel of a private opera house seating about 200. Hither would come twice a week the San Carlo Opera Company who worked their way steadily through from Trovatore to Tosca and then began again. It was not, I think, the best company, who had been caught somewhere behind the German lines; but it was conscientious even though sometimes a little pathetic. The cast was paid mainly in

N.A.A.F.I. food, for Naples was distinctly short. It was a pleasure to slip in at nights to the Royal Box for a rattling second-rate performance. Interestingly enough the troops developed a great taste for opera and I imagine that a good deal of opera's advance in favour that has taken place since the war is due to these Italian experiences.

For all that it was a busy time and Caserta was more like a monastery than a palace of pleasure. From its very nature the Italian campaign depended more for its evaluation on Intelligence than did campaigns elsewhere. The criterion of success was the calculation of enemy divisions contained. From that point of view the continuous contact all along the front meant that sources of information were constant and reliable. It was reasonable to expect that when the crisis came in May we should be able to form a pretty sound judgment of the success. of our holding operations.

One of our main tasks in the Intelligence section was of course to present the picture of the situation as it would appear to the enemy commander. We calculated that from Kesselring's point of view there were clear gains as well as losses to be reckoned. The severest loss was the mere fact that the western allies had been able to open on European soil a second front besides the eastern front. It was not, of course, anything like so extensive, but it was holding down twenty-three valuable divisions and causing the Germans a steady drain in casualties. Anzio alone had meant the equivalent of four divisions being lost to other fronts. On the other side of the account it must be admitted that only seven months before he had expected things to be much worse. Then he had expected to spend the winter defending the Apennines between Pisa and Rimini, rather than holding a strong front well south of Rome. The main land effort of the allies for 1943 had been confined in a narrow peninsula and not even their command of the sea, the thing which the Germans always feared most, had enabled them to break out. His army was in good shape, well supplied and kept up to strength most assiduously. On the average he received every month of the winter 15,000 men in drafts—the equivalent of a division per month. His ammunition and supply position was excellent. With these advantages he had just inflicted three heavy defeats on us in our attempts to break his lines at Cassino. For all that he must have reflected that the calm which descended at the end of March would be the herald of a storm greater than any he had experienced in Italy so far. Surveying his unnatural two-faced front, he must have had the most serious apprehensions.

CHAPTER XV

From Rome to the Apennines

THE spring offensive of May 1944 which culminated in the capture of Rome, was one of the most remarkable examples of generalship in the whole course of the war. Enough has already been said to make it obvious that the Italian campaign was never an affair of battering our way onwards, for we never had sufficient numbers to make such tactics possible. Success was always due to stratagems. Never was greater effort devoted to this than during March and April. The problem can be stated in fairly simple terms, as is the case with almost all military problems. First of all our landing craft had all gone home for Overlord so that we no longer had the means to mount an amphibious attack and must advance overland. Secondly, experience had shown that for a successful land attack in Italian conditions the attacker must have at least a three to one superiority in infantry. Looking at the terrain it was quite clear that a large scale offensive east of the Apennines along the Adriatic coast was quite out of the question. The country was extremely difficult and even a successful advance could not lead anywhere. The main weight must therefore be brought to bear on the west coast. To launch a large scale offensive from the Anzio bridgehead was impossible because no more troops could be maintained there than were already there. The Anzio force must admittedly go over to the attack at some stage of the offensive, and this was an enormously valuable card to play; but it was inescapable that the main effort must be made somewhere between Cassino and the sea. This reasoning seemed to us so obvious that it must, one supposed, be equally obvious to Kesselring.

Alexander's plan was accordingly to reduce the Adriatic front to a purely holding front of two divisions and to bring over the whole of Eighth Army except for those two divisions to the western sector. Fifth Army would then have a narrow coastal sector south of the Liri Valley plus the Anzio bridgehead. The main attack would be delivered by Eighth Army, now commanded by General Sir Oliver Leese, at the Cassino position once more. Fifth Army could assist with operations in the mountains to the south of the Liri Valley and at a given moment would make a strong breakout from Anzio. At one time Alexander thought of starting with the Anzio operation in order if possible to draw troops away from the main front; he decided against it mainly because it became clear from the enemy's dispositions that that was what he expected us to do. It would also not fit in with the deception plan, whose advantages became steadily more obvious. There had to be a deception plan because, after scraping together divisions from every part of the Mediterranean, Alexander could still only manage an overall superiority of one-and-a-quarter to one. This was less than half the superiority which he had laid down in his original plan as necessary.

The plan of attack on the main front involved the employment of five Corps between Cassino and the sea. From left to right they were the American 2nd Corps of two divisions, the French Expeditionary Corps of four divisions, plus about 12,000 Moroccan troops organized in Goums, 13th British Corps of four divisions, 2nd Polish Corps of two divisions and the Canadian Corps, also of two divisions, held in reserve. This was a very formidable concentration for a front of only some 25–30 miles. It was vital to conceal it. For this purpose we could rely on the generally poor performance of German intelligence, which took a long time to wake up to our moves. (One disadvantage, however, was that they were liable to overestimate our strength and invent non-existent divisions, so that our best endeavours might be frustrated by an imaginative effort on the part of one of their unreliable agents.) Secondly we put into effect right from the start of the planning a most rigid security and camouflage plan. This was very difficult because the enemy had such admirable observation. From Monte Cairo behind Cassino, and from Monte Maio on the south of the valley, they could look right into our rear areas. In the sector north of Monastery Hill, which was now being taken over by the Polish Corps, we found it necessary to erect a tall screen of hessian over a mile long to conceal movement on an important track. All dumps of course were carefully camouflaged, all moves forward were made by night and dummy tanks and vehicles were left behind in the areas vacated. 13th Corps, which was going to do the assault over the Rapido, made large numbers of tracks leading down to the selected crossing points by night and covered them with brushwood so that they should not be noticeable by day.

All this was thoroughly necessary but negative. Something positive in the way of deception was essential, otherwise the enemy would be bound to work out exactly what our plan must be. We decided that, even though it rather savoured of crying wolf once more, the only thing to do was to persuade the enemy that we were going to do another amphibious landing. He was not to know that we could hardly have transported a platoon, because all our faithful landing craft were now lining up on the north shore of the English Channel. We accordingly decided to simulate a landing at Civitavecchia; this was rather *vieux jeu* since we had already laid on a diversion there at the time of Anzio, but if we had had landing craft, and spare troops to put in them, Civitavecchia would have been a good place for a landing because it would have put us on the other side of the Tiber in a good open plain and in possession of a port of some capacity. The Canadian Corps were nominated for the notional role to carry out the landing, plus the American 36th Division. The reason for this is that the two Canadian Divisions and the 36th would all three be in reserve at the start of the offensive, and therefore there was no danger of their losing prisoners and thus blowing the gaff. Canadian Corps Signals detachment were accordingly sent down to the Naples/Salerno area where they passed a good deal of wireless traffic and spent some time splashing about in boats.

To our great delight, and surprise, these deceptive measures succeeded perfectly. It was clear that they had done so before the battle opened when we surveyed Kesselring's dispositions. Every single mobile division in his two armies was disposed somewhere on the west coast waiting for the invasion. Between their main line and Anzio was the 15th Panzer Grenadier Division, between Anzio and the Tiber the 90th Panzer Grenadier Division, and north of the Tiber, on either side of Civitavecchia, was the 29th Panzer Grenadier Division. This last was particularly gratifying; it removed a valuable and experienced formation so far from the battle front as to be almost out of the operational area altogether. The other two mobile divisions, the 3rd Panzer Grenadier and 26th Panzer, were both facing 6th Corps at Anzio; they were also earmarked as available for use against a seaborne landing. This shows, incidentally, one of the reasons why we decided against leading with the left handed punch from Anzio: that the enemy reserves were in that neighbourhood. It also shows the advantage of the deception plan in that an attack in strength on the Rapido front would be exactly what the enemy would expect as the first move in an attack even if the main move was to be a seaborne landing or eruption from the bridgehead. After all, we had done exactly the same at the time of the Anzio landing in January. Accordingly he might be expected to be slow to put in his reserves against it until we had shown our hand.

One of the reasons why the memory of this battle is dear to the Intelligence officer is not merely that we succeeded so gratifyingly in misleading the enemy but that we were so rapidly able to prove it. About three weeks after the battle started the H.Q. of 14th Army, von Mackensen's Army, was overrun and we made a haul of almost the complete Intelligence files. The most graphic items consisted of a continuous set of situation maps showing the position of the German troops at midday each day and what the Intelligence staff thought was the position of the allied troops. I might mention here a point of technique which, from the historian's point of view, worked to the Germans' disadvantage. For some reason the Germans, at all staff levels, made no use of talc and chinagraph. At a British H.Q. the Intelligence or Operations staff would pin up a map on a board, place over it a sheet of talc and proceed to draw in the dispositions of their own and the enemy's troops with grease pencils. If a mistake was made it could easily be rubbed out. The Germans for some reason liked their maps to lie flat on a table. It was Hitler's habit to be photographed leaning over a table and pointing down at a map on it. As a result they drew straight on to the map itself. At 14th Army H.Q., and as far as I know elsewhere too, it was the practice of the Chief Intelligence Officer to have a new map produced every day. This splendid series remained as an eloquent witness of how thick was the fog of war from the German side.

The most significant map was dated 12th May, the day after our attack began. This shows that even then the enemy had no idea of what was about to hit them. The French had been particularly successful in concealing their forward concentrations. They had taken over the northern sector of the existing bridgehead over the Garigliano and into this area, roughly semi-circular with a radius of only about 4,000 yards, they had packed twenty battalions, five batteries and two divisional H.Q.s. The German Intelligence had shown them with only one division forward and one well in the rear. The Canadian Corps had been completely lost sight of. 36th Division, however, had been located carrying out invasion exercises. There was an entirely mythical 18th British Division in a pointless position in the mountainous central sector. Our dispositions, in fact, as they appeared to the Germans were obviously not those of an enemy about to launch a strong attack. General Vietinghoff, who commanded 10th Army which was to be our first object of attack, had picked 11th May, which was D-Day, to go off to Germany on leave. He was under the impression that in the vital sector from Cassino to the sea we had only six divisions and that, as he had four divisions in the same sector, he was perfectly well placed to conduct a successful defensive, for his prepared defences there were extremely strong. In actual fact we were about to throw against these four divisions the equivalent of over thirteen divisions. By camouflage and deception we had succeeded in creating at the vital point a superiority of better than three to one. Not only that; so thoroughly was Kesselring convinced of the imminence of a landing in his rear that when he did send in his reserves he sent them in hesitantly, piecemeal and too late. Clearly we had thus gained strategic surprise; but Eighth Army's attack was blessed with tactical surprise as well. Things seemed so quiet on the 11th May that not only did the Army Commander go off undisturbed for his leave but his H.Q. thought that this would be a good time to reorganise the rather disjointed chain of command on the Cassino front. The Parachutists carried out a bit of a reshuffle in Cassino itself and down in the valley a more thorough reorganization was planned. The defences of the Rapido were at the time being held by five battalions from different divisions, and to introduce a bit of order a divisional H.Q. from north of Cassino was brought down to take over command. Then, when the attack went in, the plan had to be changed and the unfortunate divisional H.Q. was sent back again. It requires little imagination to picture the confusion. One striking result was that in the late afternoon of the 11th May a sudden and disconcerting silence descended on the Liri Valley front. Our own artillery had been ordered to slacken and cease fire gradually so as to avoid alerting the enemy unduly; the Germans also decided to slacken off in order to keep things quiet while the reliefs were going on. For a couple of hours there was not a sound until our artillery was ordered to start sporadic shelling to avoid arousing suspicions. At 11 o'clock that night over 2,000 guns opened up in the heaviest barrage of the Mediterranean front so far.

It must not be supposed, however, that the German soldier, even when taken at a disadvantage, gave up easily. For one thing there were no less than two extremely strong prepared positions in the Liri Valley. The Rapido River line had proved too much for the 36th Division in January and the intervening four months had seen it considerably strengthened. 4th British and 8th Indian Divisions of 13th Corps had a very severe struggle and at the end of the first 24 hours had only gained about half the objectives which it was hoped would have been taken in the first two hours. The Poles on the right had even less success; their assault on Monastery Hill had started well but by two o'clock next afternoon they had been driven back to their start line. Fifth Army had also made little progress, although on their sector they were bringing nearly seven divisions against two German, and they were not the best German divisions. Nevertheless it was clear that the Germans must soon be worn down by the weight of the attack and then Fifth Army would have a magnificent chance of outflanking the whole Liri Valley. The French Corps, besides one motorized division, contained one Algerian and two Moroccan infantry divisions and one of the latter was a mountain division. In addition there were 12,000 goumiers, irregular troops all experienced in mountain warfare. This was a great advantage though it did not last long; they were only in Italy for three months. Alexander was always asking to be allotted mountain-trained troops but without success, except that we got an American mountain division for the last three months of the campaign. There was one British mountain division, the 52nd Scottish, which we always hoped might come to Italy. It never did and when it at last went into action, towards the end of 1944, it was not in the mountains but in land below sea level in Holland.

The pattern of the battle conformed well to the plan. Fifth Army pushed forward on the left through the Aurunci Mountains, which the Germans had always thought too difficult, while Eighth Army moved massively forward up the Liri Valley. The enemy defences on that route were at their most developed and General Leese, who had not served under Montgomery for nothing, felt himself obliged to mount a deliberate set-piece attack on each one. Traffic congestion on the very inadequate road net was intense. However, the Germans also favoured a deliberate set-piece defence and suffered thereby the greater casualties. Cassino was pinched out between the Poles up above and 13th Corps down below; but it was a week from the opening of the attack before the Polish flag was raised over the ruins of the Monastery.

Two days before the fall of Cassino the Germans got their first identification of the Canadian Corps and discovered that it was not, as they thought, preparing to land behind their lines but was advancing in full strength up the Liri Valley. From then on Kesselring began to dribble in the mobile reserves which had previously been looking anxiously out to sea. They came up in detail and were defeated in detail. There was, however, a strong fortified line drawn across the Valley from Piedimonte to Pontecorvo. Its original name was 'Fuehrerriegel' which we called the Adolf Hitler Line, and continued to do so after the Germans had renamed it Dora. It had been some months in building and included a number of underground fortifications with tank turrets set in concrete. If it had been held in strength it would have been a very difficult proposition, but the troops who should have been its garrison were too severely reduced by the battles in front of it. Nevertheless, a serious operation was called for and this could not be mounted before the morning of the 23rd May.

Simultaneously General Truscott's 6th Corps began to break out from Anzio. He now had seven divisions there whereas the Germans had been drawing off their forces for the benefit of the Liri Valley front. The attack was made an hour after dawn, a time which Truscott thought would probably find the enemy in a more relaxed mood after the traditional stand-to at dawn. His appreciation was justified and considerable progress was made. By the 25th May Eighth Army was well through the last prepared defences in the Liri Valley and Fifth Army on its extreme left had joined up overland with the Anzio force.

This was a moment of acute danger for the Germans. Looking at the map it might seem that the greater part of the 10th and 14th Armies was threatened with envelopment. Critics have indeed argued that there was a possibility of an even more striking victory than the one that was gained; it is true that we captured Rome and inflicted such heavy losses on the enemy that he had to carry out a large and expensive programme of reinforcement to the detriment of the western front; but it is possible that an even larger part of Kesselring's armies might have been destroyed. There are two reasons why this possibility was not realized. One, the less important, was that Eighth Army, who faced the bulk of the enemy strength, could press forward only slowly against their determined resistance. The other is that General Clark, who had moved his H.Q. to Anzio to direct from the spot the operations of his vital left wing, changed the direction of his advance and went for Rome instead of for the encirclement of the enemy. He had been meeting very stiff resistance in his original drive on Valmontone on the vital route 6. This was natural enough since, if he could capture Valmontone, the bulk of the Germans facing Eighth Army would have been cut off from Rome and forced on to the very inferior line of communications running north either side of the Simbruini mountains. The thrust for Rome was easier, indeed at one point the 36th American Division was able to seize a vital point on the Alban Hills without opposition, but the change of direction meant that such chance as there was of a really decisive battle was lost.

Whether or not it might have been a greater victory it certainly was a great one. The two German armies were thoroughly disorganized. When Valmontone was captured on the 1st June there was little opportunity left for anything but an immediate and precipitate retreat. On the evening of the 4th June the first American troops entered Rome. The capture of Rome itself was a stimulus to Allied morale, coming as it did just two days before the landing in Normandy. It also provided us with a large number of bridges over the Tiber by means of which the pursuit of the enemy could be made easier. Alexander had prepared two armoured divisions for this task, the 6th British and the 6th South African. He signalled to General Brooke that night 'If only the country were more open we could make hay of the whole lot.' Even as it was the pursuit was speedily pressed. The South Africans made 33 miles on the first day and the Germans were unable to call a halt until they were nearly 130 miles north of Rome.

I have not made much of the fall of Rome because, although we knew it would get us a good press throughout the world, we were really concentrating far more on the destruction of the enemy. From all the evidence coming in it was clear that many of the German divisions had been reduced almost to ineffectiveness. We were then in greater strength than we were ever to be again in Italy. I confess that, having gone forward on purpose to Fifth Army H.Q., I did visit Rome on the morning of the 5th in time to see General Clark being photographed on the Capitol. On the way I was annoyed by coming under small arms fire from a methodical little street fight apparently between Italian supporters and opponents of the Fascist Republic.

The capture of Rome and the start of the pursuit north marked the first climax of the Italian campaign. In view of the defeat which the Germans had suffered, and the great preponderance which the Allies enjoyed in men, equipment and morale, there was every chance, apart from interference from outside, of driving them the whole length of the way up the leg of Italy, over the Apennines and across the Po that same summer. None of us doubted, and Alexander confidently asserts, that we could have been pushing our way into Hungary or southern Austria by the autumn. This would have had the most profound effect on the political aftermath of the war. If it had been the western allies rather than the Russians who had first captured Budapest and Vienna a great deal of the post-war difficulties with the Russians would have been avoided. Instead the victorious armies in Italy were split up and a large part of their strength was diverted to an irrelevant and unnecessary operation in the south of France.

At the time that Overlord was first planned a proposal was included for a secondary landing on the French Mediterranean coast. The original code name was Anvil, later altered to Dragoon. This operation was always strongly favoured by the Americans, and even more strongly by Stalin, who welcomed anything that would keep the western allies out of central and eastern Europe. The troops earmarked for it amounted to seven divisions, three American and four French, with a large number of Corps and Army troops. The decision to mount Dragoon was taken eventually on 2nd July and the operation went in on 15th August. It was therefore hanging over the Italian front for some time before it began to exercise its full effect. These withdrawals were a severe loss to the allied armies in Italy. Particularly regrettable was the loss of the French who included the only mountain-trained troops. Kesselring was given a reprieve, a breathing space to reorganize his scattered forces and to incorporate the heavy reinforcements which he received, and the allied armies were left with just insufficient strength to carry them across the barrier of the Apennines. The Italian theatre continued to fulfil its role of diverting German divisions, but it lost the possibility of playing a role of major strategic and political value.

These serious results would have been worth while if Dragoon itself had been an operation of outstanding value. Naturally all of us on Alexander's staff pooh-poohed the idea at the time but I have since read practically everything that has been written on the subject, including Eisenhower's elaborate apologia, and I cannot persuade myself that it was worth while. Its original purpose was to assist Overlord by holding down German troops in the south of France. Now in fact this purpose was fully achieved by the mere threat of a landing. The Germans were aware that we had the capacity to make such a landing—indeed they undoubtedly overestimated our capacity in their usual way. We could be certain therefore that they would continue to man their defences on the Mediterranean coast. They could not have stuck to that much longer than they did, for by the middle of August the front in Northern France was fluid and unless the

Germans had started quite soon to withdraw they would have found themselves entirely cut off from Germany. As things turned out, therefore, the Allied landing on the Riviera came as a signal for them to withdraw. Making very little resistance they pulled back up the Rhone Valley just in time to fall in on the left wing of the German forces now back defending the western frontier of Germany. So far therefore from drawing German troops away from the front opposite General Eisenhower, Dragoon actually accelerated the arrival there of the German garrison of the Riviera.

The next argument which is used in favour of Dragoon is that it was vital to get control of the southern French ports because in so many of the ports in northern France the Germans left strong garrisons which denied them to us. This makes better sense, because this object was at least attained, by contrast with the original diversionary object. The only thing is that all the evidence goes to show that we could have obtained the use of southern French ports very little later thanks to a voluntary German withdrawal and without having to land any troops. Finally, Dragoon did of course mean that seven more divisions, all experienced ones, came under General Eisenhower's command. Manpower, however, was not at that time a problem and against these slight advantages must be set the fact that the loss of seven divisions meant breaking the back of the Italian campaign.

The Allied directors of general strategy saw no objection to treating Italy in this way. They had from the first regarded it as a secondary theatre. The German reaction was strikingly different. At the moment that we were removing seven divisions from Italy the Germans were sending eight new divisions there. They were actually prepared to take divisions away from the western theatre for the benefit of Italy. One came from Denmark, another from Holland, two from the Balkans and one from Russia. Of the remaining three, which had just completed forming in Germany, one was earmarked for the Russian front and had already been issued with appropriate equipment. Perhaps even more striking was the fact that a battalion of Tiger tanks was withdrawn from the Central Reserve held in France at Mailly-le-Camp and sent to Italy. This was at a time when the Germans were desperately in need of armour to combat the menacing growth of the Allied bridgehead in Normandy. It must also be remembered that just at this time the Russians were for the first time threatening East Prussia. These heavy reinforcements were, of course, in addition to the normal reinforcing drafts which continued to arrive right up to the end of the campaign. They were certainly needed. Three of Kesselring's divisions had temporarily ceased to exist as effective formations. They were resurrected when their numbers were given to three of the new divisions from Germany. The 92nd Infantry Division was not considered capable of resurrection; it was disbanded and never reformed.

Kesselring also received other non-German reinforcements which were of less value. Shortly after the capture of Rome, when the Americans were advancing northwards up the west coast, their forward troops were startled to receive a charge of Cossack cavalry. This was the harbinger of the arrival of the 162nd Division, which was a regular German Army Division but made up of Russian prisoners. The bulk of them came from Central Asia and it was accordingly called the 162nd (Turkoman) Division. The Cossack charge was not a success but the infantry fought reasonably well. There had been large numbers of Russian troops in the German service in Italy since the beginning of the year. This was the only full division, but there were a number of battalions and they had been employed in the front line, in the quiet Adriatic sector, since April. All in all, before the Italian campaign was ended, something like 100,000 Russian troops were employed. I am surprised that there has not been more written about these Russian forces. The standard work on German policy in Russia by Dr. Dallin refers only incidentally to them. Plenty of people know that the Germans raised military forces from collaborators in France, Belgium, Holland and Norway, but all these were tiny compared with the Russian forces, which amounted in total to something like half a million. The Russians were in fact the greatest collaborators with the Germans. They were never used in Italy in an offensive role but they were quite reliable on the defensive though not unnaturally we picked up a certain number of deserters from them. They were thoroughly useful as internal security troops in areas where there was a danger from Italian partisans. The Turkomans were even more reliable. Their motives for enlistment included not merely dislike of Stalinism but dislike of their Russian colonizers and exploiters. This had already led in 1942 to sporadic risings in Turkmenistan, savagely repressed, and it was no doubt with memories of this that the Turkomans, when they found themselves well treated in German prisoner of war camps, were willing to respond to the call to fight on the German side.

The Russians were the only ones of the non-German forces who actually fought in the front line but there were others who were employed on internal security duties. In June the Czech Army was sent to Italy for this purpose. This was a force of about 10,000 strong; its official name was the 'the Government Troops of the Protectorate of Bohemia and Moravia'. Slovakia, a German satellite, had made its contribution even earlier. The 1st Slovak Infantry Division arrived in Italy in January 1944. It was later converted into a pioneer formation and was used for work on fortifications, particularly in the Apennines. It must not be forgotten also that the Italian Social Republic, and its leader Mussolini, remained in the war on the German side. The Germans had promised to equip its army which was commanded by Marshal Graziani, taking the field again for the first time since his defeat in 1940. The first two divisions, the Monte Rosa and the San Marco, arrived in July and August; they were used in the first place on coastal defence and for internal security. Eventually four divisions were raised.

With all these enemy troops pouring in and large numbers of ours standing by to pour out of Italy, it was clear that a brake would be placed before long on our advance. In the first weeks of June, however, it went on at an accelerated pace. The roads north of Rome were littered with the wrecks of German transport and tanks, many of which had been destroyed from the air, others of which had been abandoned when they ran out of petrol or were overtaken by our advance guard. It was an exhilarating period and not long after the capture of Rome, Alexander decided to break up his H.Q. in Caserta and take the field with a small tactical H.Q. in the style of the one he had had in Tunisia. Our first move forward was to Frascati. We set up our offices in a small building which had previously served as H.Q. for Kesselring. It was almost the only undamaged house in Frascati, and there is a connection between the two facts. Throughout the war the Air Force had rather a penchant for bombing enemy H.Q. I was never persuaded of the utility of this. It was not fellow feeling for staff officers; on the contrary I always thought that staff officers by and large were less valuable targets than others of more direct military interest. The great majority of them seemed to me to be more easily replaceable than a really good regimental officer. Of course the destruction of signal communications would be bound to cause a bit of inconvenience, but we knew from our own experience how rapidly they could be restored. I think the main reason why the Air Force favoured this kind of feat was that it made excellent headlines. They liked doing it on D-Day of an invasion—in this case Avalanche; there is never any hard news about the army on such a day and so the head-line 'Bombs blast enemy headquarters' always got a good play. The trouble was that we had no real idea whereabouts in Frascati Kesselring was. In fact he had chosen a delightful small restaurant well outside the town. It had a panoramic view over Rome with the dome of St. Peter's hovering above it like a bubble. The result was that the town of Frascati, one of the more charming places in the Alban Hills, was most violently knocked about, causing great loss of life, without blowing the dust off Kesselring's maps.

Our two armoured divisions bustled the enemy along with such briskness that Frascati was soon left too far behind and we moved, even more delightedly, to a tented camp beside Lake Bolsena. Here we were conveniently placed for the wine producing areas of Orvieto and Monte Fiascone, there were numerous sunny intervals between the normal heavy thunderstorms of an Italian summer and the sappers produced a couple of assault boats with the help of which I learnt water skiing. King George VI came to visit us; also Marshal Tito. But as the heavy hand of Anvil weighed more and more upon us it became clear that this glorious summer would fade into a dubious autumn and that we were probably committed to another winter campaign among Italian mountains.

It was about this time that I suffered my most spectacular though least serious war wound. It was the practice for officers from advanced H.Q. to be sent back to talk to staff at Rear H.Q. which was then in Rome, to give them a picture of the current situation. I went back with the G.1 Ops., Peter Miller of the Grenadiers, with whom I had a pleasant and protracted evening. The lecture was to be at eight next morning and I woke up so late that I was afraid I might not get there on time. I was staying at the Hotel Eden, an old fashioned but com-fortable one (it had only recently resumed its old name; in 1935, at the time of the abortive sanctions against Italy, it was forced to drop a name which was too reminiscent of Anthony Eden.) The lavatories were of a fairly old pattern but I was not paying much attention to this as I pulled the chain. The next thing I knew I was flat on my back. A very large brass ball had burst its way out of the cistern and fallen on my forehead. It bled like fury, which is what always happens with superficial scalp wounds. I got someone to bandage it up and dashed off for the lecture, afraid of keeping Sir Brian Robertson waiting. It was a dramatic sight, and Peter Miller was accused of having staged it, to see a staff officer tottering in as though from the front, with a blood-stained bandage round his head and fresh blood stains on his uniform.

The Germans rallied on 20th June to hold a line across Italy at the level of Lake Trasimene. The lake shore itself was the scene of one of Hannibal's brisker victories over the Roman army commanded by the Consul Flaminius. Alexander, who was always vividly alive to the historical background of Italy, signalled to General Leese warning him not to fall into the same trap as Flaminius had. The reason why Kesselring decided to stand was, first of all, simply because he discovered that he could do so. The French Corps, who were leading the pursuit, were showing less than their usual enterprise because they were all expecting every minute to be taken out of the line and sent off to liberate their homeland. It was impossible to blame them. Incidentally, Kesselring at this period won the bonus of three continuous days of heavy rain, from the 17th to 20th June, of such violence and intensity that it put a stop to all air operations and prevented any movement off the main roads. Kesselring's second motive was to gain as much time as possible for the preparation of his system of defence in the Apennines. This system is what we called the Gothic Line. The name was taken from a map captured at his H.Q. at Monte Soratte, north of Rome, and the name has stuck to it to this day. Before we made contact with it, however, in fact on 16th June 1944, the Germans changed the name to the Green Line, and it was under this name that they always referred to it. I will keep to the name Gothic Line because we never called it anything else.

A glance at the map of Italy shows the essence of the problem. About two hundred miles or so north of Rome the Apennines, which have hitherto formed the backbone of the Italian peninsula, turn west and run slanting across it, interposing a barrier between the valley of the Po and the peninsula to the south. This barrier has always been a marked one in the cultural, social and economic life of Italy. The supercilious northerners maintain that Italy finishes at the Apennines; to the Roman republic, however, the area beyond the Rubicon was a mere province. Militarily it is an obvious line to hold; if once forced off it, the next position that the Germans could have defended would have to lie in the foothills of the Alps. At the Conference at Feltre in July 1943, just before the fall of the Fascist regime, Hitler told Mussolini that he would not guarantee to hold anything further south than this. It seems likely therefore that the first reconnaissance took place then, and a great deal of work had been done on it since. If we had

had the full forces with which we fought south of Rome there seems little doubt that the Gothic Line would have marked a mere incident in our advance to the Ljubljana Gap. But in our present weakened state it represented a hard nut to crack. There were minefields and wire, anti-tank ditches, built-in tank turrets and concrete bunkers. Even more important were the advantages which geography offered to the defenders. The Allies would have to climb up to the assault up deep-cut valleys with very little or nothing in the way of lateral communications. On the German side the mountains dropped steeply fairly close to the rear of the position and there was a splendid network of roads on the flat with many side roads running up into the mountains. This meant that it was easy for the defenders to move quite large forces very rapidly from one threatened point of the line to another. No such flexibility was possible on our side.

The original idea was to attack by the shortest and most direct route up the middle from Florence on to Bologna. This would have meant that both Fifth and Eighth Armies would exert their main weight on their contiguous flanks. The plan was suddenly changed on 4th August as a result of forceful representations by General Leese. He, Alexander and Harding, Alexander's Chief of Staff, met on Orvieto airfield without any others present and talked it over while they sheltered from the sun under the wing of a Dakota plane. The gist of General Leese's remarks was that he had lost confidence in the existing plan and wanted to make Eighth Army's main effort on its right flank instead of its left, with the aim of out-flanking the Apennine barrier to the east. He argued that, with very small exceptions, Eighth Army had no mountain-trained troops, and had very little experience of large scale operations in mountains. Their speciality was the armoured battle and they hankered after the tempting stretches of flat ground which could be glimpsed round the elbow of the Apennines. Their other strong point was the handling of concentrated artillery fire power. Ever since Alamein Eighth Army commanders had had a penchant for the set piece battle and the troops were considered particularly good at it.

These were good and cogent reasons; but they were probably not the only ones. If Eighth Army made its attack on a sector of its own its success would likewise be evidently its own. There was a feeling that in the May offensive the part played by Eighth Army had not received the attention it should have done because Fifth Army had been, as planned, the first to enter Rome.

These arguments faced the Army Group Commander with a difficult decision. Both he and General Harding still favoured the plan for an attack in the centre on which they had already done a great deal of work. On the other hand it was not so obviously superior as to make it necessary to order an Army Commander to carry it out against his will. Psychological factors have as much weight in affairs of this sort as others, and it was perfectly true, leaving out of account the Army Commander's feelings, that Eighth Army had not shown up so well in the mountains and would prefer something more on the level. Moreover the new plan had the merits of flexibility. The attack up the centre looked the best bet; but if it failed and came to a standstill it would take a good bit of time to try something different and the enemy's communications gave them enormous advantage over us in the speed at which they could transfer their weight from one point to another. Contrariwise, to attack at two points would give us the chance of switching the weight from one to the other, reinforcing success and abandoning failure. So strongly did General Leese feel about his plan that he was prepared to hand over a complete Corps, 13th Corps, to Mark Clark. This would be necessary because without it Fifth Army could not keep up any serious weight of attack in the centre. It meant that Fifth Army reverted once more to being an allied army. It was only for the period May to August 1944 that it had American and French troops only; for the rest of the fighting in Italy it always had a British Corps under command.

The new plan was called 'Olive'. It involved an extremely secret transfer, postponed as late as possible, of the bulk of Eighth Army to the Adriatic shore. It also involved a hasty reversal of the plan of deception which up till then was designed to direct enemy attention to that flank. Fifth Army meanwhile prepared for an advance from Florence and Pistoia, aiming at Bologna. It now had nine divisions of which four were British. It also acquired about this time some more heterogeneous reinforcements. The first was a regimental combat team of Japanese–Americans, which gained a tremendous reputation both in Italy and later on in France. Next to arrive was the Brazilian Expeditionary Force commanded by General Mascarenhas de Moraes. (The Brazilian President of that date, General Dutra, assumed command of the force for twenty-four hours in August. His critics said that this was in order to qualify for a campaign ribbon.) This was the first, indeed the only, South American Army force to take the field in either of the two wars. It was a full division strong, magnificently equipped.

The troops were said to be the highest paid in Italy. As a matter of fact they fought quite well. To begin with they operated in the Garfagnana mountains on a defensive front where for most of the time they were opposed only by Italians. However, when the final offensive came they showed distinct capabilities in the attack. It must have been a proud moment when General von Fretter-Pico commanding the German 148th Division, descendant of one of Germany's oldest military families, with a tradition going back to the Thirty Years War, surrendered his command to General Mascarenhas de Moraes.

In addition, Fifth Army set to and constructed, as it were out of its own material, a new force equivalent in size to an infantry division made up of five American light anti-aircraft battalions, a British light anti-aircraft regiment, an American tank battalion and various other American odds and ends, such as anti-tank units and divisional recon-naissance battalions, all retrained and deployed as infantry. This was an outstanding example of 'do it yourself'. It was given the name Task Force 45. The fact was that we really had no further need for light anti-aircraft and very little need for anti-tank units since the Germans had neither low-flying aircraft nor many tanks.

The attack on the Gothic Line began on 25th August. It began with a great success, it continued with a number of hard-won tactical successes, it came very close to achieving complete success; but in the end it failed. The paradox of the Italian campaign lies in the fact that the failure was the means by which the allied armies in Italy succeeded in fulfilling their strategic mission. If we had driven the Germans off the Alps and across the Po they would have had to fall back on northeast Italy, since in the northwest they would have been between Alexander's forces and Eisenhower's forces in the French Alps. They had already prepared a number of positions in northeast Italy, one, for example, on the Adige and another on the Piave. Either of these lines would have been much shorter than the line of the Apennines and the Western Alps and they would therefore have been able to spare troops from Italy for elsewhere. An Adige Line or a Piave Line would moreover have been very formidable, and in our depleted condition it would have been difficult to mount a sufficiently strong attack on either. Of course we should not have tamely accepted so unwelcome an event and would no doubt have found another way of holding down enemy forces. Alexander had in fact a plan to meet this contingency. It was to leave Fifth Army to face the Germans on the Adige Line and transfer Eighth Army across the Adriatic for a rapid advance on Ljubljana and

Fiume. We might yet have reached Austria first. However, just as in the previous Autumn when we considered a similar strategy, this plan came to nothing because the Germans continued to hold out in Italy and thereby continued to allow themselves to be contained there.

At the time when the attack opened Kesselring had in Italy twenty-eight divisions of which two were Italian. In each of the previous three months he had received an average of twenty thousand men as reinforcement drafts. On our side there were twenty divisions and eight brigades. It will be seen that we had not even that moderate superiority in numbers which had enabled us to gain and exploit our success of the previous May. Alexander had no reserve in his hand. Each of the armies, however, had a reserve Corps; they were in fact fighting what were really separate battles. The central coordination was supplied by the fact that Fifth Army would only mount its offensive when Alexander so directed.

Eighth Army's transfer of weight to its right flank was successfully concealed. When the attack opened the enemy were still in front of the Gothic Line and as they were prepared to fall back into it they scarcely noticed the fact that our attack was now in rather greater weight. In fact it was not until 29th August, four days after we started, that the German Corps Commander realized what was afoot. By then it was already too late and the attack swept up to and through the line in one motion. By the 1st September the whole stretch from the sea to 20 miles inland was in our hands. This was one of the more elaborately fortified parts of the line because the natural defences were not so strong here. It is ridge and furrow country all the way until you get to the Rubicon; but the ridges as they slope down into the sea are not so steep or high as in the central massif of the mountains. So the concrete emplacements here were thicker together than elsewhere and there were very extensive minefields; but they did the Germans no service. The troops falling back on them were weakened and hustled by our attack, and the reinforcements coming up to man them were too late. Many of the minefields had not been armed and in one case a party of reinforcing troops who had just arrived were captured while sweeping out the bunker they were proposing to occupy.

For the first few days it really looked as though General Leese's gamble had come off and that we should soon be into the plains of north Italy—those plains which we, and particularly the armoured regiments, had looked forward to for so long. But Kesselring, as always, was quick to retrieve a difficult position. On this occasion he had greater

269

advantages than when we had caught him off balance in the past. He could bring reinforcements with great rapidity from his centre to his left flank along the great Roman Road, the Via Emilia, which runs straight as a die from Bologna to Rimini. He had one further advantage; the Gothic Line having been built on the forward slope, there was still one more ridge barring the entry into the plains. This vital fold in the ground was known as the Coriano Ridge from the village that crowns its summit. By denuding the German centre Kesselring manned the ridge with his three best divisions, the 1st Parachute, the 26th Panzer and the 29th Panzer Grenadier Divisions. It is hardly necessary to say that at this precise moment there occurred one of those periods of continuous heavy rainfall, lasting from the 5th to the 7th September, which make the Italian climate so disliked. Such weather always favours the defenders. It favoured them particularly at this time, for it halted in its tracks the 1st Armoured Division just as it was about to be thrown into the attack on Eighth Army's right. It was clear as the rain began to slacken that a deliberate attack would be necessary.

At this point, with great acuteness, Alexander decided to launch the Fifth Army attack. The enemy had been obliged to shift so many troops over to the east coast that elsewhere, particularly in the centre, he was obliged to fall back through the mountains into his Gothic Line. There was a good chance, therefore, of repeating Eighth Army's success in following up the enemy in such a way as not to reveal to him that a serious attack was about to be launched on him. This in fact took place. Fifth Army began moving forward on 8th September and on the 12th came in contact with the main positions of the Gothic Line. Simultaneously Eighth Army reopened its attack on the Coriano Ridge. Kesselring was therefore faced with a simultaneous attack on two vital points of his line. As we expected, he paid most attention to the Eighth Army attack. The reason was that this left flank was the essential pivot if he were obliged to withdraw from the Apennine position. He would have to hold fast there in order to pull back his centre and right flank through a wide arc to get them across the Po and lined up on the Adige. He may well have reflected also that his defences in the centre were strong even if his troops were fewer and that there were still many mountains for us to cross before we could look down on Bologna. The 8th Indian Division was actually the first to break through the line over on the right of Fifth Army's main attack. At the main point of thrust 1st British and 85th U.S. Divisions were successful in breaking through on the Florence–Imola road. By the end of September we were only ten miles from Imola which lay down in the plain on the Via Emilia. Eighth Army also continued to make steady progress. They captured the Coriano Ridge, taking a thousand prisoners, and on the 20th September entered Rimini. They had advanced 20 miles in 26 days, and captured over 8,000 prisoners. They had at last broken into the plain and looked forward with confidence to making more rapid progress.

I cannot now remember when it was that the realization began to dawn that the plains were going to present as difficult a problem as the mountains. Certainly up to the end of September we all thought that we had only to get out on the level and we should be able to get on. We had far more armoured divisions than we really needed; they had not been of great value so far, but we hoped that they would then come into their own. The whole of General Leese's arguments for a change of plan were based on his confidence in what he could do once he had flat ground in front of him. Perhaps we should have paid more attention to the origin of the Romagna. This part of Italy is in essence nothing but a reclaimed swamp, being a great alluvial plain formed by the Po just as lower Egypt has been formed by the Nile. Dozens of rivers, some large, some small, drain down into it from the Apennines and run into the Po. To help in carrying off the surplus water, canals parallel with the rivers have been built and added to over the centuries. With malignant perversity all these water-courses run at right angles with the axis of advance which Eighth Army was pursuing. The traveller speeding along the Via Emilia scarcely realizes that every few hundred yards he crosses a water course; if he had to travel on foot through the fields parallel to the road the fact would be brought forcibly to his notice. Nor is the military problem limited merely to the actual difficulty of getting across all these water obstacles. All swamps, when they are drained, sink. In order therefore to keep the rivers and the drainage canals within their banks the banks have to be built up. The rivers, which in their upper courses are rapid torrents, bring down silt in large quantities and deposit it on their beds so that these too begin to rise. The result is that over the centuries the embankments at either side of the river have grown higher and higher and now dominate the plain in a military sense. Nowhere in Europe, not even in the bocage country of Normandy, was there so admirable and continuous a series of ready-made defensive positions.

I was able to make this comparison because I had just returned from a liaison visit to the Western Front. Some people might have considered this a bit of a racket. I thought I was entitled to one after more than four years out of England. There were not a large number of people still in the Mediterranean theatre who could say the same, and it must be remembered that at this time, by contrast with General Montgomery's command, there had been no home leave from the Mediterranean whatever. It still required a very roundabout route to get home; first by road to Naples and then to Bizerta, Algiers and Casablanca. From Casablanca we flew well out into the Atlantic and remained out of sight of all land until with great suddenness we sighted, and almost simultaneously landed on, the extreme tip of Cornwall. The first thing I was made to do on landing was to commit perjury; because I could not prove that I had been vaccinated lately I had to sign a declaration that I had conscientious objections to it. As a reward I was given an R.A.F. operational dinner and a sleeping car to London. London was being bombarded at the time by V-1's, but only off and on. In general it looked very little changed after four years. A good many of the cities I had been in in those years had been the scene of actual fighting, which is liable to knock them about more seriously than bombing. The other striking impression was how colourful the army looked. When I left, battle dress was at its drabbest (it was after all designed to be inconspicuous) but by the summer of 1944 the taste for colour had returned. Everybody seemed to be wearing coloured regimental forage caps and sleeves had blossomed out into an extraordinary series of badges, divisional, regimental, even brigade.

It was interesting also to notice how much one was out of touch, mentally and even linguistically, with those who had spent their last four years in England. I found myself continuously asking 'Which D-Day?' and even more naughtily 'What are blits?' It still strikes me as odd to hear the invasion of France called simply by that standard military expression; I even remember being told 'We took part in D-Day' by officers of a regiment who first arrived on the western front in February 1945, or round about D plus 260. But even odder, and a question to which I still don't know the answer, is who first called bombing 'The Blitz'? The word Blitzkrieg (Guerra lampa in Italian, which sounds so much cosier) was coined to describe a certain technique. It meant the use of concentrated forces of armoured and motorized troops, attacking on a narrow front with support from a tactical air-force, mainly of dive-bombers. By some date in 1940 it was being used to describe indiscriminate, long range, high level bombing attacks on cities by night, without any connexion with any forces on the ground. It is impossible to think of any operation of warfare so totally unlike a blitzkrieg.

I had to spend a good deal of my time in England at Eisenhower's H.Q. which looked like every other H.Q. and included a large number of old friends from the Mediterranean. Before long, however, I left again for advance headquarters. Paris, as compared with London was much more familiar. It had all the characteristic marks of an occupied city recently liberated. The most noticeable differences from Italy were the odd clothes and still odder hats of the women and a bearded Mr. Hemingway holding forth in the Ritz Bar to an admiring circle of young American officers. Advance H.Q. were at Versailles with living quarters in the Petit Trianon. Here too the ribbon of the Africa Star was a useful introduction, described bitterly by palefaces without it as 'the party badge'. It went down even better in Brussels, which was my next stop, at the H.Q. of 21st Army Group. Here I was magnificently entertained by Bill Williams at a splendid black market café. It served the finest steak I had had for four years, if not in my life, and to this day I shudder to remember the price he had to pay, and did pay without blenching. The band never stopped playing Lili Marlene, except when it played the first half of the Egyptian National Anthem. This perky but banal tune was a great favourite in the Middle East, particularly with the Australians. An anonymous Australian had set it to some spirited words which are too libellous and indeed too obscene to quote; the theme was that, as the chorus maintained, the hearer's relations with a certain highly-placed personage (female) would never really be intimate unless he first came to a satisfactory financial arrangement with a second highly-placed personage (male).

Next day, in fairly sharp contrast, I was shocked to find myself being fired on when driving between Army and Corps H.Q., both of which, at least since we left the desert, should in my view have been far removed from such incivilities. I had gone on to Montgomery's advanced H.Q. at Eindhoven, where Joe Ewart represented the Intelligence Staff. It was just at the time of Arnhem, and he and I went forward along the narrow corridor which so nearly reached, but so disastrously failed to reach, the airborne landing. We got as far as Nijmegen and peered cautiously over the Waal Bridge. It was on the way back that we ran into one of the German attempts to eliminate the salient, which at that time extended only a little way on either side of the Eindhoven–Arnhem road. I complained about it to James

Nolan, G.2.I. of 30th Corps; he had been one of my people in Tunisia.

I started back for Italy about the beginning of October. The journey took some time. To begin with the aircraft on which I started refused to go beyond Dijon. This was in fact a welcome break; the Germans had intended to remove all the best wines from Dijon for the use of their troops but, owing to the rapid collapse of resistance in central France, they had been unable to do so; there were accordingly huge stocks piled up. I was one of the first British officers to arrive in Dijon. All this meant that my two days there were spent very agreeably. I then hitch-hiked a ride in a private Dakota belonging to an American General in Italy; he had sent it to Paris to make some purchases for himself or his wife and the crew were making a leisurely journey back. They flew boldly as far as Marseilles and then set out for Naples, but the cloud descended lower and lower on the sea until we were forced down very close to the waves. After about half an hour of this, while I was peacefully reading *Emma*, I was nearly thrown out of my seat by the steepest climbing turn I have ever done in a Dakota. Some very jagged rocks flashed by quite close underneath where previously there had only been grey and ghostlike sea. We had in fact nearly run into Monte Cristo. The co-pilot who was relaxing beside me was surprised by this as he had previously thought the island to be fictitious. It was too much, however, for the crew, and they turned back and landed me in Corsica. Next day I hitch-hiked once more but in very different circumstances. This time it was a South African Air Force Dakota bound from France for Italy with mail. The weather was no better than the previous day, in fact rather worse. The South Africans, as always, paid no attention to that. They were also overloaded to a fantastic degree, indeed the entire body of the Dakota was full of bags of mail almost touching the ceiling. I crawled in on top of the pile with Johnson's *Journey to the Western Isles* and had to lie flat almost up against the ceiling. We took off after an enormous run, as far as I know only by virtue of falling off the edge of the island. Thick fog persisted all the way from Ajaccio until a few miles before Naples but they hit the aerodrome right on the nose.

CHAPTER XVI

Italian Finale and a return visit to Greece

I RETURNED to find that progress was as difficult in northern Italy as it was on the Western Front. In fact the two fronts were now more closely connected than ever. As General Alexander states in his Despatch, the main factor determining his strategy was the decision by General Eisenhower, as Supreme Allied Commander in the West, that it would be necessary to fight a winter campaign on that front in order to bring about the collapse of German resistance in the spring of 1945. In other words both in France and in Italy we had missed the chance of a sudden decision. I do not know enough about the circumstances on the Western Front to say whether it would have been better to concentrate all the Allied strength on the left flank. The fact that this strategy was strongly advocated then and defended later by General Montgomery, and that it would have meant giving him the leading role, does not by any means prove that it was wrong. It seemed obvious to most of us then that the alternative strategy, of moving forward allied forces all along the line and engaging the enemy on a long front, though safe and steady, was unlikely to be speedy. We had missed our chance in Italy when the Anvil forces were removed to take their place on the right of Eisenhower's long line. Now both of us had to fight a war of attrition to keep the Germans at full stretch and wear them down until a state was reached where a decisive blow could be delivered.

This meant hard and bitter fighting in the Apennines. The Americans were now bearing the brunt and suffering severely. It is from this period I think that General Clark's unpopularity with the American troops in Italy derives, for there is no doubt that he drove them very hard, and almost beyond endurance even for such excellent troops. The American military system is, as I have said, derived from the Prussian and they have a very high concept of rigid obedience to orders. Subordinate commanders were ordered to disregard casualties and very heavy casualties were suffered. The American divisions in the attack were worn down by losses and worn out by the cruellest conditions suffered in Italy so far. The rain was continuous and of tropical intensity, the cold was bitter, there was one mountain position after another to storm. They came very close to a break-through. In the last week of October the 88th and 34th American Divisions and the 78th British Division captured three mountains which brought them to within five miles of the vital road. But this was the last effort of which they were capable. The Germans, with fresh troops, made a great reinforcing effort and on 27th October Fifth Army went over to the defensive.

Eighth Army struggled on during November and December under the new and inspiring command of General McCreery but with the capture of Ravenna and Faenza they were also brought to a stop. One important reason was a world-wide shortage of artillery ammunition, brought about by an optimistic assessment that the war was likely to end in 1944. This cessation of major efforts on our part was a blessing to us when it became necessary to send troops to Greece.

After the occupation of Greece in 1941 the Communist party had only a relatively short period during which the German–Russian pact constrained them to collaboration with the Nazis. When the German invasion of Russia set them free from this embarrassment they did not, however, think it right to dissipate their resources by attacking the occupiers. Directing their energies to establishing an unassailable post-war position they attacked instead the rival resistance movements, particularly those whose proclaimed object was to rally all patriotic persons without distinction of party or ideology. Their tactic with these was to enter into a deceptive agreement under cover of which they would suddenly attack and massacre the leaders, absorbing the bulk of the rank and file. By September 1944, when the Germans began to withdraw, they had eliminated all rivals except in the extreme northwest of Epirus.

The Communists were not likely, therefore, to pay much attention to the restored Greek Government, even though it contained representatives of the party, and they thought themselves more than a match for the scattered British troops. On 3rd December they launched an attack on all the police stations in the Athens area and next day their regular armed forces began to advance simultaneously on the centre of the city from several points.

To give the whole story of the fighting in Athens would take far too long; in any case it would call for a detailed street plan, and even with that help could only be fully intelligible if given at length in the form of a tactical narrative. It was, however, on its small scale, one of the most awkward situations that any British Commander had ever been faced with. General Alexander had just taken over the Supreme Allied Command. He knew little of what was going on, and being extremely worried about the possibilities, insisted on going at once to see for himself. The situation was worse than could have been imagined; I have often heard him describe it with more than his usual animation. To begin with there were very few British troops and most of them dismounted armoured units wholly untrained in the sort of role that they were about to be called on to fill. They were scattered about Athens and the Piraeus, not at all tactically situated. The fighting element was concentrated in the centre of Athens to defend the principal government buildings, but their food and ammunition were in dumps in areas under enemy control. The area they held in the centre of Athens was only just large enough to keep the centre of it from being under aimed small arms fire. The only contact with the outside world was through the airfield, about six miles from the centre of the city, and the Port of Piraeus at about the same distance; and communication to both of them lay through territory dominated by the enemy. Alexander flew to Athens on the morning of 11th December, the day before he actually assumed command, taking with him Mr. Harold Macmillan, then British Resident Minister and General Airey, his Chief Intelligence Officer. He found the airfield weakly held. It was cut off by land from the centre of the city and the only telephone line ran through an exchange which was in enemy hands. However, the operator obligingly put a call through and two armoured cars were sent to pick up the party. The one which carried the Supreme Allied Commander was manned by a scratch crew of batmen hastily impressed to fill the gaps caused by the ordinary crew having gone off for their tea. The batman detailed as gunner began, when ordered to test his guns, by firing a burst of 30 rounds into the window of the Corps H.Q. building. When they arrived at the aerodrome, he did not repeat this feat but jammed the belt instead. As a result the car commander decided to rely on speed alone. The most dangerous part of the journey was the main Athens Brewery on the Phaleron Road, a massively constructed building which was held by a strong force of E.L.A.S. throughout the fighting. Alexander's car went past all right at top speed but the following one drew a lot of fire. On arrival at Corps H.Q. the Field Marshal was received, not by a Guard of Honour, but by a corpse being carried out of the building, the result of shelling a few minutes earlier.

Alexander decided to make a number of changes. The British Commander in Greece, General Scobie, was a good, solid sensible man who had had two of the worst jobs in the Mediterranean, Tobruk and Malta. He was popular with his troops and with the Greeks. His staff, however, for various reasons, was not of the same calibre. Alexander sent Scobie one of his best staff officers, Brigadier Hugh Mainwaring, who had been Montgomery's G.1 OPS. at Alamein. I was asked to take over the Intelligence Branch. This was valuable when I later had the task of helping Alexander, then Governor General of Canada, with his war despatches covering all his campaigns since August 1942, the date he became Commander-in-Chief Middle East.

I don't propose to go into details about the street fighting in Athens which was ruthless and bitter. Up till Christmas we were on the defensive, and while the situation was roughly in equilibrium Mr. Churchill and Mr. Eden arrived in Athens to see what could be done in the way of a political solution. Field Marshal Alexander and Mr. Macmillan were also there. The actual political situation was highly anomalous. The King of Greece had announced that he would not return to the country until after a plebiscite had been held to ensure that this was the wish of the people. The Communists were demanding the abolition of the monarchy. General Plastiras, the Republican leader, had returned to the country and was collecting a following. There was, therefore, no fully accepted central source of authority. Alexander and Macmillan had accordingly recommended that the King should resign his authority into the hands of a Regent, and for this purpose they had been pressing the claims of the Archbishop of Athens, Damaskinos. He was a strong character, generally respected; but Mr. Churchill held firmly to the idea that his sympathies were too far to the left, and he was still resisting this appointment when he arrived in Athens. Alexander and Macmillan were convinced that the Archbishop was the only suitable candidate. It took some time to overcome Churchill's reluctance; in fact, although he had given his consent, he was still arguing as the British party arrived at the place where the conference was to be held. In a last burst of petulance he turned to Macmillan saying:

'What sort of a man is this Archbishop of yours? A typical scheming, mediaeval prelate I suppose.'

Harold Macmillan replied, 'Well, yes, as a matter of fact you could describe him as that.'

'Capital! He's our man.'

In truth this was distinctly unfair to Damaskinos, as Churchill soon recognized himself. He was a man of the utmost integrity, unselfish and indeed uninterested in his personal position. Churchill rapidly came to have a great respect for him.

The conference had no effect on the Communists, but the appointment of Damaskinos as Regent on 31st December, and of Plastiras as Prime Minister on 2nd January, were the first steps in stabilizing the political situation. Meanwhile on the military side we had cleared the Piraeus and were driving E.L.A.S. from the northern part of Athens. On the 11th January a military truce was signed with E.L.A.S. by Brigadier Mainwaring. On 12th February a political agreement was signed by the Greek Government whereby the guerillas were to be disarmed, an amnesty declared and all hostages returned. A plebiscite and general election were to be the next steps.

I was glad to be back in Greece but sorry to miss the end in Italy. I wrote up the story after the war when I was commissioned to write the first draft of the Official History of the campaign; this was after I had 'taken flannel' as a full colonel. The final battle in Italy in fact provided as fine an example of strategic skill in the planning and of hard fighting against odds in the execution as any battle in Italy. Alexander's forces had been so cut down that he had only seventeen divisions against twenty-three German and four Italian. Moreover, these were real divisions, well up to establishment in men and armaments, not the scratch formations of battalion size that were called divisions on the Western Front. For example, on D-Day of our attack the two German parachute divisions in Italy totalled 30,000 men. Their morale was magnificent. Our 'Psychological Warfare' had had no effect. Here was a large and lavishly provided organization. employing quantities of well-educated and competent men, and all their efforts met with ignominious failure. The Germans went on fighting far beyond the point at which it would be reasonable to expect them to stop.

If the propaganda arm (so-called) was to prove, as always, valueless, we got good value once more, and against all reasonable hope, from the arm of deception which had never failed us in the past. It seems almost beyond belief, but by repeating the old-established methods we persuaded the Germans that we were going to make a seaborne landing somewhere in the area of Venice. As a matter of fact such a landing would have been impossible because the water is far too shallow and too obstructed with sandbanks. The Germans didn't know this, however, and it was with rather incredulous surprise that we saw, at the end of March, their principal mobile reserve, the 29th Panzer Grenadier Division, moving from Bologna across the Po under heavy bombing and taking up a coast-watching position north of Venice. It had to come back again when the battle started, and took a long time to do so.

Nevertheless it was a tremendously hard fought battle. South of the Po the forces were very well matched and though we got tactical surprise by an attack in amphibious vehicles across the lagoon at its mouth, the Germans resisted with great stubborness. Both Fifth and Eighth Army got across the Po on the 23rd April and began to pursue northwards the fleeing remnants of Vietinghoff's forces. Two days later the Committee of National Liberation of upper Italy ordered a general insurrection. This was obeyed by numbers of Italians, a high proportion of whom were quite recent recruits to the partisan movement; they were able to seize control of a number of cities. There has been a tendency in Italy to give this rising the credit for the final German defeat and many towns and villages have renamed one of their principal streets after the 25th April. The date itself, however, serves to expose the claim. Not merely had the Germans been totally defeated by then but also it shows that this victory, like the other Italian victory of this war, Mentone in 1940, was won after the enemy had asked for an armistice. A more serious contribution was made by the Italian Combat Groups, forces of roughly divisional size, raised and armed by the British and such useful formations as G Squadron of ¡Parachutists and the Garibaldi Brigade who fought with Eighth Army.

The final act came on the 29th April at Alexander's H.Q. in Caserta. An instrument of unconditional surrender was signed by representatives of Vietinghoff as Supreme Commander and General Wolf as Supreme S.S. Commander, and came into effect on the 2nd May. It was the first surrender of German forces in the whole of the war and set a precedent for many others in northwest Europe. The story of how it was negotiated is a fascinating and in many ways amusing one.

It is given in some detail in an annex to Alexander's final despatch of the war. From this it will be seen that the opening moves took place as early as February. Wolf, the S.S. General, who had general oversight over all the rear areas in Italy, was the man who set the negotiations on foot. On the Allied side the leading man at the outset was Mr. Alan Dulles, brother of the late Secretary of State. The negotiations ran into numerous snags; one of the worst hitches was caused by Kesselring's sudden transfer to the Western Front which meant that Wolf had to start all over again with Vietinghoff. Then Himmler began to take a part, a rather ambiguous one, followed by his second in command, Kaltenbrunner. It was actually on the 24th that the final German emissaries arrived in Switzerland where the contacts had taken place with the news that they were empowered to arrange a capitulation. Then it was difficult getting them to Caserta and after they had signed there was grave difficulty in getting the instrument of surrender to Vietinghoff. This latter problem was solved by the intervention of a romantic character called Little Willie. He was a German-speaking wireless operator of Czech origin employed by the American Office of Strategic Services, who had been sent to Wolf's H.Q. quite early on. On the 29th after all other methods had failed, we eventually managed to get in wireless touch with him in his flat in the S.S. headquarters in Milan and he undertook to pass the message. Then, when the message had been passed, a dead silence descended. The trouble had arisen because Vietinghoff had been suddenly dismissed from his post and replaced by General Schultz. His chief of staff was also supposed to be replaced but refused to accept it. As a result the H.Q. at Bolzano on the 30th April and 1st May saw a series of crises during which first of all Schultz placed Vietinghoff under arrest and then Vietinghoff returned the compliment, their chiefs of staff doing the same. However, just in time, the news of Hitler's death became known. Vietinghoff, with general agreement, resumed his command and orders to the troops went out just about an hour before the time laid down for the surrender to become effective. It covered all the troops in Austria too, including some Hungarian divisions, Croats and two Cossack Cavalry Divisions. All in all, just on a million men were involved.

While all this drama was taking place I was sailing among the islands of the eastern Aegean. I had made friends with the Colonel Q Movements at 3rd Corps H.Q. In the second half of April, a fine spring month in Greece, he had been seized with the thought that he ought not to neglect his detachments in the ports of Mytilene, Chios and various other picturesque places. It occurred to me also that there was a great deal to be said for obtaining personal knowledge on the spot of public opinion in the Aegean. Hugh Mainwaring seemed sceptical about my motives until I pointed out that there was a serious security situation in Mytilene; a procession of the women of Lesbos, for some reason not stated in the report made to me, had fallen on the Subprefect of the island and had bitten him severely (the Prefect, more sensibly, had hidden under his bed). Moved by this story, he agreed that investigation was necessary and there we were sailing happily through this sparkling sea.

Our ship, almost like a private yacht, was skippered by one of the better known maritime figures of the eastern Mediterranean. He was a Spaniard, a Commander in the Republican Navy who had stuck to his ship to the last and been interned in French North Africa. Rescued from there he had commanded the *Jebel Kebir*, a rusty, antiquated tramp of Gibraltan registry which made forty-two trips into Tobruk during the siege. While better ships were being sunk all around her, she sailed unscathed. He brought with him a Greek wife and an accordion. News of the German surrender reached us in Chios. I had spent six months on Chios in 1938 and was delighted to find my old friends still well and happy; the Chians are a canny race and had given no trouble to the occupying authorities. We celebrated the news with great bursts of tracer ammunition from a British motor launch in the harbour. Our next stop was Smyrna. This was new ground to me. I had often gazed from Chios at the great black mountain of Karaburun which blocks the western entrance to the gulf; but now for the first time we sailed round the northern end into the most magnificent bay in the Mediterranean. Smyrna lies at the bottom of the bay, an amphitheatre of white houses climbing up the slopes. As we moved in to the jetty to tie up a dignified figure in top hat and frock coat was seen on shore.

'It must be the harbour master,' said Wheeler. It was indeed, and he showed the purpose of his visit by removing his hat and observing in good English and with heavy emphasis. 'The war is over.' For it was 3 o'clock of 8th May.

INDEX

283

Index

Index

Index